The Progress of

JAPAN

1853—1871

By

J. H. GUBBINS, C.M.G.

Late Secretary of Legation and Japanese Secretary of
H.B.M.'s Embassy in Japan
Lecturer in Japanese in the University of Oxford

AMS PRESS
NEW YORK

Reprinted from the edition of 1911,Oxford

First AMS EDITION published 1971

Manufactured in the United States of America

International Standard Book Number : 0-404-02939-6

Library of Congress Number:79-137237

AMS PRESS INC.
NEW YORK, N.Y.10003

PREFACE

SIX lectures given in the University of Oxford
during 1909–10 are the basis of this book. They
are published as delivered, with only that amount
of revision which publication seemed to require.
The aim in view has been to give a slight sketch
of the progress of Japan in the period of transition
which lay, so to speak, between the old life and
the new.

The appendixes include documents which I have
added in order to save the reader the trouble of
looking for them elsewhere, and others which were
accessible only in the Japanese text.

To Sir Ernest Satow my best thanks are due for
the loan of books, for information on various
points possessed by no one else, and for much
valuable criticism. For advice in the treatment
of the subject, and for many useful suggestions,
I am also indebted to Mr. S. Tuke. And the help
of every kind rendered by my wife from first to
last I gratefully acknowledge.

CONTENTS

CONTENTS 5

1. AMERICAN TREATY, March, 1854 227
2. AMERICAN TREATY, March, 1854; ADDITIONAL
REGULATIONS, September, 1854. . . . 230
3. BRITISH CONVENTION, October, 1854 . . . 232
4. BRITISH CONVENTION, October, 1854; EXPOSITION
OF ARTICLES, October, 1855 233
5. RUSSIAN TREATY, February, 1855 235
6. RUSSIAN TREATY, February, 1855; EXPLANATORY
ARTICLES (same date) 238
7. RUSSIAN SUPPLEMENTARY TREATY, October, 1857 . 239
8. DUTCH PRELIMINARY CONVENTION, November, 1855 245
9. DUTCH TREATY, January, 1856 250
10. DUTCH TREATY, January, 1856; ADDITIONAL ARTICLES,
October, 1857 255
11. AMERICAN CONVENTION (Shimoda), June, 1857 . 266
12. EXTRACT FROM CONSTITUTION (OR ARRANGEMENT) OF
1615 DEFINING SHŌGUN'S AUTHORITY . . 269
13. AMERICAN TREATY, July, 1858 269
14. NOTES ON TREATIES OF 1858 283
15. MEMORIAL ON FOREIGN INTERCOURSE PRESENTED
BY ĪI KAMON NO KAMI TO SHŌGUNATE IN 1853 . 285
16. EXTRACT FROM Bakumatsu Gwaikōdan, WITH RE-
FERENCE TO THE CONSULTATION OF THE DAIMIŌS
BY THE GOVERNMENT IN 1858 289
17. LONDON PROTOCOL, June, 1862 291
18. CONVENTION OF PARIS, June, 1864 . . . 294
19. SHIMONOSÉKI CONVENTION, October, 1864 . . 296
20. TARIFF CONVENTION, June, 1866 298
21. MANIFESTO ANNOUNCING SHŌGUN'S RESIGNATION
(1867) 305
22. MEMORANDUM, GIVING REASONS FOR SHŌGUN'S RESIG-
NATION, HANDED TO FOREIGN REPRESENTATIVES
IN NOVEMBER, 1867. 306
23. SHŌGUN'S PROTEST TO COURT, January, 1868 . . 312
MEMORIAL OF DAIMIŌS SURRENDERING FIEFS, March,
1869 313

GLOSSARY 317

SELECTED BIBLIOGRAPHY

COUNT KATSU AWA. *Kaikoku Kigen* ('The Commencement of the Opening of the Country') ; 3 vols.

SATOW, SIR E. Chapter on Japan in *Cambridge Modern History*, vol. xi.

SATOW, SIR E. *The Voyage of Capt. John Saris to Japan.* Hakluyt Society.

SATOW, SIR E. 'The Story of a Dream in the period of Genji' (*Genji Yumé Monogatari*) ; translation.

SATOW, SIR E. 'History of Modern Times' (*Kinsé Shiriaku*) ; translation.

SHIMADA, S. *Kaikoku Shimatsu* (' The Affair of the Opening of the Country ').

SANABÉ, M. *Bakumatsu Gwaikōdan* (' The Story of Foreign Relations in the last days of the Shōgunate').

HONDA, T. *Ishin Shi* (' History of the Restoration ').

KIMURA, K. *Sanjiūnen Shi* (' History of Thirty Years, 1838–68 ').

KITABARA, M. *Shichinen Shi* (' History of Seven Years, 1861–8 ').

NAKAMURA, Y. *Ïi Tairō to Kaikō* ('The Regent Ïi and the Opening of the Ports ').

KOBAYASHI, S. *Bakumatsu Shi* ('History of the Last Days of the Shōgunate ').

OKAMOTO, T. *Ōsei Fukuko* ('The Restoration of the Monarchy').

ADAMS, F. O. *History of Japan.*

MITFORD, A. B. *Tales of Old Japan* ; 2 vols.

RUNDALL, T. *Japonia.*

HILDRETH, R. *Japan as it was and is.*

CHAMBERLAIN, B. H. *Things Japanese.*

BRINKLEY, CAPTAIN F. *Japan and China* ; 12 vols.

MURDOCH, J. ⎱
YAMAGATA, I. ⎰ *A History of Japan.*

MURDOCH, J. *A History of Japan* ; vol. i.

OKAKURA, K. *The Awakening of Japan.*

IYÉNAGA, T. *The Constitutional Development of Japan.*

Tokugawa Kinreikō (' Collection of Tokugawa Enactments '), published by Department of Justice, Tokio ; 10 vols.

INTRODUCTION

THE latter half of the nineteenth and the opening years of the twentieth centuries have witnessed a startling event in the world's history, the transformation of a nation living in self-imposed seclusion in a distant and little-known corner of Asia into a great power, conspicuous for love of progress, and equipped with all the adjuncts of modern civilization. This change may be taken to have begun with Commodore Perry's arrival in Japan in 1853, and to have ended with the signature of the Portsmouth Convention in 1905—an interval of a little over fifty years.

The history of these fifty years falls naturally into two periods, the first of which seems to close appropriately with the abolition of feudalism in 1871. It is with this, the preliminary stage of Japan's development, that the present pages are concerned. It stands out in marked contrast to that which followed, for she had to disencumber herself of much before she could make a fresh start, to pull down in order to rebuild. And at the outset of this process her policy was decided for her by an impatient world, in whose economy there was no place for hermit nations.

CHAPTER I

THE CONDITIONS EXISTING IN JAPAN WHEN THE FIRST TREATY WAS NEGOTIATED

A GLANCE at the map will show that the position occupied by Japan in Asia is similar to that of England in Europe, with this difference that while the British Isles lie on the west of the European continent, the Japanese islands are to the east of the mainland of Asia. Taking them in the order from north to south, the group of islands comprised in the present Japanese Empire consist of the Kuriles, the southern half of Saghalien, Yezo, the main island known to Japanese as Hondo, Shikoku, Kiūshiū, the Loochoos, Formosa, and the Pescadores. These stretch diagonally from the 51st down to the 21st degree of north latitude, and are situated between the 120th and the 156th degrees of longitude east of Greenwich. A warm current, similar to the Gulf Stream of Northern Europe, reaches the southern extremity of Kiūshiū, and, there dividing, flows partly up the west and partly up the east coast, the latter portion of the current branching out into the Pacific Ocean before reaching Yezo. The climate is damp, like that of our own islands, but the ranges of heat and cold are much greater ; the south of Formosa is semi-tropical and has practically no winter, while the Kuriles, the portion of Saghalien, which now

again belongs to Japan, and certain parts of Yezo,
have the climate of Nova Scotia, or Iceland. It
only remains to mention that the islands comprising Japan are all mountainous, so that with
a population much the same as that of the British
Isles, and an area considerably greater, there is
less space for cultivation, and less room for the
inhabitants ; that the rainfall is greater and the
summer much hotter than ours ; and that the
rivers are short, and their gradients very steep,
causing floods and droughts to be more frequent
than with us. The area of the Japanese Empire,
as above described, was increased in August of
last year by the annexation of Corea, over which
Japan had previously exercised a protectorate.
Her authority, moreover, extends beyond these
geographical limits, for she is in occupation of
a large portion of Manchuria, formerly under
Russian control, which includes the Liaotung
peninsula.

At the time, however, at which our story opens,
the dominions over which a Mikado reigned, and
the Shōgun ruled, consisted only of an island
empire, with no territory on the continent of Asia,
and comprising neither Formosa nor Loochoo.

The history of Japan before the advent of
foreign treaty-makers may be given in a few words.
The ruler with which that history begins for the
Japanese is Jimmu Tennō, a semi-mythical personage, whose reign is said to correspond with a
date some 600 years before the Christian era.

Down to the year A.D. 1192, when Yoritomo was appointed Shōgun, the land was more or less under the personal rule of the Mikados : [1] from that date until the Restoration of 1868 the personal rule of the Mikados ceased, and the government was administered in whole or in part by Shōguns, of different dynasties, with two intervals : the period between 1199 and 1333, when the Hōjō Regents were in power ; and subsequently the short period preceding the establishment of the Tokugawa Shōgunate, when first Nobunaga, and then Hidéyoshi, took the administrative authority from the feeble hands of the last Ashikaga Shōguns. It may be well to explain what the Shōgun really was. Although the feudalism of Japan, in the form in which it finally crystallized itself under the Tokugawa rule, had distinctive features peculiar to itself, what little we know of its origin leads to the inference that it grew up under circumstances not very dissimilar to those which characterized the growth of feudalism elsewhere. The early social organization, founded more or less on a tribal basis, gave place by degrees to a more unified system, controlled and dominated by a central government, which was directed, in name at least, by an autocratic sovereign. Afterwards, as time went by, the growing weakness of the Court led to more and more authority being delegated to local governors throughout the country, whose power increased with the opportunities

[1] See p. 82.

created by the growing weakness of the government at Kiōto. The military forces of the country, which had formerly been directly controlled by the central authorities, came by degrees under the orders of the local chieftains, and were organized on a provincial basis under a system of feudal tenure. Japan thus became an armed camp, and from time to time the struggle for supremacy between these various feudal chiefs, or daimiōs, as they came to be called, led to one or other asserting his superiority, and becoming the military ruler of the country. In this capacity his authority was absolute, but the shadow of sovereignty was retained by the Crown, and he governed in the name of the Mikado, with the title of Sei-i-tai Shōgun, which means barbarian-quelling generalissimo. The Tokugawa Shōguns, or mayors of the palace, as they may not inappropriately be termed, were the last representatives of this series of administrators ; they were by far the most powerful ; their government lasted longer than those of any of their predecessors ; and their admirers base their claim to the nation's gratitude on the fact that they gave to the country what is known as the ' Great Peace ', which lasted 250 years. It was the third Shōgun of this line, Iyémitsu, who consolidated its power, and who is responsible for the closing of the country.

When Perry arrived in 1853 the Mikado was living in the strictest seclusion in Kiōto, a seclusion in which the sovereigns had remained for nearly

700 years. The Tokugawa Shōguns, however, when their turn came to administer the country, had been careful to keep up the pretence of the imperial dignity, and the Emperor in accordance with this policy was treated with semi-divine honours, and surrounded by a mock Court of *Kugé* (or Court nobles). These held meaningless administrative titles, and were the descendants of the men who had ruled the country in far-off times, when the Mikado's sovereignty was something more than a mere name. The ruling Shōgun was Iyéyoshi, and Yedo, the Tokugawa seat of administration, and not Kiōto, was the real capital. Japan was parcelled out into some 260 [1] odd fiefs, the holders of which were divided into two broad classes, those called *fudai*, who were hereditary vassals of the Tokugawa Shōguns, and others known as *tozama*. The distinction was one created by the founder of the line. In one of the posthumous papers attributed to him, the ' Hundred Articles ', better known to foreign readers as ' The Legacy of Iyéyasu ', the former are described as those *samurai* who had already declared themselves on his side before the fall of Ōsaka in 1600—the date on which his supremacy was established—and the latter as those who

[1] Japanese writers are accustomed to speak of ' the 60 odd provinces of Japan and the 260 odd daimios. The exact number is given variously by different authorities, and we know that it changed from time to time. The parliament of 1869 contained 276 members, and it was understood that each clan was represented by one member.

acknowledged his authority after that event. The distinction had no effect on precedence, and no relation to revenue. But it had a very practical significance in the fact recorded in the same paper, that the *fudai* daimiōs only, and not the *tozama*, were eligible for official posts—an arrangement which tended to the concentration of authority in Tokugawa hands. There was another classification which in the earlier days of feudalism had great importance. This was the division of daimiōs into three classes, the *Kokushiu*, or 'lords of provinces' (eighteen in number), the *Riōshiu*, or 'lords of territories', and the *Jōshiu*, or 'lords of castles'. To this last-mentioned class more than two-thirds of the feudal nobility belonged, and a few of them, known as *fuyo* were dependent on the *Kokushiu*, or over-lords, of their provinces. Towards the close of the Tokugawa rule, however, the distinction between *Riōshiu* and *Jōshiu* had lost much of its significance, and the one class which retained its original importance, and exclusive position, was that of the *Kokushiu*.

First in the precedence of those days ranked the heads of the *Gosankè*. This was the name applied to the three princely houses of Owari, Kishiū and Mito, from the two first of which, together with the Gosankiō—a family group of later institution—the Tokugawa rulers were chosen. Next came the other daimiōs of the *Kokushiu* class, the first three places being filled by the princes of Satsuma,

Kaga, and Sendai. To these succeeded the *Kugé*, or Court nobles, who in turn were followed by *tozama* and *fudai* daimiōs, not of *Kokushiu* rank. Then came the *hatamoto*, a special class of bannermen created by Iyéyasu, some of whom had estates equal in extent to those of the smaller daimiōs ; then the *Gokénin*, a sort of superior feudal gentry ; and lastly the ordinary *samurai*, who were divided into two grades. All these belonged to the military class. Outside the latter, and lower down in the social scale, came the three classes of farmer, artisan and merchant, in the order named.

The central authority was exercised in various ways. The general direction of affairs was in the hands of an upper and a lower council, the members of which were chosen from the ranks of the *fudai* daimiōs and the *hatamoto*. Decisions on grave matters of State were referred, when necessary, to the *Gosanké*, and the leading daimiōs, whose association in the work of government was, however, more nominal than real. In the Shōgun's territories, and in those *fudai* daimiates which were ruled from Yedo there were official governors (*daikwan*), as distinct from clan rulers : while the details of administration were entrusted to an army of executive and judicial officers, in town and country, with high-sounding titles, and functions having little likeness to anything known at that time outside Japan.

At Kiōto there was an official representative of the Shōgun (or Resident), called the *Shoshidai*, through whom all official communications between Yedo and Kiōto passed, the *Kwambaku*, or chief minister of the Court, and officials known as *Tensō* and *Gisō*, representing the Throne in the conduct of State business. The castle of Ōsaka was occupied by a Shōgunate official called *Jōdai*, and at Fushimi, Nagasaki, Uraga, and other places there were Shōgunate governors called *Bugiō*.

Two religions, Buddhism and Shintō, existed side by side, their boundaries at times so interlaced that they seemed to be one : while two others, Confucianism and geomancy, though hardly having the status of religions, exercised a great influence on the morality and thought of the nation.

Relations with the Spaniards had been broken off in 1824, and with the Portuguese twelve years later, and from that time, till the new foreign intercourse on a treaty basis was established, the only two nations whose ships traded with Japan were the Chinese and Dutch. The place where this commerce was conducted was Nagasaki in the province of Hizen in Kiūshiū. There the Chinese had always traded, and it was to the same port that the Dutch traders were transferred from Hirado after the issue, in 1636, of the edict closing the country. There is little doubt that in making this exception in favour of the Dutch the Japanese were influenced by the belief that they were not Christians, a belief which was confirmed by their general attitude towards Christianity, and the missionary propaganda.   There is also reason to credit the statement that the Japanese were later on very indignant when they found out that Christianity was also the religion of Holland. The curious political conditions existing at that time in Japan gave rise to much misunderstanding on the part of foreigners.   So little was known or heard of the Mikado that the Shōgun was commonly taken to be the sovereign.   Another idea was that Japan had two Emperors, one temporal and the other spiritual, and this was the view taken by the Portuguese and Dutch.   Later writers again have laid stress on the fraudulent conduct of the Shōgunate, which is accused of having deliberately concealed from the outside world the existence of the Mikado, and having falsely represented the Shōgun to be the actual sovereign of Japan.   In reality there was no wilful deception.   It would have been as difficult, if not impossible, for the Japanese officials who negotiated the earlier treaties with foreigners to explain to them the true state of things, as it would have been for the latter to understand the explanation when given. And if the Japanese who acted as Dutch interpreters in speaking and writing of the Shōgun (or Taikun) used misleading phrases conveying the idea of his sovereignty, the Japanese texts of the earlier agreements are almost equally misleading ; and it is not easy to see what other form of words would have better answered the purpose in view, which was to signify the deep veneration and respect entertained for the *de facto* ruler of Japan.

A Harleian manuscript of the sixteenth century,[1] in describing the autocratic position of Hidéyoshi, the predecessor of the Tokugawa Shōguns, towards the feudal aristocracy of those days, says :—

' To the end that he may become lord, or rather absolute tyrant, he is wont to remove the princes out of one province into another ; not ignorant that lords being taken out of their dominions and placed over strange subjects become weak . . . ; and that they may the less practise and devise any revolt he decideth their realms and dominions. Besides . . . he will have them come to yield him reverence . . . and offer him every year precious gifts. . . . For though all rivers in a kind of thankful remuneration return their waters to the sea because they draw them from thence, yet the princes of Japonia do clean contrary. They receive nothing from the Emperor ' [namely Hidéyoshi] ' and yet give all to the Emperor. . . . And that they may not grow rich and of sufficient ability to make head against him, he suffereth not their fleeces to grow, but shears them clean off by raising taxes . . . for the building of castles and the repairing of fortifications.'

What is said in the foregoing passage applies with even greater force to the power of the Tokugawa Shōgunate. Its rule, as established by its founder Iyéyasu, extended over the whole, and not, as in Hidéyoshi's case, over only a part of Japan. The opportunities for intrigue and revolt,

---

[1] Undated, but evidently written towards the end of the sixteenth century. Quoted in *Japonia* by Thomas Rundall.

already made small enough by Hidéyoshi's policy, were further reduced under the Tokugawa régime by a regulation providing for the residence of daimiōs alternately in Yedo, and in the provinces, and for the permanent detention of their families as hostages. This rule, by which the daimiōs were kept continually travelling to and fro, chiefly by land, put them to great expense, and inconvenience, besides entailing troublesome arrangements to prevent quarrels, and more serious collisions, between different processions moving along the high roads at the same time.

All-powerful as was the sway of the Tokugawa Shōguns, to outward seeming, when the early treaty negotiations commenced, the period of its zenith had nevertheless passed, and the decay which was shortly to show itself more clearly had already set in for some time. For this there were various causes. A spirit of unrest had been produced by the eager study of Western learning through the medium of Dutch books, by association with foreigners attached to the Dutch factory in Déshima, and by the news, received through the Dutch, of the proceedings of the French and English in China. And in the course of the two previous centuries the effect of three separate movements, the study of ancient learning, as it was called, the study of the Chinese philosophy of Wang-Yang-Ming—known in Japan as O-yo-mei—and the revival of pure Shintō, had been increasingly inimical to the Tokugawa Government. Each of these was in itself merely a phase of the great literary renaissance which characterized the Tokugawa period. Put very shortly, the study of ancient learning was an attempt to clothe Chinese Confucian ideas in Japanese dress, and place, as it were, Confucian teaching on a Japanese basis ; the aim of the Ō-yō-mei philosophy was to translate theory into practice ; while the revival of pure Shintō signified a revolt from subserviency to Chinese principles of ethics and administration, as well as an endeavour, by the encouragement of historical and linguistic research, to restore the ancient monarchical ideas, including devotion to the Throne, which had died out during the six or seven hundred years of Shogunate rule. The combined effect of all three, which showed, in spite of independent origin, a curious singleness of tendency, was to create a popular feeling in favour of the personal rule of the Mikado, and thus weaken the Tokugawa domination. And the operation of these various causes was strengthened by the hereditary jealousy of the more powerful daimios, who could not forget that Iyéyasu, the founder of the Tokugawa rule, had been a daimiō like themselves, by the ill-health of the reigning Shōgun at the time of Perry's visit, and by the fact that the Tokugawa family was then, owing to dissensions which arose in the Mito branch, a house divided against itself.

It should carefully be borne in mind in considering the question of Tokugawa government that

the Shōgun did not personally rule any more than
the Mikado. What for want of a better name
may be termed the figurehead system of government is noticeable throughout the whole course
of Japanese history, and is the natural outcome
of Japanese social and political ideas. Real and
nominal power are rarely seen combined either
socially or politically. The family, which is the
unit of society, and not, as with us, the individual,
is nominally controlled by the individual who is its
head. But practically the latter is in most cases
a figurehead, the real power being vested in the
group of relatives who form the family council.
And so, in the feudal times of which we are now
speaking, it was with the territorial nobility.
With one or two notable exceptions, the daimiōs
did not administer their fiefs. The administration
of these was entrusted to a group of retainers,
known as *karō*, who held office hereditarily in
their respective clans. And it was the same with
the *hatamoto*. But here again the authority was
more nominal than real, the direction of affairs
being left as a rule to the more active intelligence
of retainers of inferior rank. Similarly the Shōgun
was as often as not a mere puppet in the hands
of his Upper and Lower Councils, and these in
turn were controlled by subordinate office-holders.
So that the position of the Mikado in his enforced
retirement was simply a reproduction of what
existed in each sphere of the social and political
organization. Though very repugnant to the

court nobles, who regretted their ancient power and
wealth, this position of the Crown did not appear
startling to the average Japanese, who was accustomed by tradition and habit to the dissociation
of power from position, and regarded it, if he
thought about it at all, as perfectly natural, and,
in the circumstances, correct. With the establishment of a new line of Shōguns, or the advent to
power, in any other of the above-named capacities,
of an individual of exceptional force of character,
there might be a reversion for a time to personal
rule. But this was seldom bequeathed to a
successor. It rarely outlasted the lifetime of the
individual in question, and the frequency of the
custom of abdication, which did not necessarily
mean the relinquishment of power, shows how
innate and all-powerful in the Japanese nation
was the instinct of ruling by proxy. In what
other country would a third of the feudal nobility
have been found, as was the case in Japan not
long after the opening of the country, living in
the retirement of abdication ? Where else could
such a state of things have existed as we find on
more than one occasion when there was not only
a *roi fainéant* but a Shōgun *fainéant,* and the
government was conducted by a personage who
was neither sovereign nor Shōgun ?

The natural tendency of this system was to
hinder the development of administrative capacity,
and to keep the government shrouded in an
atmosphere of impersonality. But in another

direction it had very practical results. The weakness or incompetence of the ruler produced no violent convulsions in the body politic. The machinery of government worked on as smoothly as before, unaffected by the personality of those theoretically responsible for its control. And for the Crown there were other gains. The absence of personal rule precluded all possibility of conflict with the people, while the seclusion and mystery in which the monarch moved raised the Crown in the popular veneration and esteem. Thus was evolved a stability which has triumphed over all vicissitudes. The dual system of government in Japan has been ascribed by some writers to deep policy on the part of the usurping Shōguns. In reality it was an arrangement in thorough consonance with Japanese ideas which had its root in the social system. And, as time went by, the tendency of office to divorce itself from the discharge of the duties nominally associated with it increased everywhere, with the result that by the time Perry came all real authority both in the clans and in the Yedo Government had been transferred to members of the military class, who were the virtual rulers of Japan.

It has been the custom to represent the military class as having, when Japan emerged from her seclusion, the warlike qualities commonly associated with feudalism. This in a marked degree was true, however, only of certain clans in the south, west, and north. In other parts of Japan, and especially in Yedo and Ōsaka, and other centres of commerce and wealth, the ' Long Peace ' had instilled habits of luxury. The simplicity, frugality, and hardiness, which had formerly characterized the military class, were disappearing, and literary pursuits were being cultivated at the expense of warlike accomplishments. This movement was stimulated indirectly by the Shō-gunate through its two-fold policy of patroniz-ing Buddhism, and at the same time encouraging the spread of Confucian philosophy, each of which in its own way tended to curb the military spirit of the *samurai*.

It used to be thought at one time that all Oriental countries were barbarous in comparison with the West, and Japan was not unnaturally included in this category. Western nations in holding this view were but adopting the attitude of China and Japan, for whom the world consisted of two sets of people, themselves and ' outer barbarians ', no exception being made by either of the two in favour of her neighbour. But better knowledge revealed the fact that the term bar-barous was wholly inapplicable to the Far East ; that she possessed a civilization older than that of Europe, and superior to it in several branches of agriculture, art, and industry ; and that it was only in development along certain scientific and ethical lines that Europe could claim any manifest advantage. There is a striking unanimity of opinion among all the earlier writers on Japan

in regard to the civilization which was found to
exist. And the value of this evidence is increased
by the fact that it comes from writers of many
nationalities and different professions, was gathered
under various circumstances, and extends through
a long period of years. What the missionaries of
the sixteenth century were the first to observe
is confirmed over and over again by later comers ;
by Spex and Sergersohn, Saris and Kaempfer in
the seventeenth century, by Thunberg in the
eighteenth, and by Golownin, Siebold, and others,
in the early part of the nineteenth century. One
piece of corroborative testimony comes from an
interesting and rather unexpected source. The
date is 1815. In that year Sir Stamford Raffles,
the brilliant governor of the Straits Settlements,
was administering the island of Java, then in
British possession. In the course of a lecture
delivered by him in Batavia, the capital of the
island, he referred to a visit made to Japan two
years before by Dr. Ainslie, one of the officials
serving under him, and quoted the opinion which
that gentleman had formed of the Japanese
people during a stay of four months at the Dutch
factory at Nagasaki. Dr. Ainslie spoke of them
as a nervous vigorous people, whose bodily and
mental powers resembled more nearly those of
Europeans than Asiatics ; who had a strong
inclination for foreign intercourse, in spite of the
anti-foreign policy of their rulers ; and whose
energy of character—and, he might have added,

submission to discipline—showed itself in the extraordinary decision which excluded the world from their shores, and confined within their own limits a people who were adventurous navigators, and had formerly traded with all nations. In their apparent coldness Dr. Ainslie traced a resemblance to the stillness of the Spanish character, due, in his opinion, to the same causes, a system of espionage, and a spirit of disunion. They were, he observed, attracted by novelty, warm-hearted, and eager for knowledge and information of all kinds. Finally they struck him as being a people who were ready to throw themselves into the hands of any nation of superior intelligence. Reading this to mean a willingness to be guided by the practical wisdom of a wider civilization, wherever it might be found, this is precisely what Japan has done in carrying through the work of national development.

A similar impression, not unmixed with surprise, was produced on the foreign negotiators of the early treaties. We find constant references to the singular attractiveness of the people, their eagerness for knowledge, and the difference between them and other Asiatic peoples with whom they are compared. The advanced state of education, and its wide diffusion through the empire, were also noted.

This education was for all classes obtained chiefly in private schools. These had gradually taken the place of the *Terakoya*, or schools attached to Buddhist temples which, before the Tokugawa administration, were the only places where learning was taught. But for the special use of the military class there existed also in Yedo an academy, dating from the end of the eighteenth century, and other schools, maintained by the Shōgunate, and in the provinces there were colleges supported by local daimiōs.[1]

It should also be borne in mind that the opening of Japan to foreign trade in the middle of the nineteenth century was not the first establishment of foreign intercourse. It was the re-opening of a country which had been open before, and had then been deliberately closed. In the early years of the seventeenth century very extensive trading facilities were for a short time enjoyed by the Portuguese, the Dutch, and the English. The Portuguese carried on their trade chiefly in ports of the province of Bungo, at the island of Hirado, and at Nagasaki ; and the Dutch and English commerce was likewise confined principally to the southern island of Kiūshiū. But the trading facilities granted by the Japanese Government at that time permitted a much wider scope, of which advantage was never fully taken. Proof of this is furnished by the charter obtained by Captain

---

[1] Among the provincial towns which benefited by such establishments were Yonézawa (in the province of Dēwa), Sendai (in Mutsu), Sakura (in Shimosa), Nagoya (in Owari), Okayama (in Bizen), Hagi (in Chōshiū), Saga (in Hizen), Kumamoto (in Higo), and Kagoshima (in Satsuma).

Saris in 1613, the first article of which runs as follows :—

'We give free license to the King of England's subjects Sir Thomas Smith Governor and Company of the East India merchants for ever safely to come into any our ports or empire of Japan with their ships and merchandise without hindrance to them or their goods : and to abide buy and sell and barter according to their own manner with all nations and to tarry as long as they will and depart at their pleasure.'

The second article of this charter allowed English goods to be imported into Japan without payment of customs duty ; under the third English subjects were permitted to build houses in any part of Japan ; and in the fourth it was expressly stipulated that English subjects in Japan should not be amenable to the somewhat summary processes of Japanese law.

Could more liberal treatment have been desired ? There is nothing here of the harsh restrictions subsequently imposed on foreign intercourse, and singularly enough in the conditions respecting trade, residence, and jurisdiction, we see an anticipation of the provisions of the treaties negotiated two and a half centuries later.

This fact, therefore, that it was not the first opening of Japan to foreign intercourse, but the re-establishment of that intercourse on a formal treaty basis, must be kept in view by those who otherwise might be tempted to exaggerate the shock produced by renewed contact with Western nations.

Nor had Japan's seclusion in the interval between 1636 and 1853 been complete. The Spaniards and Portuguese were indeed expelled; Japanese subjects were prohibited on pain of death from going abroad; and submission to this decree was enforced by the provision which reduced the tonnage of ships, limited to one the number of masts to be carried, and so altered the construction of vessels that they were helpless in stormy weather, and were only fit to coast from point to point along the shore. But a small number of Chinese and Dutch trading vessels still came to Nagasaki, bringing tidings of the outside world; and foreign news trickled through from other sources—through Corea, from shipwrecked mariners of different nationalities, and in letters addressed to the Government of Japan by various foreign potentates. And, as time went on, the Japanese people acquired from Dutch books, brought in both openly and secretly, a good sprinkling of Western science, especially medicine and navigation. So that when foreigners came, demanding treaties with a show of force, the Japanese, though living for so long in a back eddy of the world's active life, were not in the position of a nation to whom the Western new-comers were total strangers. They had traditions of Spanish and Portuguese intercourse, and of an active Christian propaganda prosecuted by zealous foreign missionaries; they knew of the buccaneering expeditions and trading enterprises of their

ancestors on the coast of Asia before the edict of
seclusion ; and they were quite accustomed to the
idea of foreign trade.

And here it should be explained, by way of
excuse for much friction and misunderstanding
which subsequently arose, that the trade to which
the nation was accustomed was not a trade carried
on freely and directly by the people of Japan,
but one which, if not a Government monopoly, was
conducted under strict official supervision. State
control of foreign commerce became in the years
during which the Dutch and Chinese alone traded
with Japan an axiom of government. The principle, as we shall see later on, stands recorded
in the first treaty, and it could always be supported
on the ground that the people must be protected
from the foreigner. So it was not, perhaps, surprising that in spite of the express stipulations of
later treaties, inserted for the purpose of remedying
this state of things, the foreign representatives for
many years had much trouble in resisting official
encroachments, and in combating all sorts of
restrictions placed on the free conduct of trade.

The narratives of the negotiations bring out very
clearly the atmosphere of intrigue, suspicion and
fear in which the Japanese officials of that day
moved. Harris, the first United States representative, in his diary speaks of the agitation
shown by them in the course of business interviews.
Interpreters would lose their self-possession entirely, and shake with fear—one being mentioned as

' trembling all over his body, as though he had an
ague fit, while large drops of perspiration stood like
beads on his forehead '—and officers of higher
rank invariably supported a request for something
not to be done by the plea that, if it were, they
would lose their heads.   Of the severity of the
Tokugawa rule abundant testimony is furnished
by its laws.   For this we need not look further
than the Edict of 1636 which closed the country.
By this law it was death for a Japanese to go
abroad, for the children or descendants of Spaniards
and Portuguese to remain in Japan, or to return
there after banishment, and for a Japanese to
adopt or harbour such persons, or receive letters
from them.   In every case, too, the whole circle
of the offender's relatives were punished.   Nor,
from the lavish way in which rewards for the
detection of criminals were given, is there any
reason to suppose that these laws lost any of their
harshness in the process of application.   Of two
things there seems to be little doubt : that officials
lived in terror of the Government they served, and
that the latter were in their turn very much
afraid of the foreigners who came to make treaties,
and of what would happen when those treaties
were made.

We notice, too, in the administration of that
time a partiality for the employment of two or
more officials to do what might seem to be the work
of only one.   Thus, for instance, in Nagasaki and
Shimoda, and probably in other imperial districts,

there were two governors and two vice-governors. These functionaries were not all at their posts at the same time. It was arranged that two should be on duty during six months of the year, while the other two were in Yedo or elsewhere. When, as frequently happened, these posts were filled by daimiōs, some arrangement of this kind was necessitated by the obligation of residence in Yedo at stated times. The same superabundance of officeholders is noticeable in other branches of the State service. It is not clear whether this tendency ever extended so far as to become a principle of administration, but it was a recognized practice in the Loochoos at the time of their annexation to Japan, and to its prevalence may be ascribed the general, though perhaps mistaken, belief amongst foreigners that Japanese officials usually worked in pairs. Among the stories of those times there is one which illustrates this tendency.[1] It is said that when Lord Elgin and Kincardine came to negotiate his treaty in 1858 the double name at once attracted attention, giving rise to the assumption that the British Government had sent two envoys, and not one, to open relations with Japan; and that when, after the lapse of several days, the second envoy never appeared, inquiries were made after the missing Kincardine.

Any review of the conditions prevailing in Japan

---

[1] The Elgin treaty itself is an instance in point. On one side it is signed by Lord Elgin alone ; on the Japanese side there are no less than six signatures.

at the time of Perry's arrival would be incomplete without some reference to the well-known fact of the predominating influence of Chinese civilization, which received a great impetus during the whole of the Tokugawa period. It was apparent in almost everything. Nor is this surprising in view of the fact that at the time of what is known as The Great Reform in the seventh century, the whole administrative system was remodelled on a Chinese basis. From China the Japan of that day borrowed her written language, her court ceremonial, part of her official organization, her philosophy, her ethics, her religion, if we exclude Shintō, her arts and industries, and her laws, repeating the process later on. And, curiously enough, it is from China also that she adopted the name by which she became known to the world. The old name for herself, the use of which triumphed over that of all others, was Yamato. Originally the name of the province where the seat of Government was at an early date established, it has always appealed to Japanese patriotic sentiment, and it survives to-day in such expressions as *Yamato-kotoba*, the Japanese language, and *Yamato-damashii*, the spirit of Japan, and therefore of a Japanese. But the name Japan (or, as the Japanese pronounce it, *Nihon* or *Nippon*), which has practically superseded it, and all other names, is of Chinese origin. Long before Europe heard of the name through Marco Polo the Chinese called the country Ji-păn, or the ' origin of the

sun ', in allusion to its geographical position to the
east of China; and when Japan borrowed her
written language from China she, either unconsciously, or in deference to the great country whose
influence she was accepting, or, it may be, because
Chinese was then the fashion, adopted this Chinese
name. That, in face of an influence so overwhelming, Japan should have developed, as she
did, politically, and socially, on lines so original,
and so little like those of China, says a great deal
for the adaptive genius, and the racial vigour of her
people.

There still remain one or two points to which it
may be well to draw attention. We have seen how
insignificant Japan's foreign trade had become in
the closing years of the long period of her seclusion.
Her internal trade was also conducted under dis-
couraging circumstances. Under the feudal system
there was no such thing as free and unrestricted
movement of the population. The people of one
district could not mix freely with those of another.
The territory of each daimiate, or clan, was looked
upon as a sort of local preserve, into which the
intrusion of strangers was discouraged, even when
not expressly forbidden. And it was obviously not
easy for trade to do what was denied to individuals,
and penetrate the rigid barriers which separated
each clan from its neighbours. Nevertheless, in
spite of feudal restrictions, a considerable internal
trade was carried on by means of clan guilds,
whose operations extended beyond provincial

limits, and were conducted through the medium
of large towns like Ōsaka, which, then even more
than now, was the business centre of the country.
Trade was also hampered by the scarcity of
good roads, and the almost complete absence of
wheeled traffic. The few chief high roads, such
as the Tōkaidō and Nakasendō, which connected
Kiōto and Yedo by the sea-coast, and through the
central ranges of hills, respectively, were kept in
good order for the purpose of the daimiōs' journeys
to and from Yedo, if for no other reason. But the
other roads were little better than tracks. The
transport of commodities, and indeed also of
persons, overland was effected by means of pack-
horses and coolies, palanquins being used by the
wealthier classes.

There was also another feature of feudalism
which interfered with the development of communications and of trade. This was the position
of the farmer. In the province of Satsuma, besides
the ordinary farming class, there were *samurai*
farmers, and similarly in certain districts of the
province of Mito there was a special class of
yeoman farmers, who enjoyed some of the privileges of the *samurai*. But throughout the country
generally, the bulk of the agricultural class consisted of peasant farmers who, while cultivating
their land on conditions similar to what is known
in Europe as the *métayage* system, were in many
respects little better than serfs. The peasant farmer
could not leave his holding and go elsewhere,

as he pleased ; nor could he dispose of his interest in it, though there is reason to think that the law in this respect was sometimes evaded. He was subjected to certain restrictions both in regard to the nature of the crops to be cultivated and their rotation, and in the sale of his produce he was hampered by the action of the clan guilds. But if he belonged in a sense to the land, the land also in a sense belonged to him, and if he was transferable with it when it passed into the possession of another feudal proprietor, he was, on the other hand, under the feudal form of ownership which existed, practically free from disturbance in his holding so long as he paid his rent when it was due, and other imposts when they were exacted.

It should be mentioned also that the country suffered greatly both from the confused condition of the paper currency and from debased coinage. More than two-thirds of the daimiates had paper currencies of their own, and in many cases different issues were in circulation together. This paper money, too, was of various kinds. There were gold notes, silver notes, *sen* notes, notes representing fixed amounts in copper, brass, and iron cash, and rice notes, representing definite quantities of rice, and used in the payment of taxes, which were chiefly levied in kind ; and there were also what were called ' credit notes ', representing gold, silver, cash, or rice, as the case might be. A similar condition of things prevailed in fourteen of the *hatamoto* territories. Besides these different provincial paper currencies, there were the Government coin and paper issued by the Shōgunate, and much of the former was debased. The extent of this monetary confusion may be realized from the fact that according to an official estimate the number of different paper currencies in circulation a year or two after the Restoration was no less than 1,600.[1] It was intensified by the erroneous ideas then held as to the proper ratio between gold and silver, and between these two metals and copper, which enabled the foreign trader to make unexpected profits, and caused great loss to the country. The two classes on which the evils resulting from this state of things bore most heavily were the military class and the farmer. And other economic causes were working in the same direction, so that at the time of the opening of the country there was much distress and discontent.

The Japanese of those days seem to have had the same passion for sight-seeing and holiday-making as those of to-day. The visit of the first United States representative to Yedo for his audience of the Shōgun gave an opportunity to the population of that city for indulging their sight-seeing propensities. In his diary Harris describes the crowds which assembled on that occasion. He estimated the number of spectators at about 185,000. All the way from the outlying

---

[1] See History of Currency, published in *Kwampō* (Japanese official Gazette) in 1886 : translated by E. A. Griffiths and J. H. Gubbins.

suburb of Shinagawa to his lodgings near the castle, a distance of some four miles, the procession moved, he tells us, in a stillness which was impressive. The only sound was that made by the police in keeping the mass of people in their places; the silence of such a vast multitude struck him as having something appalling in it. The streets were packed with people standing in lines five deep on each side. There were also people in balconies, and on the tops of houses. The same dense crowds on ceremonial occasions, and their orderly behaviour, are noticed by the foreign traveller now.

Before leaving this portion of our subject, it may be well to restate briefly the position of things when Perry arrived. He found a highly organized community excelling in arts, industries and agriculture, wedded to ceremonial, and permeated by Chinese ideas, with a gift for imitation happily controlled by assimilative genius, and independence of character, and enjoying a system of government very cumbrous, and obscure, and quite unique of its kind. The central authority was nominally vested in a shadowy personage in Yedo, whose exact relationship to a still more shadowy personage in Kiōto it was not easy to determine. There was a feudal system under which the daimiōs ruled their own territories, or under Shōgunate supervision, those of their neighbours, certain localities, including what were known as the Shōgun's dominions, being reserved for the direct administration of the Yedo Government, and the central authority was exercised by means of Councils of State, and of a vast assemblage of executive and judicial officers. This central authority was weak, and growing weaker, an uneasy feeling was abroad, and the first signs of the troubles which culminated in the downfall of the Shōgunate were beginning to show themselves. Clan jealousies and feudal restrictions hindered national progress in many directions, there was much distress and discontent, and the currency of the country was in a state of great confusion. Foreign intercourse was confined to the Chinese and Dutch traders visiting Nagasaki, and, when it was not Chinese, Dutch was the medium of communication with the outside world.

CHAPTER II

THE ESTABLISHMENT OF TREATY RELATIONS
WITH FOREIGN POWERS

FOR many years after the edict of 1636 had closed Japan to all but a few Dutch and Chinese traders, it was only at very rare intervals that any other foreign vessel broke in upon her seclusion. But at the end of the eighteenth century the situation began to change, and before the first half of the nineteenth century was over new forces had come into play, making it difficult for Japan to adhere to her fixed policy of isolation. Russia was moving southwards to join her frontiers with those of Japan ; America's activity was shown by the movements of her shipping in the Pacific, and the appearance of her whalers in Japanese waters on their way to and from the Sea of Okhotsk ; while France and England were pushing their interests in the south of China in a manner which indicated that the extension of their operations to Japan was only a question of time. The trend of affairs was perceived by the Dutch. They were witnesses to the increasing frequency of the visits of foreign vessels, in connexion with which their good offices were usually required ; they knew of the growing impatience of Europe and America ; and they warned Japan that the moment was approaching when the barriers she had

raised against the outside world could no longer
be maintained with safety to herself.

These visits of foreigners were of various kinds;
some more or less accidental, as those of distressed
or shipwrecked navigators; some half-serious, as
those made with the avowed object of restoring
to their homes Japanese castaways, and the
secret hope of perhaps obtaining some advantage
in the shape of trading facilities in return; in
others again there was the declared design of
putting an end to Japan's seclusion. The two last
categories are those which claim our attention,
both from the special interest attaching to them,
and also because they form not unimportant links
in the chain of events which led ultimately to the
establishment of foreign intercourse on a treaty
basis.

After a time the method of dealing with the
visits of foreign vessels seems to have become more
or less stereotyped. If they came to Nagasaki,
they were told that Japanese law only permitted
trade with the Dutch and Chinese, and if they
came elsewhere, they were told to go to Nagasaki.
A very clear discrimination was exercised between
merchant vessels and warships. To the former
scant courtesy was shown, and they might think
themselves lucky if they were not fired upon, or
if their crews escaped harsh treatment. But
warships were treated with more respect. They
were rarely fired upon. They were towed into and
out of harbour free of charge by Japanese boats,

and they were supplied with provisions for which no money was accepted. In other respects the procedure observed was much the same. As soon as a foreign vessel had anchored, or even before she had done so, boats surrounded her. A letter in Dutch (or in Dutch and French) couched in the usual formulas, was handed on board in a cleft bamboo, and a ring, or sometimes a double ring, of guard-boats prevented all communication with the shore. Everything on board came under keen observation ; many questions were asked, and the answers carefully noted down ; but all counter-questions were evaded, and with the first favouring breeze the unwelcome guest was speeded on her way.

It was probably the Russian visits which first opened the eyes of the Yedo Government to the inconveniences of the policy of seclusion. Saghalien was held by the two countries in a sort of joint possession without any boundary line, and uncertainty existed in regard to the ownership of the Kuriles, most of which were claimed by Russia. The proximity of these islands, moreover, to the Russian mainland increased the possibilities of a collision. So it may be convenient to begin with the first Russian attempt to establish relations with Japan.

In the year 1792 a Russian lieutenant named Laxman arrived in a harbour on the north coast of Yezo. Here he passed the winter, and in the summer of the following year sailed round to

Hakodaté. He was charged with a mission from the Empress Catherine to hand over to the Japanese Government the crew of a Japanese vessel, which had been wrecked in 1780 on one of the Aleutian islands then belonging to Russia, and he was instructed to utilize this opportunity to establish friendly relations. But the Japanese authorities at Hakodaté had no idea of entering into any negotiations of the kind. To have done so would in all probability have meant signing their own death-warrants. They explained to the Russian commissioner that by the law of Japan his life, and those of all the Russians on board his vessel, were forfeit for coming there, as the only port in Japan not closed to foreigners was Nagasaki. But as they had come on an errand of mercy, and had saved the lives of Japanese, their fault would be pardoned. They must, however, return to Russia at once, and come to Nagasaki, if they came again. As for the shipwrecked crew, they might leave them, or keep them, as they liked, for they were regarded as belonging to the place to which their destiny had carried them.

When a second mission under the leadership of a chamberlain named Résanoff was dispatched some years later, the advice of the Japanese was followed, and it came to Nagasaki. The reception given, however, was not encouraging. The unlucky chamberlain was put into a caged enclosure, and he returned without having effected anything. On his way back to Russia he conducted a raid on some Japanese islands in the North, in revenge for the rough treatment he had experienced.

In May 1811 Lieutenant Golownin was sent to survey the Kuriles in the Russian frigate *Diana*. This at least is the Russian statement. Probably he had a roving commission, in the execution of which much depended on circumstances. Whether the local Japanese knew the reason for his presence, or would have understood or respected it had they known it, is very doubtful, as doubtful indeed as the nationality at that time of many islands in those northern latitudes. But at any rate they remembered Résanoff's raid ; and here was an opportunity for reprisals. So Golownin was enticed on shore and captured. Like Résanoff, he was put into a sort of cage, but he was otherwise not unkindly treated, and in the summer of the following year he was released and taken on board the *Diana*, which had come to look for him.

In dealing with the visits of British vessels it may be useful to refer in passing to the few cases which occurred before the nineteenth century.

In 1673, during the reign of Charles II, and fifty years after the English trade with Japan, which only lasted ten years, had been discontinued, an English ship, the *Return*, came to Japan and asked for permission to trade. Owing, it is said, to Dutch intrigues this permission was refused on the ground that the English king had married a Portuguese princess, and that the Portuguese were the enemies of Japan.

From that date till the beginning of the nineteenth century only two British ships visited Japan. One was the *Argonaut,* a merchant vessel engaged in the Alaska fur trade. She put into a harbour on the west coast of Japan in 1791, and tried to trade, but was warned off. The other was H.M.S. *Providence,* which visited Yezo a year or two later, and was civilly treated by the authorities.

In 1803 an English merchantman, the *Frederick,* was sent to Nagasaki from Calcutta with a cargo of goods, but she was refused admittance to the harbour, and was compelled to leave at once.

Five years later, England being then at war with Holland, which had become a part of the French Empire, H.M.S. *Phaeton* found herself in the neighbourhood of Japan in need of supplies, and resorted to an artifice to obtain them. She hoisted the Dutch flag, and stood into the harbour of Nagasaki. She was boarded by two men from the Dutch factory, who were promptly made prisoners. Through them and the superintendent of the factory the commander eventually received the supplies he needed, payment for which was declined, and he was allowed to leave unmolested. On this occasion the local authorities were blamed for not having everything in readiness to meet force by force, and several Japanese officials committed *harakiri.*

In the summer of 1813 the same superintendent, whose name was Hendrick Doeff, went on board one of two ships, the *Charlotte* and *Mary*, which came into Nagasaki flying, as the *Phaeton* had done, the Dutch flag, and showing a private Dutch signal. On arriving on board he found that he had fallen into a trap, and that the ships were British, and not Dutch. He was also astounded to learn that Holland had been taken by the French, and Java, whence his instructions reached him, by the English; and that the Governor at Batavia was Sir Stamford Raffles, who had sent these vessels in charge of two commissioners. These were Dr. Ainslie, whose opinion of the Japanese has already been quoted, and a Mr. Waardenaar, a former superintendent of the Déshima factory. In these difficult circumstances Doeff showed great courage. When asked to obey the instructions of the new Governor of Java, he refused to do so, on the ground that they came with orders from the Government of a colony in possession of the enemy, and that neither Japan, nor the Dutch factory there, was in any way affected by what might have taken place in Java. It would probably have gone hard with the English ships if the Japanese had got wind of the situation, but they were saved by the friendship between Doeff and Waardenaar. The fact that the ships were not Dutch was kept secret, the trading transactions followed the usual course, and the vessels sailed on the return voyage to Java, leaving Dr. Ainslie behind as physician to the factory.

The fluctuating character of the relations of the

Dutch and English about that time puzzled the Japanese a good deal. This was only natural, for owing to the course of events in Europe these relations were for some years rather involved. During the continuance of hostilities between the two countries the Dutch communications between Java and Japan were maintained with difficulty by the charter of vessels of other nationalities, and were frequently interrupted for long periods. Between 1810 and 1813 no ships reached Nagasaki from Batavia, and on the occasion when the above-quoted incident occurred the Dutch factory had been without news for several years.

In the course of the following year (1814) Sir Stamford Raffles made another attempt to reopen intercourse with Japan, sending the *Charlotte* again to Nagasaki with a Dutch agent on board. But the attempt was unsuccessful.

Four years later, in 1818, Captain Gordon sailed up the Bay of Yedo in a small brig of sixty-five tons. He explained that he had come to ask for leave to bring to Japan a cargo of goods for sale. The officials who came on board insisted on the rudder being unshipped and taken on shore,[1] and the removal of the ship's arms and ammunition. This having been done, various questions were put through interpreters speaking Dutch, some words of Russian, and a little English. The visitors were especially anxious to know if the

[1] The practice of removing a ship's rudder was not confined to Japan.

vessel belonged to the East India Company, and
if the English were again friends with the Dutch.
On the subject of trade they had but one answer
now familiar to our merchants : it was impossible.
Some trifling presents were offered to them but
declined, and eventually the rudder and other
things were restored, and thirty boats towed the
vessel out of the bay.

In 1845 H.M.S. *Samarang,* a surveying vessel,
called at Nagasaki to ask for supplies. These were
given readily, but no payment was accepted for
them.

The last British ship to visit Japan before intercourse was reopened was another surveying vessel,
H.M.S. *Mariner.* She came in 1849 to Uraga, the
port visited by Perry four years later. The usual
letter was handed on board, and the captain was
asked not to cruise in the bay, but as he kept
on his course, the Japanese officials gave way, and
boats towed the ship to an anchorage ; and they
towed her out again, when, a few days after, she
went away.

The French seem to have made only one attempt
to establish friendly relations before their treaty
negotiations of 1858. This was in 1845. In that
year Admiral Cécille visited Nagasaki with two
ships, but he left without having succeeded in his
object.

We now come to the visits of American vessels.
Though mostly later in date than those we have been
considering, they showed a more serious purpose.

The question of establishing commercial relations with Japan had occupied public attention in the United States for more than twenty years before Perry's arrival in 1853. Both in official and business circles the matter had been much discussed. A resolution in favour of a mission being sent to Japan had been proposed in the House of Representatives. And as early as the year 1832 the United States Government had sent to Commodore Roberts, then in command of the American squadron in Chinese waters, instructions regarding a mission to Japan ' for the purpose of opening a trade ', which were to be acted upon if he thought advisable. If he decided to undertake this mission, he was to charter a private vessel, and letters of credence, in which the proper title of the Emperor was to be inserted, when ascertained, were furnished to him. In view of the defiant attitude adopted by Japan, and the reception usually accorded to unarmed vessels, it is hardly surprising that it was not considered advisable to act on these instructions.

Apart from the desire to forestall the French and English in gaining a footing in Japan—a point to which the United States Government attached some importance—the execution of the new and vigorous policy decided upon at Washington was doubtless hastened by the harsh treatment received on various occasions by the crews of American whalers wrecked on the coasts of Yezo and neighbouring islands, and by the experience of the

Morrison in 1837. This was a British merchant vessel, called after a well-known missionary in China, and chartered by an American mercantile house at Macao, for the purpose of restoring to their country seven shipwrecked Japanese. The *Morrison* was received with undisguised hostility. She was not allowed to communicate with the shore, and she was twice fired upon, first in Yedo Bay, where she arrived, and afterwards at Kagoshima.

In 1845 the *Mercator*, an American whaler, rescued some Japanese sailors at sea and took them to the Bay of Yedo. On anchoring she was surrounded by several hundred armed boats, and deprived of her arms and ammunition. After a detention of three days, orders for her release came from Yedo. But the captain was told that Japanese castaways could only be returned through the Chinese and Dutch, and that in future no more Japanese would be received under similar circumstances.

In the same year Commodore Biddle endeavoured under instructions from Washington to open relations with Japan. He came with two men-of-war, for by this time the United States Government had evidently realized the futility of trying to negotiate with unarmed vessels. Avoiding Nagasaki, as Commodore Perry did later on, and probably for the same reasons, he anchored in Yedo Bay, and at the request of the Japanese explained in writing the reason for his visit. But his mission was a failure. The Yedo Government, in a written reply, refused definitely to enter into trading relations, and with this answer Commodore Biddle withdrew.

Four years later the American man-of-war *Preble* was sent to Nagasaki to fetch away the shipwrecked crew of a whaler. She had some difficulty in accomplishing her object, which was only effected after a show of force. It was this incident, perhaps, which led to the procedure subsequently followed by the Japanese in all cases of shipwrecked foreigners. They were handed over at Nagasaki to the Dutch, who forwarded them to Batavia, whence they were eventually repatriated.

In no way discouraged by the result of Commodore Biddle's visit, the United States Government persevered in their policy of opening Japan to foreign trade. In 1851 instructions with that object were sent to Commodore Aulick on the China station, together with a letter from President Fillmore addressed to the Emperor of Japan. For some reason which does not appear these instructions were not acted upon, but in the following year the matter was again taken up; fresh credentials were prepared; and Commodore Perry received orders to proceed to Japan on a mission which assumed almost the dimensions of a naval expedition.

The objects of his mission were explained by the State department to be threefold: to make an arrangement for the more humane treatment of American sailors who might be shipwrecked on the coasts of Japan ; to obtain the opening of one or more harbours as ports of call for American vessels, and the establishment of a coal dépôt; and to secure permission for trade at such ports as might be opened.

No secrecy surrounded the intentions of the United States. They were known in Europe as well as in America. Macfarlane, writing in London in 1852, says, with some exaggeration perhaps : ' The attention of the whole civilized world is now fixed on the American expedition.' What Europe knew the Dutch of course knew, and through them the Japanese.

The late Count Katsu Awa in his book *Kai-Koku Kigen*, ' The commencement of the opening of the country,' reproduces a communication addressed in the summer of 1852 by the out-going and incoming superintendents of the Dutch factory at Déshima to the Governor of Nagasaki. In this the strength of the American naval forces under Commodore Aulick in Chinese waters is mentioned ; also the rumour that Commodore Perry was to replace Commodore Aulick, that the American squadron was to be largely reinforced, and that the new Commodore would proceed to Japan with an expedition in the coming spring, or possibly a little later, all preparations for landing a force, if necessary, having been made. The Governor's report to Yedo asking for leave to receive this communication, which is given in the same work, states that this step was taken only at the repeated request of the factory superintendents, who represented the matter as being of urgent importance for Japan, and drew attention to the fact that the information had come a long way, direct from the Governor of the Dutch East Indies. The Governor of Nagasaki adds that he had at first, in accordance with the law of Japan, declined to receive the communication, but had finally consented to refer the matter to Yedo. In another report, presented by officials entrusted with the defence of the coast, it is pointed out that the communication from the superintendents, though addressed to the Governor of Nagasaki, is drawn up in the form of a memorandum, and not a letter. This is held to diminish its importance, and the contents, it is suggested, may be treated as what they profess to be, namely, mere rumour. Nevertheless, the possibility of an attempt to establish commercial relations being shortly made by some foreign country or other ought not to be overlooked. Reference is also made to the Dutch having previously advised the relaxation of the restrictions placed on foreign trade. Their attitude is regarded as puzzling, since they would be the first to suffer by the change ; and it is hinted that the English, ' who have conquered more than half the world and whose orders the Dutch have at one time obeyed,' may possibly be at the bottom of the whole business.

Permission to receive and transmit the document was granted by the Yedo Government on the understanding that it was to be treated simply as a statement of what was rumoured, and that the superintendents of the factory should be informed accordingly.

The action of the local authorities on this occasion shows how strict were the orders relating to foreign intercourse. It reveals at the same time no little anxiety in the Japanese official world, which doubtless felt that the country was confronted with a situation more serious than any it had yet been called upon to face.

On July 8, 1853, Commodore Perry with four men-of-war anchored in Uraga harbour. The letter from the President with which he was entrusted dwelt on the advantages to be derived by both countries by the establishment of commercial intercourse. His instructions were to obtain the facilities desired by persuasion, if possible, but if necessary by force, and there is evidence to show that he was ready, if authorized to do so, to take such strong measures as the occupation of territory to effect his object. With his arrival the Shōgun steps upon the scene under a new title, that of Tycoon (or Great Lord). This, a term first used in correspondence with Corea, is the word chosen to designate the Shōgun in the earlier treaties and in official correspondence, and is the name by which he was commonly known to foreigners until the Restoration fifteen years later. Once or twice, however, in treaties and correspondence, he is also called *Kunshiu*, sovereign or ruler, a term never applied to the Mikado, for whom a loftier designation was reserved.

Perry was asked by the Japanese at Uraga to go to Nagasaki, this being, he was told, the only place where foreign ships were allowed to come. He refused, and asked for an interview on shore, at which he could deliver the letter he had brought. After a few days' negotiation the Japanese gave way. The interview on shore was granted, and Perry delivered the President's letter, and his own credentials as envoy. In the formal receipt given to him it was admitted that the letter had only been accepted under compulsion.

The envoy also handed in a letter from himself. The vigorous terms in which this was couched must have been as embarrassing to the Japanese translators as they were surprising, even in their softened Japanese form, to the ministers who read it. For he said, amongst other things which must have seemed somewhat unusual as coming from an envoy in those days, that he was there to receive a written assurance that Japan would treat humanely the crews of American vessels wrecked on her coasts, or driven by stress of weather into her harbours. He pointed out the folly of persistence in the present policy of seclusion, and the importance of avoiding a quarrel. Great warships were on their way from his country to Japan. For these he had not waited, preferring to show his friendly intentions by coming with only four small vessels. He would return, he added, next spring with a larger squadron, and hoped that before then the Japanese Government would have decided to adopt the just and friendly policy indicated in the President's letter. We are prepared, therefore, for the complaint of the Japanese, in the course of the later negotiations of the following year, that the Americans were not long-suffering, like the Dutch and Russians, but quick-tempered, and did not understand the principles of benevolence and good faith—two, it may be noted, of the five cardinal virtues adopted by Japan from the moral code of China.

On July 17, three days after the interview, Perry sailed for the Loochoos, where he had called on his way to Japan. These islands professed a sort of double allegiance to China and Japan, and as the Japanese had made no attempt to enforce in them their policy of seclusion, they served as a convenient base of operations.

In December of the same year Perry received a letter from the Governor-General of the Dutch East Indies, written at the request of the Japanese Government, telling him of the Tycoon's death having occurred soon after the receipt of the President's letter, and asking him to postpone his return to Japan as everything there was in confusion. Perry in his reply thanked the Governor-General for the news, but announced no change in his plans.

On February 12, 1854, he arrived in Japan again, this time with six ships, and on the following day sailed up the Bay of Yedo and anchored at a spot twelve miles above Uraga. He was urged by the Japanese to go to Uraga, or Kamakura, and hold a conference there. This, however, he declined to do, and on the 25th he moved further up the bay, anchoring off Kanagawa, then a small posting town on the Tōkaidō, the high road leading from Yedo to Kiōto through the maritime provinces. The Japanese then proposed that the conference should take place at Yokohama, a village quite close to Kanagawa, and opposite to the squadron's place of anchorage. To this Perry agreed, and about a month later his negotiations were brought to a successful issue by the signature of the Treaty of the 31st of March,[1] which opened the ports of Shimoda and Hakodaté to American vessels, the former at once, the latter at the end of a year. From the time of this treaty the Shōgun figures under two titles. To foreigners he appears as Tycoon ; to the Japanese he remains the Shōgun.

In the following September additional regulations [2] dealing with the limits within which excursions might be made at the two open ports, and other minor points, were agreed upon at Shimoda ; and in February, 1855, the ratifications of the treaty were exchanged at the same place.

This treaty, it should be noted, was not a regular commercial treaty, like those of later date. It was an agreement for the concession of certain limited facilities for navigation, and facilities of

[1] Appendix 1.   [2] Appendix 2.

a still more limited character for trade, which simply amounted to this, that an American vessel might, through the medium of the local authorities, dispose of cargo at two Japanese ports, and obtain cargo there in exchange. In other words, what trade there might be would be done, under the supervision of Japanese local officials, by a supercargo on board of a vessel, and not by American merchants on shore. It provided very fully for cases of shipwrecked or distressed vessels, and it contained an unconditional most favoured nation clause, but it did not concede even the right of residence. If, however, it was far from granting all that was wanted, it was a step, and, under the circumstances, a long step, in the desired direction ; the express stipulation for treatment different from that accorded to Dutch and Chinese traders placing foreign relations at once on an altered, and a more dignified, footing.

According to the account of the discussions given in Count Katsu Awa's book already mentioned the Japanese negotiators took credit to themselves for having conceded so little, besides making it appear that they had conceded even less. In their report on the treaty to the Yedo Government they are careful to mention that a memorandum on the subject of the trade regulations agreed to between America and China was handed in with the suggestion that a beginning might be made on this basis. 'But we pointed out,' they go on to say, 'that nothing was known about foreign trade in Japan, and that, therefore, it would be difficult to allow it. The chief point the Americans had raised was the humane treatment of their countrymen. This we had taken into special consideration, and had agreed to furnish ships with supplies, but on the question of trade, which is conducted for profit, and at the traders' own risk, we were not prepared with an immediate answer. Since then the matter has not been mentioned.' The negotiators also prided themselves on the fact that a settlement had been reached between themselves alone and Perry, without any answer being given to the President's letter, and without the members of the council being called upon to affix their seals to any document. This they thought was a worthy upholding of Japan's dignity.

The choice of open ports was unfortunate. Hakodaté was selected because of its convenience for American whaling vessels frequenting the Sea of Okhotsk. It had nothing else to recommend it, for the extensive coal deposits since worked were not known of at that time, nor, with a fringe of population only on the south coast, could Yezo be regarded as offering great prospects for trade. As for Shimoda, there was nothing in its favour, except from the Japanese point of view. The harbour was bad, and the town stood at the end of a wooded peninsula, shut in on every side but that facing the sea by ranges of hills, and remote from high roads and markets.

The praise bestowed on Perry for the firmness, patience, and tact displayed in his negotiations was certainly deserved. As his correspondence with the United States Admiralty shows, he had made up his mind to demand as a right the courtesy due by international usage, to suffer no petty annoyances to be inflicted on him, and to jealously maintain the dignity of the American flag. He would allow no guard-boats to be stationed near his ships, nor was any one, except those who came on business, allowed on board. His initial advantage was scored when on his first visit he persuaded the Japanese to receive the letter he had brought. But there is no doubt that his diplomacy was assisted very largely by the weakness and confusion existing in Japan. In spite of the brave appearances kept up, both the Yedo Government and the Court at Kiōto were overawed by the force with which Perry's demands were backed. This they felt powerless to resist. All that they could do was to try to gain time ; to postpone the evil day, Micawber-like, as long as possible, in the hope that something might turn up. And so we see them in the course of the negotiations falling back on the argument, already urged through the Dutch, that the pressure of State business caused by the death of the late ruler and the appointment of his successor, made it impossible for the Government to attend to anything else ; when this excuse did not answer, expressing their readiness to give supplies to vessels, but not

to permit any closer intercourse ; then suggesting
Nagasaki as the only port of call for some years ;
putting forward the excuse that so important
a matter could not be settled without reference
to Kiōto ; and finally, when the treaty had
become a *fait accompli*, asking that the appointment of a consul should be held over for five years.

The signature of Perry's treaty was shortly
followed by the conclusion of arrangements with
other powers—with the British, the Russians, and
the Dutch.

First in order comes the British convention.
This was negotiated at Nagasaki in October of
the same year, 1854,[1] by Admiral Stirling, who
came with a squadron of four vessels, and it was
ratified a year later. The Crimean War had
broken out, and the British Government, who were
aware of the efforts of Russia to effect an understanding with Japan, were anxious that British
ships should be at no disadvantage as regards
access to Japanese harbours. The convention
simply opened the two ports of Nagasaki and
Hakodaté to British vessels for the purpose of
supplies and refitting ; and, as in the case of Perry's
treaty, no right of residence was conferred. The
omission of Shimoda may mean that its useless-
ness even as a port of call had already been
recognized. The last article contains the singular
provision that after the ratification of the convention ' no high officer coming to Japan should

[1] Appendix 3.

alter it '. This was evidently intended to place
on record the fact that the terms of the convention
represented the high-water mark of Japanese concessions. Another curious feature is the exception
made in the most favoured nation clause that this
was not to apply to ' the advantages accruing
to the Dutch and Chinese from their existing
relations with Japan '. The American negotiator
had, as we have seen, expressly stipulated for
treatment in the matter of trade different from
that accorded to the subjects and vessels of the
two countries in question. The British Admiral
was not concerned with trade at all.

When ratifications were exchanged, the meaning
of certain articles of the treaty was more clearly
set forth in a supplementary document.[1] In this
was recorded the general right of ships of war,
as distinct from merchant vessels, to enter ports
of friendly powers, but it was added that the right
would not be exercised in Japanese waters without
necessity, or without offering proper explanations
to the imperial authorities.

Four months later the Russian admiral, Poutiatine, concluded a treaty at Shimoda,[2] the ratifications being exchanged in the following year.

This was his second visit to Japan for that
purpose. He had previously (in August, 1852)
gone to Nagasaki, and the Russians made much of
this point, as showing their respect for the law
of Japan. From Japanese sources we learn that

[1] Appendix 4.   [2] Appendix 5.

his visit on that occasion caused some consterna-
tion, for he came with four vessels. He said he
wished to go to Yedo, and had brought letters and
presents. The local authorities were afraid to
obey their standing orders, and send him away,
for fear he might go to Uraga. So they wrote
to Yedo asking for instructions. Should they
receive the letters, and tell him to go away, naming
a date when he might return for an answer ? If
they received the letters, what was to be done
with the presents ? If an interview was granted
to him, should ceremonial dress be worn; and how
big a suite might the admiral bring ? The reply
which came said : The letters might be received.
This, though contrary to the law of Japan,
seemed to be unavoidable. As for an answer, if
there was nothing about it in the letters, nothing
need be said, but if the Russians insisted on having
one, they might be told that the Government were
too busy to give it at once, but that it would be
sent later through the Dutch superintendent of the
factory. Poutiatine should be requested to leave.
They should be civil to the Russians, but careful
to maintain the dignity of the country. With
regard to the question of dress, they need not wear
ceremonial garments if an interview took place ;
ordinary attire would meet the case.

On his second visit—this time to Shimoda in the
late autumn of 1854—Poutiatine came with only
one ship, and this he lost owing to a tidal wave.
But in the interval between the two visits Perry's

treaty, and also Stirling's, had been concluded, and this seems to have made all the difference in his reception. The treaty he signed in February, 1855, which opened the three ports of Shimoda, Hakodaté, and Nagasaki to Russian vessels, and the first two to Russian trade, was more on the lines of later treaties than the two preceding conventions. Russia's chief concern, according to the letters brought by Poutiatine, was for her frontier with Japan. This is the first subject mentioned. In the Kurile islands it was determined, but the boundary in Saghalien was left purposely undefined. The treaty is, moreover, in some respects bilateral, and the principle of exterritoriality, of which there is no mention in either the American or British convention, is recognized.

Additional articles [1] explaining the meaning of the treaty were signed at the same time, and a further supplementary treaty was negotiated by Poutiatine at Nagasaki in the autumn of 1857.[2]

The Dutch benefited very soon by the new direction given to foreign relations. The treaties made by America, Great Britain, and Russia had, as we have seen, left them in the undisturbed enjoyment of their trading privileges at Nagasaki. Perry had designedly overlooked that port, and the rights of the Dutch there had been carefully respected by the other negotiators. But the position into which they had drifted, so to speak,

[1] Appendix 6.   [2] Appendix 7.

in their eagerness for trade, was rendered almost intolerable by the humiliating restrictions which accompanied it. To name only a few of these, a gate and guard-house barred all passage over the bridge connecting Déshima with the mainland; no one was allowed out or in without a permit, nor, when allowed out, were the Dutchmen permitted to go anywhere without an escort. Any Christian books found on board ship, or in the possession of persons who had landed, were taken away and kept during the vessel's stay in port, or confiscated. Every one landing from a Dutch vessel was strictly searched, and could only come on shore at what was called 'the water-gate of Déshima' to distinguish it from the land-gate guarded by the Japanese; no Dutchman, even with an escort, was allowed to go beyond the limits of the town of Nagasaki, or to hold any communication with Japanese except through the recognized channels; and Dutch vessels were deprived of arms and ammunition, and were obliged to give hostages, before being supplied with boats to tow them into harbour. Some relaxation of these restrictions it was desired to obtain, and the concessions newly made to the three other powers gave the Dutch the needed opportunity.

In November, 1855, Mr. Donker Curtius, whose original title of factory superintendent had been raised to the more important one of Netherlands Commissioner in Japan, concluded with the local

authorities at Nagasaki what was termed a Preliminary Convention of Commerce.[1] The term is
a little misleading, for it was simply an arrangement for altering the conditions of Dutch residence
and trade at Nagasaki. Though never ratified,
it went into operation in the manner agreed upon,
and it was replaced by what was called a Treaty
of Commerce, but was in reality nothing more than
an expansion of the previous arrangement, negotiated by the same commissioner in January of
the following year.[2] By these two agreements the
Dutch position was materially improved. They
obtained full personal freedom ; exterritoriality
was formally recognized ; the commanders of
Dutch vessels were exempted from search by the
Customs ; communication with the Japanese,
except through certain channels, was no longer
forbidden ; Dutch women and children were
allowed to live in Déshima ; Dutch ships were
allowed to retain their arms and ammunition ;
both crews and vessels received better treatment ;
and the Dutch were allowed to send letters abroad
by Chinese and other vessels, and to correspond
with the commanders of foreign ships in the port
of Nagasaki.

When the ratifications of this treaty were exchanged, in October, 1857, certain additional articles
were agreed upon.[3] These gave to Dutch relations
with Japan for the first time more of the character
which distinguished those of other powers. Trade

[1] Appendix 8.   [2] Appendix 9.   [3] Appendix 10.

at Hakodaté as well as Nagasaki was permitted under regulations of the usual kind; most favoured nation rights were conceded ; limits within which excursions beyond the town of Nagasaki might be made were fixed; the custom of making presents, at stated times, to 'the Emperor and other great personages ', and, annually, to the local authorities, was abolished ; and the Dutch were allowed to practise in their houses, and at burying-places, ' *their own* or the Christian religion.' The curious wording of this last provision, occurring as it does in a document signed by the Dutch representative, and ratified by his Government, seems to prove that the Japanese had originally thought that the Dutch were not Christians, and that the Dutch had not discouraged the idea.

About the same time, the autumn of 1857, the orders in force with regard to trampling on Christian emblems were rescinded, the abolition of this practice being notified to the Netherlands commissioner by the local authorities of Nagasaki.

The advantages secured by the Dutch in this series of arrangements give some idea of the extent of the disabilities under which they previously laboured. There was still some difference between their position and that of other foreigners, but this only lasted a year or two. With the operation of the treaties of 1858 the nation which had prided itself on its exclusive trading privileges with Japan for more than two centuries came in on the same footing as other Western powers.

The American treaty had stipulated for the
appointment, at any time after the expiration of
eighteen months from the date of its signature,
of a consul-general to reside at Shimoda, provided
either of the two governments (or both, according
to the Japanese text) deemed such arrangement
necessary. Mr. Townsend Harris was selected
for the post, and arrived in Japan in August, 1856,
in an American man-of-war. This appointment
of a consular official was the point of all others
which had provoked opposition during Perry's
negotiations. With the course of events in China
during the previous fifteen years the Japanese
were tolerably familiar, for news of what was going
on reached them through the Chinese and Dutch.
They knew of the constant turmoil surrounding
foreign intercourse in the sister country, of the
disputes which had resulted in the opium war,
and the British occupation of Hong Kong, and
of the general effect of the activity of foreign
official agents. When driven at length to acquiesce
in the residence of a consular official in Japan,
they had hoped that this provision of the treaty
might remain a dead letter, and this expectation
was encouraged perhaps by the delay of eighteen
months arranged for in the treaty. It can readily
be imagined, therefore, how unwelcome the arrival
of Mr. Harris was. The Japanese begged him to
return, urging—and the Japanese version of
the treaty certainly supported this argument—
that it was intended that a consul should be

appointed only if difficulties arose. None had
arisen ; so a consul was not required. Besides,
the Dutch and Russians would ask for one too.
When these entreaties had no effect, they turned
to the commodore who had brought him, and asked
him to take him away. Their contention, however,
was not borne out by the American text, and
Mr. Harris remained to negotiate subsequently at
Yedo his treaty of 1858.

The United States Government were as fortu-
nate in the selection of their first representative in
Japan, as they had been in their choice of Commodore Perry. The task which confronted him was
one of peculiar difficulty, for he was the first foreign
agent to deal *on equal terms* with the Government
of Japan. In that capacity he had to bear the
brunt of obstruction so ingeniously and constantly
exercised that had he not been plentifully endowed
with patience, he must have relinquished his task
in despair. He had been forced upon the Japanese.
They retaliated by practically boycotting him.
He could get no trustworthy information ; if he
asked for anything, his request was either referred
to Yedo, which meant a delay of many weeks, or
he was told that it was contrary to the law of
Japan ; and his dispatches were unanswered
because ' it was not customary to reply to the
letters of foreigners '. To add to his difficulties, he
was for long periods without news from his Government, and neither he nor his secretary had received
any training for the special work they had to do.

The details of his long negotiations, which began as soon as he arrived, are recorded at length in his diary. Like Perry, he had brought a letter from the President of the United States. This he was determined to present to the Tycoon himself, and he requested an audience at Yedo for this purpose. The Japanese, on the other hand, wished him to deliver the letter at Shimoda, as Perry had done. He was also anxious to make some further arrangements in respect to residence and trade, in amplification of Perry's treaty. Several months having elapsed without any real progress being made in any of the matters under discussion, he was instructed to warn Japan that any attempt to evade treaty obligations would render it necessary for the United States Government to adopt strong measures. This threat, assisted doubtless by the success of the English and French forces in China, had the desired effect. In June, 1857,[1] he was able to report the signature of a convention opening Nagasaki (the port which Perry had thought it prudent to overlook) to American vessels, conceding the right of residence at Shimoda and Hakodaté, providing for the appointment of a vice-consul at the latter port, regulating the question of the exchange of American and Japanese currency, and affirming the principle of exterritoriality. Four months later he was received in audience by the Tycoon.

Long before his visit to Yedo the United States

[1] Appendix 11.

representative had recognized the desirability of concluding a convention with Japan on a much wider basis than that covered by the Perry treaty, even when amplified by his own convention of June, 1857. Accordingly on his arrival there he at once opened negotiations with the Japanese ministers on this subject. He found them more open to persuasion than before, a change of attitude due, partly at least, to the growing influence of Ïi Kamon no Kami, who not long afterwards became the Shōgun's chief minister. To his arguments that Japan had danger to fear from the aggressive policy of European powers, as instanced by the war then in progress in China ; that it was wiser for her to come to an understanding with him than to wait for demands from others which would immediately be backed up by force ; and that an arrangement satisfactory to the United States would probably be accepted by other powers, they yielded. The terms of the new treaty were finally settled in February, 1858, but it was decided to refer it before signature to Kiōto for the approval of the Throne.

There was no necessity for this reference. The supremacy of the Shōgun in all administrative matters is clearly laid down in the constitution, or arrangement, established in 1615.[1] Long custom had confirmed the rule then made. And before that date the Crown's concern in such matters had never extended beyond a formal

[1] Appendix 12.

recognition of accomplished facts. Moreover, the treaty had not yet been signed, so reference to Kiōto was in any case premature. But on the occasion of Perry's first visit the Shōgunate, in order to conceal its embarrassment, had revived the obsolete formality of imperial concurrence, extending at the same time its application. The same course was pursued now, and the minister who had taken the most prominent part in the negotiations, Hotta Bitchiū no Kami, was sent to Kiōto to obtain the imperial consent. Hayashi Daigaku no Kami had been sent a month previously to explain matters, but the court had signified its disapproval of the negotiations.

In June Hotta returned, having failed in his mission. Anti-foreign feeling was too strong. The discussions over the treaty in Yedo had been viewed with disfavour by the court party in Kiōto, and by the large majority of influential daimiōs, who welcomed any pretext for opposing the action of the Shōgunate. The leader in this opposition was Tokugawa Nariaki, ex-chief of the Mito branch of the Tokugawa family, and ex-prince of the clan of that name, a man of strong character and great ability, who had already made himself conspicuous by taking the side of the Kiōto Court party against his relative the Shōgun.

The signature of the treaty was accordingly postponed till September, on the understanding that, whatever happened, it should have precedence over that of any other, and the American nego-

tiator returned to Shimoda to await the result of
further overtures to Kiōto. Very soon after his
return, however, an American man-of-war arrived
with the news that the war in China had terminated,
and that the English and French ambassadors to
China were on their way to Japan to negotiate
treaties. He at once proceeded in this vessel to
Kanagawa, and urged from there by letter the
necessity for the immediate signature of the treaty.
His representations, assisted by the presence of
Ïi Kamon no Kami at the head of affairs, had the
desired effect, and without waiting any longer for
consent from Kiōto, the treaty was signed at
Kanagawa on board the American man-of-war
on July 29.[1]

The ice having been broken, other treaties
followed in rapid succession, all on the same
general lines, thus proving the correctness of the
opinion given by Harris that what was satisfactory to the United States would be acceptable to
other powers. The Dutch signed theirs on the
18th of August, the Russians on the 19th, the
British on the 26th, and the French on the 7th
of October. The British treaty was negotiated at
Yedo by Lord Elgin. All four followed more or
less closely the lines of the American convention.

[1] Appendix 11. Although the wording of the other four treaties
is not absolutely the same it has been thought unnecessary to
include them amongst the appendixes. Choice has been made of
the American treaty because it was the first, and became the
model for all the rest.

The new features of these treaties, which served as a model for later conventions, were the opening of additional ports, the establishment of a tariff, and the introduction of tonnage dues ; the concession of the right of travel anywhere in Japan to diplomatic agents and consul-generals ; the obligation, on the side of foreigners, to refrain from erecting fortifications or places of strength, and, on the Japanese side, to refrain from enclosing the foreign residential area ; a slight modification of the unilateral character which distinguished the previous treaties ; and an understanding in regard to revision. In other respects they merely confirmed, or amplified, the provisions of earlier arrangements. Thus, to quote a few instances, the right of appointing a consular agent at a particular port was expanded into general diplomatic and consular privileges, including the right to appoint a minister at Yedo ; for the port regulations of previous arrangements general trade regulations were substituted ; the right given the year before to the Dutch in regard to religious matters became a right to the free exercise of religion and the erection of places of worship ; the concession of exterritoriality was more explicitly defined, and was made to apply to civil as well as criminal jurisdiction ; and the prohibition of the importation of opium, mentioned in previous Dutch and Russian treaties, was confirmed.

It has been already explained how, in spite

of the statements to the contrary made in the report of the Japanese commissioners who signed the Perry treaty, certain trading facilities were granted by that instrument. But the treaty stipulation conceding the privilege in question remained a dead letter. One or two American vessels did call at Japanese ports, but no trade of any importance was carried on. Far-reaching in other respects as were the effects of the first treaties, the result, so far as trade was concerned, was insignificant. It was only after these earlier agreements had been amplified and expanded by the treaties of 1858, to which a fifth power, France, became also a party; after provision had been made for the residence of foreigners in treaty ports, within reach of domestic markets, for trade regulations, and for a tariff, that the way was finally cleared for the development of foreign intercourse and trade. The year 1858 is, therefore, an important date in the history of Japan's foreign relations.

In addition to enlarging the scope of foreign relations, and thus aiding the process of Japan's development, the new treaties conferred a great benefit by simplifying Japan's position, and replacing a number of scattered and complicated engagements, made at different times to meet different cases, by a series of practically uniform agreements. Modified later on by tariff changes, and supplemented from time to time by regulations regarding quarantine, travelling, and other matters, the treaties of 1858 governed Japan's foreign relations for over forty years. It is important to notice that the rights of residence and trade acquired under them by foreigners applied only to the so-called treaty ports, and that the right of travel, except by special permission not readily granted, did not extend beyond a certain area, known as 'treaty limits', in the neighbourhood of each port. The rest of the country remained closed as before—an arrangement which, however unpalatable to foreign residents, was, in the then temper of the Japanese people, a wise precaution. The limitation of facilities for commercial intercourse was moreover accentuated by the fact that the choice of treaty ports was not always the best that could have been made. Strongly opposed as the Japanese were to the establishment of any intercourse of a general kind, it was only natural that they should prefer to open places as far from markets as possible, and useless for other reasons, and that when, as in the case of Kanagawa and Hiōgo, they were driven to consent to better localities, they should seek to nullify the effects by selecting the worst sites available.

With the conclusion of the new treaties Japan's progress assumes a more definite shape. It had begun long before. The first seeds had been sown in the time when Dutch and Chinese traded under such difficulties at Nagasaki. The new ideas which then crept in, especially towards the end of that long period, when many earnest students of foreign things in Japan read Dutch and French, German and English books, had made an effect, not perhaps noticeable at the time. The study of ' Dutch Learning ', as it was called, which was a general term for all Western knowledge, was encouraged for official purposes by the Yedo Government, and had prepared the way for later changes by stripping them of the terror of the unknown. And so, when Perry signed the first treaty, many things came with a rush. The year which saw his treaty signed saw the issue of a decree removing the restrictions on the construction of Japanese vessels, which could once more trust themselves on the high seas. Twelve months later the position of the Dutch in Déshima ceased to be one of undignified confinement. Other changes affecting foreigners followed quickly. It is a striking fact, that with all their dislike to foreign intercourse, the Japanese in the course of five years from the date of Perry's treaty had entered into no less than thirteen elaborate agreements of one kind or another, not to speak of other arrangements of a less formal character.

CHAPTER III

IN the preceding chapter some account was given of the visits of foreign vessels during the fifty or sixty years preceding the advent of Commodore Perry, and of the circumstances attending the negotiation of the treaty of 1854. It was also shown how quickly, once the barrier of seclusion had been broken down, agreements with other foreign powers had followed, one on the heels of another; and the main features of these various agreements were explained.

Before leaving this part of our subject it may be useful to glance in passing at what the Japanese had been doing to keep the country closed to all foreigners, except the two nations which were allowed to trade at Nagasaki.

In consequence of the apprehensions aroused by the visits of foreign vessels, the Japanese Government, towards the end of the eighteenth century, decided to establish a system of coast defence. The duty of organizing and maintaining this system was entrusted to the daimiōs and hatamoto of maritime provinces, who were called upon to pay all the attendant expenses; but in districts ruled directly by the Shōgunate, such as those which included the ports of Uraga and Nagasaki, this duty was assigned to officials appointed from

Yedo for that purpose, and the expenditure for coast defence was defrayed by the Government, who recouped themselves for this outlay by levying contributions on the merchants of Yedo and Ōsaka.

Those who were thus made responsible for the protection of the coast were called *Kai-bo-gakari*, or coast defence commissioners, and stations in communication with each other were established at suitable points along the sea-board. The bay of Yedo, and its vicinity, the inland sea, and the harbours in Kiūshiū, including the immediate neighbourhood of Nagasaki, were places to which special attention was given. Although the duty of participating in the work of coast defence was at first limited to the feudal lords whose territories bordered on the sea, later on even those whose fiefs had no sea-board were ordered to lend assistance, in proportion to their resources, in the event of a foreign vessel arriving anywhere in the vicinity of their domains. The system was in force only in the spring and summer months, during the prevalence of the south-west monsoon. For the rest of the year the coast defence establishments went into winter quarters, since there was little likelihood of their services being required so long as the north-east monsoon lasted.

It is clear from the experience of foreign ships which accident or enterprise carried into Japanese waters, from the detailed instructions issued periodically from Yedo, and from the reports concerning the movements of foreign vessels appearing off the coast which were constantly being received from the local authorities, that there was no lack of vigilance in the working of the system of coast defence. But the manner in which the instructions were carried out seems to have varied to some extent from time to time according to the degree of apprehension existing in official circles at Yedo in regard to the intentions of foreigners. And in the instructions themselves we can discern the anxiety to evade responsibility, the tendency to face both ways, so typical of the Government of that day.

Two sets of these instructions, issued at different dates to the coast defence commissioners, are quoted in Mr. Kimura's *San-jiū-nen Shi*, or ' History of Thirty Years'. In the first, which was issued in 1806, two years after Résanoff's visit to Nagasaki, this visit is referred to, and the opinion is expressed that the Russian ship in question will not return, since she was told that her request for trade could not be granted, and that she was not to come again. The coast defence commissioners are nevertheless enjoined to be always on their guard. Whenever a foreign vessel is seen preparations for defence are to be made, and the militia assembled. If, it is added, the ship is Russian, steps are to be taken as quietly as possible for her departure. Vessels taking shelter from bad weather are to be given whatever supplies are needed, but should a ship refuse to leave when ordered to do so, she is to be driven away by force, in accordance with the orders issued in 1791.

The second of these instructions is dated 1842, five years after the *Morrison* incident. It begins as follows :—

' In the year 1819 orders were given that foreign vessels coming to Japan should be driven away without hesitation. But everything has now been revised, and the (Shōgun's) gracious wish has been expressed for a return to the system of government in the periods Kiōhō (1716–36) and Kwansei (1789–1801), and for the adoption of a benevolent administration in regard to all matters. Should foreign vessels which come for the simple purpose of asking for provisions, fire-wood, and water, be driven away, without the circumstances of the case being understood, such action may, it is considered, be interpreted as a hostile or retaliatory act towards all countries generally. Accordingly it is the (Shōgun's) gracious wish to revert to the humane policy in regard to the treatment of foreign vessels announced in the instructions issued in 1806.'

The order then goes on to say that a foreign vessel must in all cases be asked the reason for her visit ; it repeats what was said before, in the instruction already quoted, with regard to giving supplies to vessels in distress ; it enjoins upon those in charge of coast defence the exercise of constant vigilance and the avoidance of undue intimacy with foreigners ; and it ends with a warning against panic, and with the injunction, which we have heard before, that there must be no hesitation to use force if necessary.

It would appear from these instructions that at one time there was a disposition to refrain from pushing matters to extremity, and perhaps a wish to perform a disagreeable duty as pleasantly as possible, that afterwards a policy of stronger measures came into favour, and that finally more prudent views again prevailed. But these plausible exhortations to benevolence, emanating from a Government of distracted counsels, do not seem to have been intended very seriously, nor indeed, judging from subsequent incidents, to have had much effect. The system of coast defence, elaborate, but singularly ineffective, continued in operation even after the negotiation of Perry's treaty, and, if it failed to accomplish the object for which it was instituted, it probably did much to strengthen anti-foreign feeling throughout Japan.

In the brief remarks on Japanese history made in the opening chapter, it was stated that down to the year 1192, when Yoritomo was appointed Shōgun, the country was more or less under the personal rule of the Mikado. This statement expresses the general idea on the subject, and is convenient for marking the great change introduced by the establishment of feudalism; the transfer, that is to say, of the seat of power from Kiōto to the provinces, and of authority from the Court and Court nobles to the feudal nobility, as representatives of the military class. But it must not be taken too literally. As a matter of fact the personal rule of the Mikados ceased at a much earlier date.

Though instances of the usurpation of the imperial authority by the representatives of great houses occur before the introduction of the Great Reform in 645 A. D., the elimination of the sovereign from all active share in the work of government may be said to have begun with the rise to power of the Fujiwara family in the seventh century. From that time on, though the country was still ruled from the capital, the sovereign's influence in the administration grew less and less, until by the middle or end of the eighth century the Mikados were little more than puppets in the hands of the Fujiwara statesmen. For nearly five centuries, allowing, it should be explained, for the short interval in the twelfth century, during which the Taira family controlled the Court, the offices of regent (*Sesshō*), during the minority of the reigning Emperor, and of prime minister (*Kwambaku*), at other times, were hereditary in the Fujiwara family. If we look at the list of sovereigns who reigned during this period, and compare the average length of their reigns, and the number of abdications,[1] with those of the later period, between the establishment of feudalism in 1192, and the Restoration of 1868, the comparison—if shortness

[1] So common was the custom of abdication amongst Japanese sovereigns that many instances of three Mikados being alive at the same time occur in Japanese history, and occasionally the number rose to more. The language, moreover, has special words to designate the exact order of monarchs who have abdicated.

of reign and frequency of abdication may be regarded as proofs of the weakness of the sovereign's influence—is in favour of feudalism.   In other words the monarchical influence, judged by this criterion, was, if anything, stronger in the feudal period than before.   The average length of the reigns of forty emperors who occupied the throne during the four and a half centuries of Fujiwara supremacy, and the short Taira period, is only twelve years ; of these forty, no less than twenty-three abdicated after reigning for an average period of not more than nine years.   In the longer feudal period of nearly seven centuries which followed, there were thirty-seven sovereigns.   The average length of their reigns is over eighteen years ; but, while the frequency of abdication shows little variation, the average length of the reigns of the sovereigns who abdicated in the latter period rises from nine to fifteen years.   Further study of these reigns brings out other points.   We find that of the first twenty emperors who reigned during the period of Fujiwara ascendancy, that is to say, during the 250 years from the beginning of the eighth to the middle of the tenth century, only four were minors on their accession to the throne ; whereas in the latter half of the same period, including the short interval of Taira supremacy, there were no less than twelve.   We notice also that with the establishment of feudalism this tendency in favour of the accession of minors to the throne increased.   Of the first fifteen sovereigns

who occupied the throne after Yoritomo's appointment as Shōgun, only four (including one of only
seventeen), were not minors, and these youthful
sovereigns were mostly children under twelve, the
youngest being a baby of two years old. The same
feature, the large proportion of minors who came
to the throne, characterizes the Tokugawa rule.
Only one of the first nine emperors who succeeded
to the throne during this period was not a minor,
and he was a boy of only eighteen. It does not
seem unreasonable to associate such frequent instances of the occupation of the throne by minors
with a weak grasp of power by the sovereign, and
in this respect the comparison is in favour of
the earlier Fujiwara period, when, if reigns were
shorter, whether the sovereign abdicated or not,
and abdication was not less common than later on,
there were, at any rate, fewer cases of sovereigns
reigning as minors. The conclusion to which we
are brought is that so far as the weakness of the
position of the sovereign is concerned there is
not much to choose between the two periods,
the monarchy gaining in one respect what it lost
in another, and also that the withdrawal of the
sovereign from participation in the work of government was of very ancient date, beginning, not with
feudalism, but far back in Fujiwara times, and
gradually developing during the course of twelve
centuries into a fixed principle, which resulted in
feudalism and the dual form of government.

The frequency of abdication, and of the appoint-

ment of minors to the position of ruler of the
State, is even more noticeable in the case of the
Shōguns, down to the beginning of the seventeenth
century, than in that of the sovereigns of Japan ;
although it must be borne in mind that the abdication of a Shōgun did not mean quite the same
thing as the abdication of an Emperor. Some of
the former really did rule, and their abdication
did not necessarily signify the relinquishment
of their interest in the work of government. On
the contrary, it often meant a tighter grasp of
power, their influence in the administration being
greater after abdication than before. Of twenty-
five Shōguns succeeding Yoritomo who ruled, or
nominally ruled, from 1202 to 1603, no fewer than
sixteen were minors at the time of their appointment, and the number of abdications was the same.
When we come to the Tokugawa Shōguns, we find
a change in both respects. Of the sixteen Shōguns
of this line only four were minors when they were
appointed, and only five abdicated. This change
must not be taken as meaning that the personal
rule of these Shōguns was in reality more marked
than that of their predecessors—the Shōguns who
were controlled by the Hōjō regents, and those of
the Ashikaga line. It is, on the contrary, safer to
assume that the principle of figure-head government, to which we have previously referred, had
taken such firm root that neither abdication nor
the rule of minors made any difference to the
working of the administration.

It should be noted that the two features in the reign of sovereigns, and the rule of Shōguns, to which attention has been called as weakening the principle of personal government, were both part of the family system in its peculiar Japanese development. And a third factor, which also plays a conspicuous part in the social structure of Japan, lent its influence in the same direction. This was the custom of adoption. In Japan, as has already been explained, the family, and not the individual, is the unit of society. Everything centres round the family.[1] The individual has little importance except in his association with it, the continuity of the family being the thing which matters most. It is only natural that a state of things which is the normal condition of society at large should be reflected in governing circles. It will therefore be readily conceived that the failure of a direct heir in the imperial house, or in a line of Shōguns, presented no insoluble difficulty. It was a matter to be arranged by the Council of State, just as in less exalted spheres such questions were referred to the family council. So long as adoption could be relied on to provide a successor, the question of succession was greatly simplified, and the risk of friction very much reduced. In these considera-

---

[1] The importance of this fact comes out even in the case of legal punishments. The extinction of his family was the severest sentence which could be pronounced on a member of the military class. This was the sentence passed on the leaders of the raid on Kiōto in 1863.

tions we find the key to what to us seems the strikingly incongruous and artificial system of government evolved by the Japanese for themselves. That so often in the course of Japanese history abdication should have occurred, that the failure of direct heirs should have led to no difficulty, that, in the same way, the machinery of government should have worked smoothly on, whether the occupant of the throne, or the ruling Shōgun, was a minor, or not ; and that neither sovereign, nor Shōgun, should have taken an active part in State affairs, may seem to the Western observer unusual and even startling. To the Japanese mind there was nothing surprising about it. It was simply the normal condition of things to which every Japanese of that day, and his father before him, were accustomed. At the same time we must not overlook the peculiar prestige attaching at all times to the Throne. In spite of, and partly, too, because of, its early relinquishment of administrative power, it retained intact, together with its sanctity in the eyes of the people, the jealously-guarded prerogative of conferring Court dignities and empty titles, which never ceased to be objects of ambition to all the leading members of the feudal hierarchy. Thus, as has already been explained in the opening chapter, in its very aloofness from political life, in its having the shadow without the substance of power, lay the monarchy's greatest strength. This accounts for its hold on the people, and its unbroken survival, of which the Japanese nation is so proud.

An appreciation of the foregoing facts is necessary in order to understand the events which marked the closing years of the Tokugawa Shōgunate, and to rightly apprehend the course of internal affairs, which will occupy our attention in this and the succeeding chapter.

At the time of Perry's visit more than half of the country was practically under the direct rule of the Shōgunate, for in many of the lesser *fudai* daimiates little latitude was left to the clan authorities, even when the governors were not Tokugawa officials. The remainder of the country was governed by the feudal nobles, the degree of dependence on Yedo varying according to the situation and importance of the fief. Though the nominal allegiance of these daimiōs to the Shōgun remained unchanged, the influence of the central authority was gradually decreasing, especially in the south and west of the country, owing to the growing weakness of the Shōgunate.

During the twenty-nine years of the rule of the eighth Shōgun (1716–46), a slight relaxation of the anti-foreign policy which prevented the study of all Western learning had resulted in some knowledge of the Dutch language being acquired by those who wished to qualify as Dutch interpreters, and by doctors who were curious to know something of the methods of the West. But in this direction, as in that of trade, the Yedo Government pursued the same selfish course, being anxious to retain for their own benefit any advantage which could be derived from either. The principle on which they acted was to keep the people ignorant of everything relating to foreign countries and things. A different spirit was shown by some of the leading feudal nobles, notably those of Mito and Satsuma, who quietly encouraged for their own purposes the introduction of Western knowledge in regard to military matters, shipbuilding, and other things. But the country generally—thanks to the jealous and short-sighted policy of the Shōgunate—knew nothing of anything going on outside of Japan. This ignorance, so Mr. Shimada tells us, is strikingly apparent in the literature of those days, which he describes as being full of denunciation of foreigners, and extravagant laudation of everything Japanese.

Under conditions such as these, when everything appertaining to administration was being conducted strictly in accordance with Chinese ideas, it would have been surprising if the visits of foreign vessels, and the signature of the first treaties, had not produced much popular commotion. This was increased by the action of the Yedo Government. Had they, when Perry came in 1853, acted with the promptitude and decision they showed on the occasion of the Russian visit to Nagasaki in 1804, the nation, it is generally held, would have accepted their decision without demur, the Shōgun's au-

thority being ample to meet the case. And this
decision must have been in favour of the opening
of the country, for the simple reason that Japan
was not prepared for war. But the Shōgunate,
instead of taking the course expected of them
under the circumstances, referred the matter to the
Throne, and asked the advice of the feudal nobles.

The latter were as much embarrassed in coming
to a decision as the Shōgunate, and the memorials
giving the advice called for by the Shōgunate
showed little knowledge of the situation, nor can
they have given much assistance to the perplexed
Government. 'I would venture to point out,'
said one daimiō, 'that the title of the Shōgun
is " Barbarian-expelling generalissimo ", and that
these words " barbarian-expelling " have been in
use from time immemorial.' Similar language was
used by another feudal noble, who—forgetting, or
perhaps ignorant of, the fact that this title had
been adopted by the second Shōgun in his correspondence with the Spaniards and Portuguese in the
seventeenth century—said that the title of ' barbarian-expelling generalissimo ' was altogether incompatible with the policy of maintaining friendly
relations, and concluding treaties with foreigners.

In a letter in the collection of Lettres Édifiantes,
written from China by a Jesuit missionary, Père
de Fontaney, in 1703, he alludes to the unfavourable answers given by Chinese officials of the
Board of Rites when reference was made to them
by the Emperor, suggesting the stoppage of a

Christian persecution in a certain province. He explains that when the Emperor asks a question of the tribunals, and they return an answer *agreeably to the laws*, they cannot be blamed ; whereas, if the contrary is the case, the censors of the empire have a right to impeach them, and the Emperor is authorized to punish them for pronouncing an opinion in opposition to the laws.

There was a similar reverence for the law ('the honourable country's law' as it was called) in Japan, at the time in question, and some allowance for this feeling must be made in arriving at the true value of the opinions given by the daimiōs when consulted by the Government.

The majority of the daimiōs who were consulted, little as they understood the question, were in favour of resisting the foreigners' demands. Their opinion was adopted by the Court, which had no views of its own, and the Shōgun received instructions from the Throne to drive away the foreigner. Accordingly in the autumn of 1853 the Government issued a proclamation which purported to express the decision of the Throne. But in reality this proclamation meant nothing. It said, what every one knew, that there was much divergence of opinion in the advice offered by the feudal nobles in their memorials, and added, what was equally patent to all, that the outcome of the deliberations was that there must be peace or war. It dwelt on the necessity of strengthening the defences of the country, and of fighting, if necessary, to preserve the country's honour ; but it also urged the importance of giving no definite answer, and at the same time of doing everything that was possible to avoid a collision. As a declaration of policy such a document was worthless. Its effect was only to increase popular excitement, and to strengthen the hands of those who were working with the Court party against the Shōgunate.

The chief of these was Tokugawa Nariaki, the ex-prince of Mito, one of the three Tokugawa houses known as the *Gosanké*. It was a Tokugawa tradition that the Mito prince should act as adviser to the Shōgun, and on this ground the representatives of this branch of the family were usually excluded from the succession to the Shōgunate. Nariaki was a man of very strong character. He seems to have resembled in many ways his more famous ancestor Tokugawa Mitsukuni, who from the encouragement he gave to literature in the latter half of the seventeenth century, has been called the Maecenas of Japan. In 1844 Nariaki was obliged to abdicate because he had destroyed the Buddhist temples in his province, and made their bells into cannon. The reason he gave for thus acting was his desire to be in a position to render effective assistance in repelling a foreign invasion, but the Shōgunate suspected him of entertaining other designs. Like his ancestor, he was a great patron of learning. He promoted the study of foreign languages, and he took an interest in many new things of foreign origin, especially the science of shipbuilding. From his ancestor, too, he seems to have inherited a bias in favour of the Kiōto Court, and his imperialist tendencies were increased by his marriage with the daughter of an imperial prince. Early in his career he was given the high rank of *Chiūnagon*, and after his death this was altered to the still higher rank of *Dainagon*. He is one of the many instances in Japanese history of the power wielded by political personages after abdication. The policy pursued by him was somewhat inconsistent even for an age of inconsistency. He encouraged ' Dutch Learning ', and nevertheless supported the party who clamoured for the expulsion of the barbarian. He was an avowed imperialist, and an opponent and detractor of the Yedo Government. Yet at the same time one of his chief objects was to secure the succession to the Shōgunate for his son Hitotsubashi Keiki, who, having been adopted into the Hitotsubashi family, was eligible, in spite of his parentage, for appointment as heir. Had his ambition been gratified by his son's succession to the Shōgunate in 1858, instead of nine years later, the course of events would probably have been very different.

In the history of those times two figures stand out with special prominence. Nariaki is one of these. The other is Ïi Kamon no Kami Naosuké, the daimiō of the province of Ōmi. His castle town was Hikoné, and he is also known as Ïi Tairō, the Regent Ïi. The events of the period between

1853 and 1860 resolved themselves into a struggle
between these two statesmen. The Ii family was
ancient, tracing its descent back to the Fujiwara
administrators. Its founder Ii Tomoyasu forsook
the pleasures of the Court for a country life, and on
the shore of Lake Biwa, at a spot called the valley of
Ii, whence the family took its name, he built himself a castle. His successors took an active part
in the civil wars, and other more local disturbances, which took place in the twelfth, fourteenth,
and fifteenth centuries. At one time the fortunes
of the family were brought to a very low ebb
through the treachery of a retainer, but they
were subsequently retrieved by Ii Naomasa, who
was one of Iyéyasu's most famous generals. As
a reward for his services he was confirmed in the
lordship of Hikoné, and to the family were given
certain hereditary privileges. Amongst these were
the duty of guarding the Court, and sheltering the
Emperor in the castle of Hikoné, should it become
necessary for His Majesty at any time to leave
the capital, a permanent position in the Council
of State, and the first seat in the Tamari-no-ma,
the second highest of the antechambers of the
Shōgun's castle in Yedo. The house of Ii also
prided itself on other distinctions. The head of
the family was qualified to go to Kiōto as the
Shōgun's representative to thank the Court for
Imperial Orders, and to worship at the Nikko
shrines on behalf of the Shōgun ; and he alone
of all the nobles had the honour, when the Emperor

went out of his palace, of carrying a spear and a box in the imperial procession. This privilege, and the fact that red was the battle colour of their chiefs, gave them the soubriquets of the 'Single Spear Holders' and the 'Scarlet Demons'. The future regent was born in 1815. He was one of nineteen children, and had thirteen brothers older than himself. It was a rule in the Ïi family, as in others, that younger sons should be adopted, if possible, into other families, where an heir was lacking, to the headship of which they might succeed. This was, and is, the universal practice in Japan, as much pains being taken to establish younger sons in this way as is taken in Western countries to arrange suitable marriages for daughters. Failing such arrangements, younger sons were either brought up as retainers of the family, or were given a small allowance, barely sufficient for their maintenance. The latter course was adopted in the case of Naosuké, who for several years lived a very retired life in Hikoné. His eldest brother had succeeded his father in 1832, and, having no children, had adopted another brother as his heir. The latter dying in 1845, Naosuké was adopted as heir in his place, and he was taken to Yedo and presented at the Shō un's court. Five years later the head of the family died, and was succeeded by Naosuké. During his five years' residence in Yedo, Naosuké had heard a good deal about the visits of foreign vessels, which had become one of the pressing questions

of the day, and he had had many opportunities
for making himself thoroughly acquainted with
the subject. From the first he seems to have made
up his mind that Japan could no longer persist in
her policy of seclusion. The reasons he gave in
writing in support of this view, when the opinions
of the daimiōs were sought by the Government
in 1853, do not suggest any special enthusiasm
for foreign ideas, but they show more practical
wisdom than the advice tendered on the same
occasion by others.

His memorial [1] called attention to the fact that
in 1636, when the country was closed by the
third Shōgun, Iyémitsu, there were nine government vessels suitable for navigating the high seas.
All vessels above a certain tonnage being then
destroyed, there were at present none which could
use heavy guns in a fight with foreigners. It was
a maxim of war that the advantage lay with those
who attacked. Owing to the want of proper ships
Japan could not take the offensive, but could only
defend herself against attack. ' Our ancestors,'
the memorial went on to say, ' in closing the
country left a Chinese and Dutch bridge. Japan
should make use of this bridge for the conduct of
foreign relations, and follow prudent counsels for
the present, postponing hostilities till we are in a
position to obtain certain victory.' The memorial
proceeded to urge the advisability of giving way
to the American demands in regard to the supply

[1] Appendix 14.

of coal, and the treatment of shipwrecked mariners, and of adopting the bold policy of carrying on commerce with both America and Russia, and, in pursuance of this policy, sending Japanese ships once more into distant seas. A modern navy, it was suggested, might be gradually created with assistance from the Dutch as instructors, and then Japan would be in a position to go out to meet difficulties, and not wait for them to come to her. And, in accordance with the procedure customary in times of national emergency, the memorial ended by recommending the consultation of certain Shintō shrines and Buddhist temples by the Court and Shōgunate, in order that the Government might be fortified by the knowledge that their decision had been submitted for the approval of the gods.

The sincerity of Naosuké's convictions has been questioned. His memorial at any rate gave no uncertain sound. It contained a distinct declaration in favour of treaties with foreign countries. The early associations of his family, moreover, made the rising statesman a strong supporter of Tokugawa rule. On both of these points he found himself, when he joined the Council of State in 1853, in conflict with the ex-Prince of Mito, Tokugawa Nariaki. The death of the Shōgun Iyéyoshi in that year created a new ground of discord.

It arose in this way. The new Shōgun Iyésada was childless, and, in accordance with custom in these cases, it was necessary for him to choose, and adopt, a successor. The wish of the ex-Prince of Mito was, as we have seen, that his son Kéiki should be chosen. But the Shōgun Iyésada was only twenty-nine on his accession, and he was in no hurry to choose a successor from another house, hoping still for a family of his own. Moreover, his relations with the ex-Prince of Mito were not cordial, and he seems to have objected to Kéiki as a successor, because he was too distant a relation, and also on the grounds that he was not young enough, though he was only fifteen at the time, and that if he were chosen, it would lead to his own (the Shōgun's) abdication. If he were obliged, against his own wishes, to nominate a successor, his choice would, it was known, fall on his nearer kinsman, the young Prince of Kishiū, a boy only nine years of age. The Shōgun's views with regard to the succession was shared by Ii Naosuké, by four or five other members of the Council of State, and by Prince Kujō and his party in Kiōto. The ex-Prince of Mito was supported by the Prince of Owari, the daimiōs of Satsuma, Échizen, Tosa, and Sendai, and many other feudal nobles, as well as an influential group of Court nobles headed by Prince Konoyé. The weight of family prestige and territorial influence was with the ex-Prince of Mito, while the strength of the other side, the party of Ii Naosuké, lay chiefly in the two facts that they held the reins of government and were in the Shōgun's confidence. The struggle lasted for some five years, and at one time (in 1855) the ex-Prince of Mito gained the upper hand. But it was only for a moment. Ïi Naosuké and his party regained their ascendancy in the administration, and held it until, in 1858, the question of the succession was finally settled in their favour by the appointment as heir of the Kishiū candidate Iyémochi.

We have seen how vague and contradictory was the proclamation issued in 1853, after the question of permitting foreign intercourse had been first referred to Kiōto by the Yedo Government. If any inference could be drawn from so colourless a pronouncement, it would be that the policy to be pursued should be non-committal. It certainly gave no authority for negotiating treaties. But since foreigners were clamouring for admission to Jᵒpan, and pressing for a definite answer, a policy of the nature indicated was obviously impossible. So, in spite of the proclamation, and in direct opposition to the instructions received, the Yedo Government took the only possible course, and went on with the negotiation of foreign treaties. And this course was justified by the result ; for with delightful inconsequence, the Throne, in spite of its previous attitude, and in contradiction to its non-committal policy, formally approved, in February, 1855, the conclusion of the first treaties with America, Great Britain, and Russia. The Shōgun's Resident in Kiōto, in reporting this approval to Yedo, stated that copies of the treaties had been submitted for the Emperor's perusal, that His Majesty had expressed his warm appreciation of them, and that his mind was at ease. His Majesty, it was added, was fully sensible of the great trouble which the work of negotiation had given to the Shōgun, of the strenuous labours of the Council of State, and of the services rendered by all the officials concerned.

It might well have been supposed that the issue of this imperial approval would be conclusive, and would put an end to the contentions existing with regard to foreign relations. But this was not so. The struggle over the succession was becoming more acute, and presumably, in view of the strong anti-foreign feeling of the time, the treaty question was too convenient a weapon for use in the contest to be discarded. So the strange and almost incomprehensible farce was continued. In theory foreign intercourse was condemned ; in practice negotiations were pursued uninterruptedly, and the silent procession of treaties went on amidst a chorus of official and popular disapproval.

The period of four or five months preceding the signature of the American treaty was a period of busy intrigue at Kiōto, each of the two parties in the State trying to gain the advantage in the contest over the succession, and the ex-Prince of Mito losing no opportunity of opposing the treaty policy of the Shōgunate.

In June, as was mentioned in the previous chapter, Hotta returned to Yedo, having failed

in his attempt to gain the imperial consent to the
American treaty.   The answer of the Throne, which
brought his mission to an end, was drawn up after
no less than seventy Court nobles had been
consulted.   It said that the Court had from the
first viewed with disfavour the idea of concluding
treaties, and changing the sound policy followed
ever since the beginning of the Tokugawa administration.   It had been decided, therefore, to call
upon the feudal nobility, from the *Gosanké* down-
wards, for their advice on the following points :—

1. How best to give tranquillity to the imperial
mind.

2. What measures were necessary to avert
calamity from the State.

3. The devising of a scheme of national defence,
to be adopted in the event of the refusal of the
Court to consent to any other treaty with the
Americans.

If the advice received pointed to no definite
conclusion, an imperial messenger would be dispatched to the Isé shrine, and as soon as a decision
had been arrived at, it would be communicated
to Yedo.

As was only to be expected, there was some
divergence of opinion in the advice tendered in
answer to this summons, but as compared with
the result of the first consultation of notabilities,
when Perry arrived five years before, there was
a great difference.   From many of those consulted
came answers showing that they, or the retainers

directing clan affairs, took an intelligent interest in the question, and had ideas of their own.

The Prince of Owari said that if the request of the foreign barbarians were granted there would be no limit to the concessions demanded, and the country would be disgraced.

The young Prince of Kishiū, the future Shōgun, and one of the candidates for the succession, excused himself from offering an opinion on the ground of his youth.

The ex-Prince of Mito, and his son, who had succeeded him in the chieftainship of the clan, were of opinion that the demand of the foreign barbarians for the opening of Kiōto and Ōsaka could not be granted, nor could they be given access to the province of Kii, or the island of Awaji. As for trade, it should be limited to articles useful for Japan.

The Lord Tayasu (one of the *Gosankiō*, and later on guardian of the young Prince of Kishiū after he became Shōgun) said he had no opinion to offer, but suggested that a conference should be held, and a joint decision adopted.

Prince Kéiki, the other candidate for the succession, and afterwards the last of the Shōguns, then known by the official title of *Giōbukiō*, or Minister of Justice, suggested that the Shōgun should be careful not to bring shame on the country by neglecting his duty as ' barbarian-queller ', and that officials should be chosen for their merit.

The Prince of Kaga explained verbally that he

had no special opinion to offer, but that if it was a question of deciding between peace and war, he would be in favour of the first.

The Prince of Échizen, a noble of great character and influence, spoke strongly of the Shōgunate's treaty policy. He advocated the encouragement of navigation and commerce ; the introduction of a new system of foreign trade ; and military and educational reforms. He objected to the opening of Kiōto to foreigners, but thought three ports, including Ōsaka, should be opened, that foreign ministers should reside in Yedo, and that Shinagawa (a suburb of the latter) should be made a commercial port. He was also in favour of three other things, the connexion between which is not obvious, the purchase of arms from America, the granting of permission to foreigners to travel, and the creation of Ōsaka as a place of residence for all the feudal nobility.

The Prince of Awa was in favour of foreign trade, and the immediate opening of Shinagawa and Yedo, but not of Kiōto. He also advocated military reform and the encouragement of navigation.

The Prince of Satsuma attached the greatest importance to reverence for the Throne, a sound condition of military defence, currency reform, naval construction, the raising of the rank of the governors of places opened to foreign trade, and the encouragement of navigation.

The Prince of Mutsu would wait and see what

advice was tendered by others before expressing any opinion.

The Prince of Mikawa objected to the residence of foreign representatives in Yedo, and to open ports being established in districts where men's minds were disturbed, but he was in favour of foreign trade with limitations, of preparations for defence being completed in order that the country might not suffer disgrace, of military reform, and of the existing system of the residence of daimiōs in Yedo in alternate years being made less rigorous.

The Prince of Étchiū was opposed on general grounds to the demands of the foreign barbarians being granted, but he was not prepared to offer any special suggestions on the subject, so long as measures were taken for the defence of the country, and for preventing men's minds from being disturbed, and the clans from falling into decay.

The Prince of Sendai was in favour of military reform, and the encouragement of commerce and navigation.

A group of dignitaries which included Ii Naosuké and other members of the Council were of opinion that the proposals of the American representative should be reduced as much as possible, that Yedo, Shinagawa, Kiōto, and Ōsaka should not be included in the list of places to be opened, the number of which should be made as small as possible. But they could not undertake to say how far it might be possible to carry out these suggestions.

The Baron Inaba of Mino said that the foreigners ought to be driven away at once, but as Japan's military preparations were not yet completed, the American demands should be granted for the present.

The Baron Sataké of Hitachi suggested that the limit of concession had been reached. If more were conceded, more would be asked. Let the foreigners be content with the three ports of Nagasaki, Hakodaté, and Shimoda.

Another daimiō, one of the many Matsudairas, thought, like several others, that the opening of more ports could not be prevented. He suggested, however, that steps should be taken to prevent a rise in prices ; that gold and silver should not be exchanged weight for weight with foreign coin ; and that paper money should be used instead.

One or two of those consulted suggested the conclusion of the proposed treaty for a term of years, at the end of which period it was hinted that the foreigner might be expelled ; others dwelt on the necessity for reform, and the impossibility of persisting in the policy of seclusion ; while a fourth of the whole number (sixty-five) from whom answers were received had no opinion to offer.[1]

The results of this second consultation of the territorial nobles ought to have strengthened the Shōgunate's hands, and shaken the Court's objections to the conclusion of the treaty, for there was

[1] See also on this point Appendix 15.

a clear preponderance of opinion in favour of the extension of foreign intercourse—and this too came mostly from the same men who a few years before had spoken in a very different sense. But it is doubtful if all this reference and consultation of which we read had much influence on the situation. The part of the game of politics that counted was being played by other hands in ways of which the public did not hear so much.

Since the crisis of 1855, already mentioned, the influence of Ïi Naosuké in the Government had gradually increased, and on June 5, 1858, he was appointed *Tairō*, a title which may be rendered by the word Regent. The office of *Tairō* was to the Yedo Government not unlike what the office of *Sesshō*, a term which more closely corresponds to our word Regent, had been to the Kiōto Government under the Fujiwara administrators. Whereas, however, the latter office was tenable only during the minority of an Emperor, that of *Tairō* was not limited in this way to a Shōgun's minority, but could also be created at any time at the pleasure of the ruling Shōgun to meet occasions of emergency.

On the 16th of July the ex-Prince of Mito, whose association with his son in a written opinion on the treaty question—which though unfavourable to the Shōgunate's policy was moderate in tone— has already been noticed, addressed to the Regent and Council of State a letter, or memorial, enclosing the well-known memorandum called ' the fourteen points '.

In this letter he explained that when asked for his advice on a recent occasion, in regard to the nature of the imperial answer to be made on the subject of the proposed new treaty, he had given a hasty opinion without learning the views of the Shōgunate, which was a very wrong thing to do. He had thought of attending at the Shōgun's palace, and learning the sentiments of the Council of State, and the ideas of the coast defence commissioners, but he thought it would not look well for one who had withdrawn from public affairs to put himself forward so prominently. He was, therefore, obliged to express his opinions in writing, and this he did not feel the same reluctance in doing, since on the Shōgunate was laid the duty of administration, and the Court acted on the advice it gave.

The first four clauses of this memorandum, which may serve to show the nature of the arguments used by the Jō-i, or anti-foreign party, in support of their views, may be summarized as follows :—

' The American barbarians made representations last winter, and after interviews had been held treaties were concluded. I understand it is the Shōgun's intention to complete military preparations with the profit made out of commerce. In my opinion military preparations should be completed first. If this be done, commerce will be developed later. I beg the Government will consider this.

' It is said that the northern barbarians have

made a request, and that, if this be not granted, all countries will unite and attack us. This is quite probable, but assisted only by hearsay, and maps, they will not be able easily to penetrate far into the interior of our country. Everything now is quiet, but by means of trade and their bad religion the barbarians will become intimate with our people, and they will learn thoroughly the geography of the country, and the feelings of the nation. Then, if war should break out, the situation will be much more dangerous. I beg the Government will consider this.

'It is said that a Minister is to be placed in Japan, and that he will have charge of all matters, and communicate with the Minister in charge of foreign business. If this should happen, he will ask for changes in all sorts of things relating to foreign countries, besides commerce, which he may regard as inconvenient. And it is impossible to say what harm may not be done. They (the foreigners) say, that in the case of the opium war in China, the matter would have been amicably arranged had there been a Minister in Peking. But if there was not a Minister in Peking, there was one in China. I beg that the Government will deal with the matter after they have carefully examined the action taken by the Chinese Government. The foreigners ask for a speedy decision, but I beg the Government will carefully consider this point.

'With regard to the request for the opening of several ports, is this only for the American barbarians? The others may come and say it is difficult for them to live in the same ports as the American barbarians, and may ask for more ports to be opened.'

Other points in the treaty criticized in the memorandum were the treaty limits, and the right

to build Christian churches ; the policy of making
treaties at all was assailed on the grounds that
the indiscriminate introduction of foreign learning
would have a demoralizing effect, that if once this
new departure were made, and the ancient laws
(closing the country) disregarded, everybody would
do as they liked, and there would be no longer any
discipline ; stress was also laid on the desirability
of keeping the foreigners away from the National
Shrines at Isé, and the Five Home Provinces
surrounding the capital.

That a communication of this kind could have
been addressed to the Government four years after
the signature of Perry's treaty, and after several
other agreements had been concluded, and were
in operation, shows what a singular condition of
things then prevailed. We shall probably be
right in regarding it as a demonstration directed
as much against the Shōgunate, as against the
Shōgunate's foreign policy.

It was doubtless due to the authority attaching to
the appointment of *Tairō*, added to the ascendancy
he had acquired over his colleagues in the Council
of State, which made it possible for the Regent
to conclude, on the 29th of July, the American
treaty of 1858, without waiting any longer for the
imperial sanction asked for in the spring.   To the
same causes was probably due the final triumph
of his party a week later in the matter of the succession.   On the 4th of August the young Prince of
Kishiū was proclaimed heir.   Ten days later the

Shōgun Iyésada died. The new Shōgun, Iyémochi, being still a minor, a Tokugawa prince became his guardian, and the Government was conducted by the Regent.

The day after the signature of the treaty an explanation in writing of the reasons for its signature was sent to the Shōgun's Resident in Kiōto, for the information of the Throne.

The reasons given were the arrival of more Russian and American ships, the defeat of China by the English and French, and the news that the two latter were on their way to Japan determined to carry matters with a high hand. The American Minister had advised the immediate signature of the treaty as the best way to meet the new demands, and the Government had, after much anxious consideration, decided to adopt this course, in spite of the fact that the question was still under considera⁺ion by the Throne. The report added that a member of the Council would shortly be sent to Kiōto to offer further explanations.

At the same time the fact was notified to the daimiōs in a circular letter, which quoted the terms of the report to the Throne.

The signature of the American treaty was the signal for a fresh outburst of real or simulated indignation from some of the feudal nobles. The ex-Prince of Mito was, as before, the most conspicuous. In the remonstrance which he addressed two days afterwards to the Council of State, he ignored the fact of the treaty having been already signed, and insisted on the Court's being consulted beforehand. For the Shōgunate, he said, to act without reference to Kiōto would be to fail in its high duty of respect for the Throne, which had been the guiding principle of all Shōguns, and to be guilty of disobedience to the imperial commands.

The Regent's reply was to strike at once at his enemies. This his newly acquired authority, and his triumph in the matter of the succession, enabled him to do in vigorous fashion. The ex-Prince of Mito and the Prince of Owari were confined in clan *yashikis* in Yedo, while the latter and the daimiōs of Échizen, Tosa, and Uwajima were forced to abdicate. And when the Court, growing uneasy at this sudden reassertion of authority on the part of the Shōgunate, summoned the Regent, or one of the *Gosanké* (the Kishiū Prince being only a boy at this time), to come to Kiōto to report on the situation, a reply was sent to the effect that the Regent was detained by State affairs, and that the princes of Owari and Mito were confined to their clan *yashikis*.

The confinement of the latter Prince in Yedo did not stop the intrigues of the party in Kiōto. On the 15th of September their allies there arranged for the issue of a secret imperial decree, addressed to the Shōgunate, and signed by six of their number. Accompanying the decree was a separate paper addressed to the ex-Prince as doyen of the daimiōs, and ordering the immediate publication of the imperial wishes.

The decree censured the Shōgun for his presumption and disrespect in concluding the treaty in defiance of the imperial wishes duly notified to Yedo. Leaving aside the question of foreigners, it said, the Throne was troubled to think of the disorder in the country which might result from this action. It expressed the astonishment of the Court at the reasons given for the inability of the Regent, or one of the *Gosanké* princes, to go to Kiōto in obedience to the imperial summons, and it concluded by calling for a further consultation of the dignitaries of the Empire. These papers duly reached the ex-Prince of Mito in Yedo towards the end of September by the hands of the retainers in charge of the Mito *yashiki* in Kiōto. Whatever expectations may have been formed by the Mito party as to the favourable results of this manœuvre were not realized. In Mito itself much mischief was caused. The ex-Prince's successor had not inherited his father's political prejudices, and when, later on, the return of the decree was demanded by the Court, serious disturbances broke out in the clan, and it was with the utmost difficulty that the Prince of Mito was able eventually to comply with the Court's request.

And the only result so far as the Shōgunate was concerned, was to hasten the departure for Kiōto of a mission charged with the formal report of the conclusion of the American treaty, which had been delayed by the death of the Shōgun Iyésada. The mission was composed of two members of the Council of State, Manabé and Sakai.

This, it will be noted, was the third mission within a year, sent by the Yedo Government to Kiōto in connexion with the negotiation and signature of the same treaty. The previous missions of Hayashi and Hotta had both failed to obtain the approval of the Court. By the time, however, that the third mission under Manabé was dispatched, the aspect of affairs had been changed by the Regent's appointment.

At the end of three months Manabé succeeded in accomplishing the main object of his mission, an interesting account of which is given by Sir Ernest Satow in vol. xi of the *Cambridge Modern History*.

It has been already suggested that the treaty question was a very minor issue in the struggle between the parties led respectively by the Regent and the ex-Prince of Mito. The author of the *Bakumatsu Gwaikodan*, 'The story of Foreign Relations in the last days of the Shōgunate,' thinks also that this treaty question was merely a secondary matter in Manabé's negotiations; that the Shōgunate's agents were directed to make no difficulties in regard to wording, but to accept any decree which clearly established the fact that an understanding between the Court and the Shōgunate had been effected.

However this may be, the imperial decree, which was eventually handed to Manabé, is as singular a document in its way as the memorandum of the ex-Prince of Mito, to which reference has already been made.

Beginning with the statement that previous sovereigns had been much troubled in mind by matters concerning friendship and trade with barbarians, and that the Throne had repeatedly expressed to the divine ancestors its feelings of apprehension and distress lest this reign should be the first to witness the establishment of foreign relations, the decree went on to say that the two councillors from Yedo had represented to the Throne that the Shōgun, the Regent, and the whole Council of State were in favour of keeping foreign barbarians at a distance, as the Throne had decreed, and that the imperial mind was accordingly at ease. And it concluded by urging on the attention of the Shōgun the Throne's deep concern in regard to the sea in the neighbourhood of the imperial Shrines and Kiōto, and the safety of the sacred insignia—which, put into plainer language, meant that no port should be opened near Isé, or the capital.

The generally accepted explanation of the issue of this decree, which deliberately ignored the progress already made in foreign relations, and talked of closing the country again, is that Manabé, in the course of his negotiations at Kiōto, succeeded in persuading the Court that though the signing of this particular treaty was unavoidable, the Yedo Government were really not in favour of foreign intercourse, but would welcome the first opportunity that presented itself for the expulsion of foreigners. In any case the fact of the Mikado's approval having been given to the earlier treaties does not appear to have caused any embarrassment to the Court in coming to its new decision. This, it should be noted, in spite of its anti-foreign tone, contemplated, as was so often the case throughout the period we are considering, doing nothing for the moment.

In order to enable the reader to follow the complicated course of political events during this period it has been thought necessary to give many wearisome details from the State-papers of those days. The reader who has the patience to peruse them will form some idea of the tortuous methods adopted, in the course of the long struggle between the rival factions, by each side : by the anti-foreign party in order to discredit the Shōgunate, and by the latter in order to come to some arrangement with the Court, which, however openly it might sacrifice the name for the reality, and seem to give way to the wishes of the Throne, might justify in practice the policy upon which the Government had embarked.

Both in the affair of the succession, and in regard to the treaty question, the Mito party had been defeated, for, strange as it may seem, the anti-foreign decree issued by the Court was regarded everywhere as a triumph for the Regent. He took full advantage of his victory. Hotta, the State

Councillor who had originally supported the Regent against the Mito party on the treaty question, in connexion with which he had gone to Kiōto, but had opposed him in the matter of the succession, had already been dismissed from the post of minister in charge of foreign business, and other changes were made in the Council of State. Many arrests were made in Kiōto and elsewhere, and sentences of banishment and execution were carried out on a scale which surprised even the officials of those days.[1] By the end of the year the Regent had disposed of all his opponents, and was master of the situation. His triumph was, however, short-lived. The long struggle he had waged with the anti-foreign party, which had ended in the defeat and disgrace of the ex-Prince of Mito, had roused feelings of bitter hostility in the clan ; and in the spring of 1860 he was killed in Yedo by Mito swordsmen on his way to the Shōgun's palace.

There can be little doubt that the Regent's direction of affairs greatly assisted the work of re-opening Japan to foreign intercourse. What is not so clear is whether he was guided in his action by the conviction that this was the only safe policy for Japan under the circumstances, or whether he adopted it as the best means of strengthening and maintaining the Tokugawa régime. For the

[1] Count Katsu Awa says in his book to which reference has already been made, ' The prisons were filled to an extent unknown before, even in remote times.'

vacillating and contradictory behaviour of the Yedo Government and the Kiōto Court during his tenure of office it would be unjust to blame him. For this he was not responsible. It was part of the system of government in his time. Nor in the apparent inconsistency of his actions was he doing more than following the tendency of the age. He seems to have been willing to allow the Court and nation to believe in the nominal triumph of the anti-foreign policy, so long as he remained free to secure practical results by the negotiation of foreign treaties, and to have been content to leave the future to work out the complicated problem presented by a State which was saying one thing and doing another. He saw, and for the moment checked, the beginning of the political movement which shifted the centre of gravity in the administration from Yedo, where it had remained for three centuries unchallenged, back to Kiōto. After his death the fall of the Shōgunate was only a question of time.

When looking at Japan during the period we have been considering from outside—from the point of view of the foreign countries seeking to establish commercial relations—we are struck by the evidence of sudden and rapid progress afforded by the number, and increasing scope, of the treaties and agreements negotiated in so short a space of time. A survey from within gives a less favourable impression. We notice, it is true, the existence of a current of progressive thought, but we see, dominating everything, in Government circles as elsewhere, unreasoning anti-foreign prejudice, which threatened to undo all the good that had been done.

How this wave of hostile sentiment subsided without doing the mischief expected must always remain something of a puzzle. The same mystery of inconsequence attaches to the imperial decrees, which said so much but effected nothing. It may be that here again we simply see the working of the Japanese tendency towards make-believe, that much of what was said and done at that time was intended simply for effect, and was never meant seriously. But perhaps the truer explanation is that Japan was being drawn, with or against her will, into the stream of the world's progress, and that against the forces thus drawing her no reactionary influences, however exalted or powerful, could contend with any prospect of success.

CHAPTER IV

In the preface to his book *Kaikoku Shimatsu,* 'The Affair of the Opening of the Country,' Mr. Shimada gives an account of what happened after the Regent's assassination, which is also the story of how the materials for the book came to be preserved. It gives so clear a picture of the times in which the Regent lived, and of the political methods of those days, that we are tempted to reproduce it nearly in full.

' Almost immediately after the Regent disappeared with the spring snow,' writes Mr. Shimada, ' the aspect of affairs underwent a great change. The voices which denounced the policy of the Shōgunate were heard everywhere, both at Kiōto and throughout the various clans, and in the end this clamour resulted in an outburst of " posthumous censure " against the Ii family. The Shōgunate thereupon confiscated the territories of the Hikoné fief, in order to give the Court at Kiōto a proof of the reformed character of the Government. The people of the Hikoné clan were much incensed, and there were many who wished to call the Shōgunate to account for this injustice, and dispute the matter with their lives. But they were calmed by appeals to the instructions left behind at his death by one of the Regent's ancestors, Ii Naotaka. According to the Shōgunate regulations, if a *samurai,* or *karō,* or *daimiō* died a violent death, his hereditary income ' (if a *samurai* or *karō*) ' or his territories ' (if a *daimiō*)

' were confiscated. When the Regent was murdered a cry was raised in the Hikoné clan for vengeance on the Mito clan, which had done this thing, and two of the clan *karō* presented a letter to the Government declaring that they could not rest happy until the assassins had been apprehended. But the Shōgunate, fearing trouble between the two clans which might grow into more widespread disorders, rejected the petition, and sent secret instructions to the Hikoné clan to conceal the murder, and to report that the Regent had died (in his palace) from the effects of a wound. This having been done, the Regent's son Naonori was acknowledged as his successor (in the lordship of Hikoné), and the matter was settled in this way. Soon after, however, political feeling changed ; the Regent was accused of having conducted the administration badly during his lifetime, and his retainers were blamed for not having reported the murder of their master ; and on these grounds the fief was sequestered. Thereupon the whole clan was thrown into commotion. Kato, a *han-sotsu*, went to the Yashiki in Yedo of a member of the Council of State, the daimiō Inouyé Kawachi no Kami, and there disembowelled himself, leaving a paper complaining of the injustice of the Government. Many others sympathized with this act, and matters were in a disturbed condition. It was then that the authorities bethought themselves of the instructions bequeathed to the clan by its former chief Ii Naotaka, who laid down the rule that however heartless and cruel the orders of the Council of State might be, they must always be obeyed. The first duty was to serve the State. Then the public mind gradually quieted down.

' Previous to this, however, the *karō* of the clan, fearing lest it might be punished by the Shōgunate, executed two faithful retainers of the Regent named Nagano Shiuzen, and Utsunoki Rokunojō, hoping

thereby to lighten the punishment which they felt
was coming.'

Nagano, it should be explained, had been the
secret agent of the Regent in Kiōto, and the latter's final triumph in the long contest with the
ex-Prince of Mito was largely due to the ability
and courage with which Nagano penetrated and
defeated the intrigues of the Jō-i party in the
capital.

'Things had now come to such a pass that it
was not only impossible to bring the Government
to book for the injustice they had perpetrated, but
the *karō* feared lest further calamity should fall
upon the clan through information obtained from
the Regent's private papers, and the records kept
by his personal retainers. So it was decided to
burn all these documents, and thus destroy all
traces of the past. The task was assigned to two
men, a priest of the Buddhist temple of Riō-hō-ji,
and a retainer of the Ii family called Ōkubō Shōnan;
and it was generally understood that the papers
had all been destroyed by these two. But when
after the Restoration public opinion again changed,
and the Ii family was praised for loyalty to the
Throne; and when later on, with the lapse of time
and the progress of events, the feeling even with
regard to the Regent changed, and finally the nation
ceased to condemn him, then it became known
that the two persons entrusted with the burning
of the Regent's papers had held different views.
The priest of Riō-hō-ji had been of opinion that
to burn the papers was the best way to secure the
welfare of the Ii family. Ōkubō, on the other hand,
had argued that although the policy of his deceased
lord had perished with him, it rested with these
documents alone to prove in the future the true

state of things at the time, and the difficulties he had had to contend with. If from inability to bear patiently present trouble the papers were burnt, how could the injustice of the charges brought against the Regent ever be proved ? He would therefore secretly preserve them and report their destruction to the clan office. Should the matter come prematurely to light, he would accept all responsibility, and, destroying himself with the documents, prevent the implication of his old lord in the affair. If happily, however, an aupicious age arrived, when it was possible to make the papers public, the happiness would not be theirs alone. If, again, the auspicious moment did not come in his lifetime, he would charge his descendants to preserve the papers in the family. The priest was unable to dissuade him from this course, and so the papers were kept by Ōkubō, who guarded against all eventualities by keeping them stored with some gunpowder. Nobody save the priest and he knew what had been done, and, the former dying not long afterwards, the secret remained with him. His cherished hopes were not in vain. In 1887 the happy time he looked for came. In the spring of that year the anniversary of the Regent's death was celebrated with every mark of respect for the deceased statesman, whose reputation in the eyes of the nation was completely restored. Ōkubō's thoughts returned to his old friend, the priest, whose solicitude for the welfare of the Ii family had been as great as his own. He visited his friend's grave, and explained what he was going to do. Then he published the papers. They are now in the custody of the Ii family.'

Six months after the Regent's assassination his old enemy the ex-Prince of Mito died. The deaths of the two rival statesmen may have had the effect of diminishing to some extent the bitterness of party feeling, but it is doubtful if the country was the gainer in the end. Their removal from the scene left Japan without any master mind to control a difficult situation. So long as the reins of government had been in the strong hands of the Regent, the Court, eager though it was to regain the authority which the weakness of the Shōgunate seemed to place within its reach, hesitated to run counter to the custom of centuries. And the same feeling restrained the territorial nobility, which had welcomed the anti-Shōgunate policy of the ex-Prince of Mito. But the set of the tide of popular feeling was in the direction of change of some kind, and favoured the aspirations of the Court, and the ambitions of the feudal aristocracy ; and while, on the one side, the Shōgunate was deprived of its strongest supporter, on the other, the movement initiated for his own purposes by the ex-Prince of Mito had gathered such strength that the Court felt more and more encouraged to try conclusions with the Kwantō administration.

Hitherto there had been three centres, as it were, of political action, the Regency, which meant the Yedo Government, the Court, and the Mito party. With the disappearance of the Regent and the ex-Prince of Mito the situation was simplified. What had been the Mito party joined the Court, and Kiōto became the open rival of

Yedo. Hitherto it had been more or less a conflict of parties, the overthrow of the Shōgunate not being yet contemplated as part of a realizable programme. Henceforth it was a struggle between Kiōto and Yedo, between the Court and the Shōgunate, between the west, as it was called, and the east.

In describing geographical situation in Japan we naturally talk of north and south, east and west, as the case may be. And so do the Japanese themselves. But in Tokugawa days, politically speaking, and in a sense geographically too, there was for the Japanese one broad division of the country which overshadowed all the others, that, namely, between east and west, the line of separation passing not through the centre of the country, nor through the capital, but through the mountains in which lies the Hakoné pass. For the Japanese all was east—*Kwantō* or *Tōgoku* it was called—which lay to the east of the guard-house at the top of the Hakoné pass, and everything to the west of that was west, being termed *Kwan-sai* or *Sai-koku*.

The growing excitement and unrest in the country gave an opportunity to a class of persons, of which in ordinary times little was heard, though it existed as a feature of feudalism. This was the class of *rōnin*.

Readers of *Tales of Old Japan* will recall the explanation of this class which is given by the author in a note to the story of ' The Forty-seven Rōnin '.

'The word *rōnin*,' he says, 'means literally a " wave-man ", one who is tossed about hither and thither as a wave of the sea. It is used to designate persons of gentle blood, entitled to bear arms, who, having become separated from their feudal lords by their own act, or by dismissal, or by fate, wander about the country in the capacity of somewhat disreputable knights-errant, without ostensible means of living, in some cases offering themselves for hire to new masters, in others supporting themselves by pillage ; or who, falling a grade in the social scale, go into trade and become simple wardsmen.[1] Sometimes it happens that for political reasons a man will become *rōnin*, in order that his lord may not be implicated in some deed of blood in which he is about to engage. Sometimes, also, men become *rōnin*, and leave their native place for a while, until some scrape in which they have become entangled shall have blown over ; after which they return to their former allegiance. Nowadays it is not unusual for men to become *rōnin* for a time, and engage themselves in the service of foreigners at the open ports, even in menial capacities, in the hope that they may pick up something of the language and lore of western folks.'

To this description, written, it should be remembered, when feudalism was in its death-throes, we may add that the adventures of these *rōnin* knights-errant, both real and imaginary, have a special place in Japanese literature, and that their number varied with the circumstances of the day. They were the stormy petrels of Japanese feudalism, increasing, like the *sōshi* of recent years,

---

[1] *Chōnin*, a Japanese term applied to all townspeople who were not *samurai*.

in turbulent and unsettled times, and diminishing again whenever stricter conditions of law and order prevailed. The troubled period which ensued after the deaths of the Regent and the ex-Prince of Mito favoured the increase of these clanless *samurai*, and they played a by no means inconsiderable part in the history of that time. The cry of ' Honour the King and expel the barbarian ' appealed to their adventurous, if lawless instincts, and singly, in groups of two or three, and in larger bodies they found their way to Kiōto, drawn thither, like many of the feudal nobles, by an instinctive feeling that there, and not in Yedo, was the centre round which forth- coming events would group themselves ; that the hereditary seat of imperial power, and not the capital of the ' usurping Shōguns', would furnish the stage on which the last scenes of the approaching political drama were to be enacted.

These *rōnin* posed as the protectors of the Court against foreign intrusion. They bid for public esteem in their character of *rōnin*, and also in a rôle to which they had no claim, that of *otokodate*, a kind of citizen knight-errant, who, somewhat after the fashion of the city apprentice in the Middle Ages in Europe, figured as the champion of the weak against the strong, of the burgher against the military class. Their acts soon showed that their sympathies were enlisted on the side of the Court, and in opposition to what by this time, in spite of the bewildering tenour

of the Yedo proclamations, had come to be regarded as the Shōgunate policy with respect to
foreign intercourse.   Their hands were against
every man who was identified in any way with the
Government, but they specially singled out for
attack the retainers of men in high positions, who
had distinguished themselves as the instruments
of the late Regent in the severe measures taken
against the members of the Mito party.   Among
their earliest victims were two well-known retainers
of Prince Kujō, the ex-Prime Minister of the Kiōto
Court, one of the Regent's staunchest allies ; and
not a week passed without the murder of some
of their political enemies, Government officials,
police officers, or spies ; the usual course followed
being to expose the head of the murdered person
on a pole in the bed of the river which flows through
Kiōto, a placard stating the reason for the murder
being attached thereto.

In the year 1861 they extended their operations
to Yedo, where they attacked the British Legation,
and two years afterwards they destroyed the
official residence which was being built for the
British Minister.   The general effect produced in
official circles by their reckless audacity is mentioned by the author of ' The Story of a Dream
in the period of Genji ', who says :—

' In consequence the *Bakufu* officials were in
a great state of alarm. . . . Some abandoned their
hereditary appointments, their household goods
and families, and fled far away to hide their

shadows from sight. They dreaded the *rōnin* as if they had been tigers, or wolves, and remained shrivelled up with fear.'

The people of Kiōto, on the other hand, in whose eyes the cry of ' expel the barbarian ' was justified by its connexion with that of ' honour the King ', if by nothing else, welcomed them as the champions of the Court and the popular cause, and spoke of them in grateful terms as 'the righteous *samurai*', 'the loyal *samurai*', and 'the avengers of heaven'.

This *rōnin* movement eventually assumed such serious proportions as to embarrass the Court, whose protection was the chief object in view, as much as it alarmed the Shōgunate, which was so openly defied ; and an appeal was made to the daimiōs of Satsuma, Chōshiū and Tosa, who by the Court's desire had established a sort of head-quarters for themselves at the capital, to take steps for their control. In this matter the Prince of Chōshiū took the leading part by enrolling large numbers of the *rōnin* as an auxiliary force with the Chōshiū troops. The Shōgunate, after a time, recognizing the advantages to be derived from securing their co-operation, followed his example, and from that time, until the Restoration was finally accomplished, considerable bodies of *rōnin* were employed on both sides, those enlisted in the Chōshiū ranks being called the *Seigishi*, or ' Righteous Samurai ', while the name of *Shinchō-gumi*, or ' New Levies ', was applied to those in the service of the Yedo Government.

Before leaving the subject of the *rōnin*, to whose influence on the events of this particular period it is necessary to draw special attention, it may be interesting to give one or two instances of their lawless behaviour, which will serve also as an illustration of the disturbed condition of affairs. From ' The Story of a Dream in the period of Genji ' we learn that in the spring of 1862 the father of the young Prince of Satsuma, Shimadzu Idzumi, on whom, though he was a less adroit politician, the mantle of Tokugawa Nariaki, as leader of the anti-foreign and anti-Shōgunate party had fallen, was on his way to Yedo. He was met at Himéji a castle-town on the northern shore of the inland sea, and the capital of the province of Harima, by several hundred *rōnin*, ' assembled,' as our author tells us, ' like a flight of crows, to complain of the crimes of the Tokugawa officials, and to declare their noble purpose of laying the facts before the Mikado, and urging His Majesty to set forth to subjugate and expel the barbarians in person.' Their leader presented to Shimadzu Idzumi a document, for transmission to the Throne, stating amongst other things that, since the violation of the fundamental laws of the Empire by the Yedo Government, Japan was in great peril from the foreign barbarians with whom treaties had wrongfully been made ; that the patriots of the western provinces had secretly consulted and desired to perform some noble deed. Unfortunately their numbers were small, and without the assistance of some great daimiō, they felt they could not succeed. They had ascertained that the province of Satsuma was animated by the most ardent zeal, and, hearing of Shimadzu's visit to Yedo, they had waited for him, hoping for his assistance in restoring the old state of things. They wanted him to at once attack and destroy the Shōgun's castles in Ōsaka and Kiōto, and the castle of the Ii family at Hikoné, to drive out all the Shōgunate officials from Kiōto, and then, escorting the Emperor to Yedo, to put an end to the Tokugawa Government. Shimadzu Idzumi, we are told, praised these 'low-class *samurai*' for their loyalty and honest feelings, and, not perhaps seeing his way to refuse, acceded to their request, and proceeded with the band to Ōsaka, and thence to Fushimi. But the band of *rōnin* arrived without their leader. The daimiō of the clan to which he owed allegiance happened to be also travelling in the same direction, and when the *rōnin* leader, in accordance with feudal etiquette, sought an audience to announce his intentions, he was promptly arrested, and sent back to his native place.

Some weeks later the daimiō of Ōka in the province of Bungo was passing through Fushimi, a suburb of the capital, on his way to Yedo to fulfil the duty of periodical residence. It was not customary in those days for daimiōs to stop at Kiōto on their way to and from Yedo, but the Court, with an increasing sense of its importance, affected to be indignant at what it professed to regard as a want of respect to the Throne.

'At a time like the present,' it was said, 'when all the daimiōs of the West who were devoted to the Throne were hastening to Kiōto, and exerting themselves on behalf of the State, to pass so close to the capital without the slightest intention of asking after the Mikado's health was a slight offered to the Court, and therefore a crime. The Prince Awata (one of the imperial princes), and the *Kwambaku* gave orders that his conduct should be rigidly inquired into, and in consequence a number of *rōnin* patriots proceeded at once to Fushimi, intercepted the daimiō of Ōka, and demanded an explanation. The daimiō obeyed the orders of the Court, and, entering Kiōto, took up his residence in a temple on the west of the city.'

This last instance seems to point to an understanding between the Court and the *rōnin*, and there is little doubt that this was often the case, and that the assemblage of *rōnin* in the neighbourhood of the capital was hastened by private advices received from persons in palace circles. The Court had no troops of its own, the military element in the capital being represented only by the Shōgun's forces. It is only natural, therefore, that it should welcome armed support from any quarter. We read, for example, of a retainer of the daimiō of Settsu collecting a number of confederates, and marching openly to Kiōto 'in order to work there for the good cause'. For his loyalty he was rewarded by the Emperor—in what way is not stated—but on returning to his native province he was put in prison, like the other *rōnin* leader we have mentioned, lest his chief should be suspected in Yedo of being in sympathy with the Court. This, too, was the pretext for Shimadzu's first visit to Kiōto, at the end of which, in addition to the Emperor's thanks, he received a sword and the name of Saburō, in place of his original name of Iduzmi; the young Prince of Chōshiū, on his way back to his province from Yedo, was persuaded to arrest his journey at the capital for the same object; and it was also for the same reason, and in answer to secret requests for aid, that so many of what were called the western daimiōs flocked with large retinues of armed followers to Kiōto.

It must not be supposed that the *rōnin* had matters all their own way. This was by no means the case. Always objects of suspicion to the Yedo Government, their movements were closely watched, and, when arrested, they usually received a short shrift, for the Shōgunate laws were severe, and at that time, as a measure of self-defence, they were administered in the harshest spirit. Sometimes, too, the tables were turned upon the *rōnin* in an unexpected manner, their own methods being used for their discomfiture. A dramatic incident of this kind occurred during the visit to Kiōto of Shimadzu Saburō—henceforth to be known by his new name—to which reference has already been made. A formidable band of Satsuma *rōnin* was already in the capital. Dissatisfied with what they regarded as the too cautious policy of the clan authorities, they were determined, in spite of all efforts to dissuade them, to strike a blow against the Shōgunate at once. A few Satsuma men in the suite of Shimadzu resolved to risk their lives in an attempt to defeat this design. So they went one evening after dark to the inn where the *rōnin* were staying. The latter were lodged in rooms upstairs. The party of Satsuma men, at the head of whom was Narabara, who has since held high official positions, established themselves downstairs in a part of the building some distance away from the quarters occupied by the *rōnin*, and invited their leaders to a consultation. At a given signal the lights were put out, and each man of the party struck at the *rōnin* he had singled out beforehand, crouching down after each stroke to avoid the sweep of the swords in the air. After a few minutes of desperate fighting all of the eight *rōnin* leaders were killed, and only one of their assailants. The survivors of the *mêlée* then went upstairs, and told the rest of the *rōnin* what they had done, expressing their willingness to die now that their object was accomplished. Their case seemed desperate, but the fury of the *rōnin* was appeased by the sudden championing of the opposite cause by one of their number, the younger Saigō, brother of the famous Saigō Takamori, and afterwards for many years a prominent member of the Tōkiō Ministry. He succeeded in persuading his comrades that the others had understood better than themselves their duty to the clan, and the State, and the affair ended without further bloodshed.

This is the popular account of what took place. The official version, which is given in the *Shichinen Shi*, ' The History of Seven Years,' is less romantic. This connects the incident with Shimadzu's meeting with the *rōnin* on his way to Kiōto, and says that, in accordance with the promise made to them, he memorialized the Throne, asking, amongst other things, for the dismissal of one of the two Councillors of State, who, since the Regent's death, had had the chief control of affairs, for orders summoning the other to Kiōto, and for the appointment of Prince Kéiki to be guardian to the young Shōgun, and of the ex-daimiō of Échizen to be regent ; that certain Satsuma *rōnin*, wishing to precipitate matters by attacking the palaces of Prince Kujō and of the Shōgun's residence were met and defeated by Narabara's party, seven of whom were wounded and one killed. The Court's answer to the memorial of Shimadzu was an order to him to remain at the capital to control the *rōnin*, but this incident, and the stern repressive measures subsequently taken by him, caused the Court, it is said, to regret its decision, and to rely afterwards more on the protection of the Prince of Chōshiū, whose lenient attitude towards the lawless bands of *rōnin* suggested his being, for the moment, a more amenable and useful ally.

After the death of the Regent the growing power of the Court showed itself in many ways. The Mito party held up its head again, and the Regent's friends were in their turn dismissed from office, fined, imprisoned, or banished, For a time indeed there seemed to be some prospect of a complete reconciliation between the Court and the Yedo Government. The latter had not hesitated to sacrifice the Regent's family and allies for this purpose, and, as a further means to this end, a marriage between the Mikado's sister and the young Shōgun was arranged. Moreover, advantage was taken of the general amnesty which was proclaimed on this occasion to restore to favour the chief members of the Mito party, who had been involved in the disgrace of their leader. But the concord was of short duration.

The Shōgun's marriage took place in the spring of 1862. In the summer of the same year an imperial messenger, escorted by Shimadzu Saburō, presented what was practically an ultimatum, demanding the presence of the Shōgun at Kiōto to consult with the Court in regard to the expulsion of foreigners. To this the Yedo Government after some demur consented, and the triumph of the reactionary party was emphasized by concessions on two other points, the appointment of Prince Kéiki to be guardian to his young cousin the Shōgun, in the place of Prince Tayasu, and the selection for the post of President of the Council of State of the ex-Prince of Échizen, the head of one of the numerous clans related to the Tokugawa family, a statesman noted as much for his persistent hostility to the late Regent as for his political association with the ex-Prince of Mito. As a further sign of the Court's displeasure, the Shōgun's Consort, who on her marriage had, in accordance with custom, assumed the title of Midaidokoro, always borne by ladies in her high position, was obliged to revert to her original title of Imperial Princess. At the same time the new turn given to the conduct of affairs was apparent in the more uncompromising tone assumed in regard to the question of foreign intercourse, despite the fact that Portugal in 1860, and Prussia in the following year, had been added to the list of 'treaty powers'. In its anxiety in 1858 to arrive at an understanding with the Court at almost any price, the Shōgunate had, as we have seen, made many concessions in point of form, concessions indeed which, strictly interpreted, might have been regarded as stultifying its own actions. And in the course of the negotiations conducted at Kiōto with this object the impression had undoubtedly been conveyed that the treaty with America of 1858, and consequently, by implication, those which followed it, the tenour of all being the same, were simply provisional arrangements, which might be cancelled at the pleasure of Japan in the time to come. This idea lay at the bottom of the Court's attitude in regard to this question, and to some extent explains the futile proceedings for the expulsion of foreigners which continued to be taken from time to time in subsequent years.

But in the midst of much that was futile the determined hostility of the Court and conservative party to everything foreign led to one practical result in the direction of their wishes. In their perplexity, placed as they were between the devil and the deep sea, the Yedo Government appealed through special envoys to the Treaty Powers, and also to the representatives of those powers in Japan, not to abrogate the treaties, which was what the Court wanted, but to postpone for five years the opening of the ports of Hiōgo and Niigata (or some other harbour on the west coast) and the towns of Yedo and Ōsaka. The governments addressed consented on the conditions recorded, so far as Great Britain was concerned, in the London Protocol of June 6, 1862.[1] The grounds on which this appeal was based were frankly stated in the protocol to be ' the difficulties experienced by the Tycoon and his ministers in giving effect to their engagements with foreign powers having treaties with Japan in consequence of the opposition offered by a party in Japan which is hostile to all intercourse with foreigners '. The conditions, stated shortly, were the cessation in future of official interference of all kinds with trade and intercourse. The wording of this instrument shows that the position of the Tycoon was becoming better understood in Europe. The

[1] Appendix 17.

title of royalty does not appear, as in the earlier treaties. The protocol also records the intention of the Japanese negotiators to recommend to their Government the opening, as a treaty port, of Tsushima, an island in the channel between Corea and Japan, which Russia had temporarily occupied the year before. The recommendation, if ever made, was never acted upon, and very wisely, for the position of the island is not favourable to trade. The idea in the minds of the envoys, due, it seems, to a suggestion made in London, was probably that the opening of the island to foreign trade might protect it against aggression on the part of any single foreign power.

In the autumn (October 1862) a momentous decision, indicating in itself the feebleness of the administration, was taken by the Shōgunate in regard to the periodical visits of the daimiōs to Yedo, to which reference was made in the opening chapter. The system known as *San-Kin Kō-tai*, ' taking turns in official attendance at Yedo,' was introduced by the third Shōgun, Iyémitsu, in the middle of the seventeenth century, as a political measure to strengthen the Shōgunate. It drew the feudal nobles in alternate years from the provinces to Yedo, where they stayed for fixed periods, leaving their wives and families behind as permanent hostages when they returned to their fiefs. The arrangement was troublesome, besides being inconvenient, and led to the loss of much time in journeying to and fro. It was also very costly, for in addition to the expense of the journeys, performed with every accompaniment of ostentatious luxury, it was the rule for each daimiō, on arriving in Yedo, to offer valuable presents to the Shōgun, who bestowed gifts in return. The details of this exchange of gifts, which never varied, was regulated with minute precision, the things to be given and received on these occasions being in each instance duly noted in the *bukan*, or manuals of the peerage. The changes now introduced made the conditions, both in regard to these periodical visits and the giving of the customary presents, much lighter. Though professedly made in the interests of the feudal nobles, who, it was said, would be enabled to attend more closely to the administration of their territories, and to the work of coast defence, we can see in them the hand of the Court and of the daimiōs who had previously belonged to the Mito party. From various authorities, which are not always in agreement, we gather that attendance at Yedo was regulated for the future somewhat as follows :—

The heads of the three Princely Tokugawa Houses of Owari, Kishiū, and Mito were required to visit Yedo only once every twelve years, in the years of the wild boar, the rat, and the dog, respectively, according to the calendar then in force, the period of residence at the seat of government not being stated. The great nobles, lords

of provinces (*Kokushiū*), such as the daimiōs of
Satsuma, Choshiū, and Tosa, who were privileged
to sit in the *Ōbiro-ma*, the highest of the antechambers of the Yedo Castle, were required to
attend at Yedo for only a hundred days every
third year. In the case of the daimiōs of Mino,
Tsushima, and Hizen, who, for some reason which
does not appear, seem to have occupied a special
position, attendance at Yedo was limited to only
one month in three years. The daimiōs who sat
in the *Tamari-no-ma*, the second ante-chamber, of
whom the late Regent was one, those of equal
rank but without that right, certain *fudai* daimiōs,
and the *tozama* daimiōs, were called upon to pass
one year out of three at Yedo; while the rest
of the feudal nobility, including the *hatamoto*,
were required to spend two hundred days there
every year. Things were made easier for them
in other respects, the general tendency being in
favour of relaxing the stringency of all ceremonial
observances and etiquette as between the Shōgun
and the feudal aristocracy. Those, for instance,
whose official duties kept them in Yedo might
apply for permission at any time to go to their
territories. Daimiōs were encouraged while in
Yedo to go to the Shōgun's castle at any time to
discuss ·State business, to talk over things with
other daimiōs, or in order that they might be
consulted by the Shōgun. They were asked to
bring small retinues with them when they came
to Yedo, to leave their mansions there in charge

of as few retainers as possible when they left, and
to avoid unnecessary trouble and expense in their
journeys to and fro.

But the greatest change of all was the abolition
of the rule under which the wives and families of
feudal nobles were detained permanently in Yedo
as hostages. Henceforth they were free to reside
in the provinces. The effect is thus described in
the ' Story of a Dream in the period of Genji ' :—

' In consequence all the daimiōs and hatamotos
who owned lands sent their wives and children
to their country residences, and in the twinkling
of an eye the flourishing city of Yedo became
like a desert ; so that the daimiōs allied to the
Tokugawa family, and the Tokugawa family
itself, and the vassals of the Shōgunate of all
ranks, and the townspeople too grieved and
lamented. They would have liked to see the
military glory of Kwantō shine again, but as the
great and small daimiōs who were not vassals of
Tokugawa had cut at the root of this forced
residence in Yedo, and few of them obeyed any
longer the commands of the *Bakufu*, they also
began to distrust it, and gradually the hearts
of the people fell away. And so the prestige of
the Tokugawa family, which had endured for
three hundred years, which had been really more
brilliant than Kamakura in the age of Yoritomo
on a moonlight night when the stars were shining,
which for more than two hundred and seventy
years had forced the daimiōs to come breathlessly
to take their turn of duty in Yedo, and had day
and night eighty thousand vassals at its beck and
call, fell to ruin in the space of one morning.'

What Yedo lost, the provinces and the capital

gained. Recovering something of its long-vanished greatness, the population of Kiōto increased, and trade and industries revived.

' From this time until the spring of 1863,' says the book from which our last quotation came, ' the daimiōs from all parts of the country came up to Kiōto to about the number of seventy, and besides them the number of vassals of the Shōgun was also very considerable. As none of them had residences in the capital, they hired temples as temporary head-quarters, so that all the temples and monasteries within and without the city were occupied in this way. The clans, anxious not to be behindhand in appearing at Kiōto, at last bought houses . . . and built barracks. The streets were crowded with *samurai* on foot and on horseback ; pleasure and sightseeing became the order of the day, and the capital flourished as it had never done in any former reign.'

In the spring of 1862 the Court had issued one of its many anti-foreign decrees, insisting on the expulsion of the foreign barbarians, and reminding the Yedo Government of the provisional nature of the treaties concluded by the Shōgunate. Early in the following year another stage in the futile protests of the Court against foreign intercourse was reached, when at a council held in Kiōto and attended by the Shōgun's guardian, Prince Kéiki, and many feudal nobles, it was decided that a date should be fixed for the expulsion of foreigners, and the cessation of all foreign intercourse.

In the meantime complications had occurred.

One of a party of four British subjects was killed
on the high road a few miles from Yokohama by
Satsuma men belonging to the retinue of Shimadzu
Saburo. The Satsuma leader was on his way back
from Yedo, whither he had escorted the imperial
messenger carrying the ultimatum to which reference has already been made. The confessed inability of the Government to punish the murderers
led to the bombardment of the Satsuma capital
by the British fleet in August of the same year.

This Richardson affair, in which Great Britain
was the only foreign country concerned, was
followed by a more serious incident, in which the
other clan, whose close connexion with the *rōnin*
movement has been mentioned, that of Choshiū,
were the aggressors, and several foreign powers
were involved. But this falls more naturally into
its place if dealt with as one of the results of the
anti-foreign movement, at the head of which the
Court had placed itself.

In the spring of 1863 the Shōgun, in compliance
with the imperial summons, went to Kiōto, which
had not seen a Shōgun for two hundred and fifty
years. There is something unusual, even for those
days, and almost pathetic, in the circumstances
under which the present visit was made. Iyémochi
had become Shōgun at the age of twelve, had
married three years later, and was now seventeen.
He was still, however, a ward under guardianship,
according to the etiquette of the time, and the person selected for the post of guardian was no other

than his cousin, who had been the rival candidate for the post he now occupied. Moreover, he was going to the capital against his wish, or at any rate against the wish of the Government he represented, and while, on the one hand, it was desired in Yedo that his visit should be very brief, the intention of the Court was to keep him as long as it could.

The Shōgun reached Kiōto on the 21st of April, and on the 24th he was received in audience by the Mikado. Four days later there appeared an imperial edict saying it was very natural for the Shōgun to wish to return to Yedo at once, for the purpose of organizing the defence of the country in the crisis occasioned by the visit of English ships, but that it was necessary for him to give personal orders for the defence of the capital and the adjacent seas. At the present moment, too, when it was a question of deciding upon warlike operations for the expulsion of the barbarians, it was important that there should be a complete understanding between sovereign and subject.

If the Shōgun returned to Yedo, he would be at a distance from the Court, and relations might be disturbed by misunderstandings due to defective communication of views, with grievous and irreparable consequences to the State. The imperial mind could not entertain without anxiety the idea of the Shōgun's return to Yedo. He must therefore allay this anxiety by staying in Kiōto, and giving his earnest attention to plans for the defence of the capital, and the adjacent seas.

On the same day the Emperor, accompanied by the Shōgun and his guardian, visited the Kamo Shrines in connexion with the measures to be taken for the expulsion of foreigers. A month later the Emperor paid a visit to other shrines in the neighbourhood, where it was arranged that the Shōgun should receive from the Emperor a sword in token of the part he was to play in the approaching campaign against the barbarians. But at the last moment the Shōgun pleaded sickness, and Prince Kéiki, his guardian, who took his place in the imperial procession, became also suddenly indisposed before the shrine was reached. So the ceremony of presenting the sword was never performed, much to the indignation of the anti-foreign party, who said that the Yedo Government did not after all intend to drive out the barbarians.

On the 5th of June the question of expelling the foreign barbarians was discussed in council, the Shōgun and his guardian being present, and a date for their expulsion was solemnly fixed. The date chosen was the 24th (or 25th, according to some accounts) of June. Preparations for hostilities were at once made by the Court, and the Yedo Government found themselves in the impossible position of appearing to acquiesce in measures for the expulsion of foreigners, knowing all the time the futility of the proceedings. In this new crisis we find them, as before, trying to face both ways at once ; yielding to the imperative messages from the capital, and at the same time welcoming any opportunity for shelving the orders received. Some suspicion of their attitude being entertained in Kiōto, the Prince of Mito was sent to Yedo to see that the Mikado's orders were carried out. He was followed later by Prince Kéiki, and on the appointed day, the 24th of June, Ogasawara Dzusho no Kami, a member of the Council of State, having conferred with two of his colleagues, Matsudaira Buzen no Kami and Inouyé Kawachi no Kami, who, during the Shōgun's absence from Yedo, had been left in joint charge of affairs, delivered to the British, French, and American ministers a letter informing them of the Government's decision to close the country again to foreigners, and of his readiness to open negotiations at once for that purpose. The reception given to his communication was disquieting. It looked, indeed, as if Japan might be forestalled in the commencement of hostilities ; for the British authorities were still pressing the question of Richardson's murder, and an intimation was given by the powers concerned that suitable steps would be taken to protect foreign interests. So the Shōgunate in its alarm paid the indemnity asked for by the British, and insisted on Ogasawara's explaining to the Court that ' it (the Court) knew nothing about foreign affairs, and that if hostilities once broke out it would not be easy to make

matters quiet again '. Accordingly the Prince of
Mito and Ogasawara reported that the two
questions of Richardson's murder, and the closing
of the country, must be kept separate ; as to the
first, an indemnity had been paid ; as regarded
the latter, negotiations would be continued.
Prince Kéiki, too, at this juncture memorialized
the Throne, saying that on the question of the
expulsion of foreigners no two Councillors of State
were agreed, and that the imperial mandate
could not be carried out. He also tendered his
resignation, but it was not accepted.

While the Mikado's decision was being communicated to the foreign ministers at Yokohama,
the Shōgun had left Kiōto on a visit to Ōsaka,
and Kishiū, his native province. He was back
in the capital at the end of June, and a month
later returned by sea to Yedo. His return, which
seems to have taken the Court by surprise, was
hastened by the action of the Yedo Government,
who, becoming anxious at his long absence, sent
two steamers with troops to bring him away.

Meanwhile, on the 24th of June, the day on which
Ogasawara had delivered his letter in Yokohama,
the Chōshiū forts at Shimonoséki fired on an American vessel—the reason assigned being that this
was the date fixed for the expulsion of foreigners.
A fortnight later other foreign vessels were fired
at. Reprisals followed, and the Chōshiū clansmen
were worsted in engagements with the Americans
and French. But the straits remained closed

till the autumn of the following year, when the batteries were attacked and destroyed by an expedition in which Great Britain, France, the United States, and Holland took part.

A great deal of false sentiment has been manufactured in connexion with this incident and the indemnity exacted by the four powers concerned under the Shimonoséki Convention signed at Yokohama on the 22nd of October, 1864.[1] One writer on Japan, the author of *The Mikado's Empire*, even goes so far as to call it ' a needless and wicked act of war '. The truth is that nothing helped Japan more, or did so much to save the situation for her at a critical time, than the destruction of the Shimonoséki forts and the bombardment of Kagoshima. A sharp lesson was needed in each case. Nothing else would have answered the purpose.

The action of the Chōshiū Prince in precipitating hostilities with foreigners before preparations everywhere were completed gave great umbrage in Kiōto, and the fact that his troops had been unsuccessful did not improve his position with the Court. Eventually the Chōshiū clansmen, who had figured so prominently in the protection of the Court, and the encouragement of the *rōnin*, were forbidden to stay in the capital, and accordingly they left in a body, being accompanied by seven of the leading Court nobles. One of these was Prince Sanjō, who was afterwards Prime

[1] Appendix 19.

Minister in the first Cabinet formed after the Restoration.

No sooner had the Shōgun returned to Yedo than he addressed a memorial to the Mikado on the subject of foreign relations, which confirmed the reports previously received by the Court from the Prince of Mito, Prince Kéiki, and Ogasawara. In this he said that he had come to the conclusion that the present was not a suitable moment for expelling foreigners, and that the measures to be taken for that purpose should be postponed. He advised, therefore, that it should be left to him to fix a suitable date later on. To this the Court reluctantly consented.

The attempt to persuade the Foreign Representatives to consent to the closing of the port of Yokohama had thus failed completely, its only result having been to bring fresh discredit on the Shōgunate, and to suggest to the British and French Governments the advisability of making special arrangements for the protection of their subjects. Thinking, however, that they might find foreign governments more amenable, if approached in Europe, than the diplomatists on the spot, the Shōgunate decided to send a mission to London and Paris ; and the murder of a French officer near Yokohama in the autumn of that year (1863) furnished a pretext for its dispatch. The mission effected nothing in the desired direction, and it did not go further than Paris. But when its members returned, in August, 1864, they brought with them a convention they had signed in Paris [1] for the reopening of the Shimonoséki straits. This contained a stipulation providing for its immediate operation, without ratification by either party. The Shōgunate, however, conscious of their inability to carry out this provision, repudiated the agreement, and it never came into force ; but the mere fact of its signature delayed for a short time the destruction of the Shimonoséki forts.

The threatening attitude of the Court, and the inability of the Yedo Government to restrain the growing hostility of the anti-foreign party, made it necessary to take precautionary measures for the protection of the foreign community. Towards the end of the year 1863, with the full approval of the Japanese authorities, French and British troops were quartered in Yokohama, where they remained until 1875.

The history of this short period, which calls for rather detailed treatment, is written in proclamations, memorials, and political correspondence. All three have a strong family resemblance. Under the influence of Chinese culture men think in grooves and formulas. And this is also how they speak and write. So the same stock phrases did duty on each occasion. The Court and the Shōgunate, which issued proclamations, the memorialists, who addressed themselves to each in turn, or, when

[1] Appendix 14.

they were simple *samurai*, to their feudal lords, and the inditers of political epistles, which were often manifestos, were all equally distressed at the perilous condition of affairs ; all equally concerned for the safety and honour of the State, and the sanctity of the country's laws ; all burning to get rid of the foreign barbarian ; all equally convinced of the vital importance of giving rest to the country, and tranquillity to the imperial mind. We hear of little else.

Conditions such as those described did not admit of much progress. On the whole, nevertheless, things were moving forwards in spite of anti-foreign sentiment and administrative chaos. The saving factor in the situation was the presence of the foreigner, who had come to stay. This fact was gradually becoming recognized. The fighting at Kagoshima and in the Shimonoséki straits brought it home to the mind of the Court at Kiōto, and led also, as more than one writer has pointed out, to the creation in each of the two clans concerned of a small but influential group of men, who were thenceforth in favour of foreign intercourse, seeing clearly that therein lay the only salvation for Japan.

CHAPTER V

THE FALL OF THE SHŌGUNATE

IN the midst of the political confusion of the short period dealt with in the last chapter we notice two things : the beginning of the formidable coalition of western daimiōs which subsequently overthrew the Shōgunate, and the lead taken thus early by the two clans of Satsuma and Chōshiū. In the first of these clans the chief figure is not that of its ruler, but Shimadzu Saburō, the father of the ruling prince, and the brother of his predecessor. He it was who succeeded the ex-Prince of Mito as the moving spirit of the party opposing the Shōgunate ; who became the adviser and protector of the Throne ; who alternately encouraged and held back the *rōnin* ; and who, like the statesman he replaced, while secretly favouring the study of foreign learning for clan purposes, figured to the last as a determined opponent of everything that was foreign.

Japanese writers take different views as to the actual date from which the authority of the Shōgunate became so seriously impaired as to justify the conclusion that its downfall had begun. Some think that this date should be placed at the time of the issue of the proclamation which so greatly changed the system of the attendance of the daimiōs at Yedo, and did so much to restore the ancient glory of the capital at the expense of its eastern rival ; others hold that the overthrow of the Tokugawa rule did not suggest itself as a realizable project until the failure of the Shōgunate expedition against Chōshiū. To us it seems that the first weakening of Tokugawa authority is to be seen in the reference to Kiōto when Perry arrived, and that the turning-point of its fortunes came with the death of the Regent Ïi in 1860. After that occurrence the Shōgunate's authority was never the same. Little by little the Court encroached on the administrative sphere in which for centuries the Shōgun had ruled unchallenged, and one by one the privileges it had enjoyed for so long were withdrawn. Its authority was impaired by the relaxation in 1862 of the rules for the attendance of the daimiōs at Yedo, and by the concessions made in regard to investiture and other matters in 1864 ; and the Chōshiū campaign exposed its military weakness. The point to be noted is the gradual waning of its influence. Its end did not come all at once, but by slow degrees. When the Restoration took place it was not so much that the Shōgunate was overthrown, as that the institution bearing that name had fallen to pieces, having outlasted its time.

Our attention must now be given to the struggle between the Shōgunate and the Chōshiū clan, which was the final stage in the undoing of the existing order of things.

It was in the summer of 1863 that this clan, by reading too literally the Court's pronouncement against foreigners, had involved the Government in complications with foreign powers, and brought about the expulsion of its clansmen from Kiōto. Smarting under this rebuff, and anxious, perhaps, to anticipate the operations of the Shōgunate, which had received orders to punish it for firing on foreign vessels at Shimonoséki, the clan planned a sudden raid on the city of Kiōto. The instruments for the purpose lay ready to its hands.

It has already been pointed out how the Court at one time was disposed to rely more on the support of the Chōshiū clan than on that of Satsuma, owing to the former's more lenient attitude towards the bands of lawless *samurai*, who, as *rōnin*, were a doubtful asset to their employers. The attitude of the Court had, however, changed. A reconciliation, good for the moment at least, had been effected with the Shōgunate, and the Satsuma leader, Shimadzu Saburō, was in favour both with the Court and with the Yedo Government. The capital, therefore, being no longer a safe place for those *rōnin* whose patron was the Chōshiū Prince, the territory of the latter, and not Kiōto, became the centre of their activity, and large numbers were enrolled into a force called the *Kiheitai*, or ' Irregulars '.

The object of the clan's raid was to gain possession of the person of the Emperor, and then proclaim their opponents rebels (*Chōteki*), a favourite device resorted to during the civil wars of earlier times in order to enlist popular sympathy, and at the same time act with the weight of imperial authority.

The details of the affair are recorded at length in two books, ' The Story of a Dream in the period of Genji,' already quoted, and the *Kinsei Shiriaku*, ' A History of Modern Times,' both of which have been translated by Sir Ernest Satow.

Towards the end of July two detachments arrived at Ōsaka by sea from Suwo, the nearest to the capital of the two Chōshiū provinces, one slightly in advance of the other. The first was a mixed force, some 400 strong, composed of Chōshiū *samurai* under the command of Fukuhara Echigo, a karō of the clan, and *rōnin* irregulars ; the second, and more numerous, body was under the leadership of two retainers of the Prince of Chōshiū, named Kunishi and Masuda. These forces moved on Kiōto from Ōsaka, and established themselves at three different places in the suburbs, Fukuhara, the most prominent of the leaders, addressing a petition to the Court. In this it was stated that ever since the Prince of Chōshiū and his son [1] had obeyed His Majesty's desire for the

---

[1] A characteristic feature of the documents of this time relating to Chōshiū affairs is the frequent association of the names of the prince and his son. The prince not having abdicated, there was no reason for the son's name to be coupled with the father's. Nor did the association of names impart any strength to the clan administration, for both princes were completely in the hands of *karō*, or other clan *samurai*.

expulsion of the barbarians (by firing on foreign vessels in the Straits of Shimonoséki) they had passed their days and nights in ceaseless anxiety lest they should fail in carrying out the imperial will ; and that the clan was unable to understand why the Court should attribute guilt to Prince Sanjō, and the other Court nobles, who had taken refuge in Chōshiū. The clan, therefore, humbly prayed that the seven Court nobles might be' restored to their functions, and the Prince of Chōshiū and his son might be permitted to re-enter the capital. A similar petition was presented a day or two later by the leader of the *rōnin* irregulars.

To the first of these petitions the reply of the Court was to the effect that Fukuhara might remain at Fushimi with a small number of men, send the petition quietly through the proper hands, and wait for the Emperor's orders. As for the rest of the Chōshiū forces, they must return at once to their own territory. Fukuhara, who was at Fushimi, expressed his readiness to obey these instructions, but it soon appeared that he had no authority over the other leaders. Accordingly, after a delay of several days, a notification was issued by the Court to the Chōshiū clansmen at the two other places in the suburbs, referring to the orders already given to Fukuhara, and adding that the Court had decided to take vigorous measures at once for the chastisement of the rebellious clan. The Court's firm attitude put an end to negotiations, and the raiders, one of whom, Kido, played a prominent part afterwards in the Restoration, forthwith delivered their attack. This was directed from three different points, and was designed to converge on the imperial Flower Garden. Here the Prince of Aidzu, the guardian, or military governor, of the city, had established himself for the double purpose of directing the defence, in which task he was assisted by Prince Kéiki, and seeing to the personal safety of the Emperor.

And here it should be mentioned that, when the order of the Court expelling the Prince of Chōshiū and his son from the capital was issued, a certain number of Chōshiū clansmen had been allowed to remain in the city in charge of the clan *yashiki*. The leading *samurai* of this garrison of caretakers took part in the discussions at which the policy to be adopted towards Chōshiū was decided, and as soon as the notification above mentioned was issued, they evacuated the *yashiki*, and joined their comrades outside the town.

The forces in Kiōto at the disposal of the Shōgunate consisted chiefly of *samurai* of the Aidzu, Kuwana, Satsuma, Échizen, and Hikoné clans, with a sprinkling of *rōnin*, and considerably outnumbered the assailants. The fighting which ensued was fierce, and for some time the advantage lay, if anything, with the assailants ; but eventually superior numbers, and the courage of the Aidzu and Satsuma men gained the day, and the raiders, being completely routed, fled in all directions. The Court having commanded the instant chastisement of the rebellious clan, the Shōgunate embarked upon the campaign against Chōshiū which, by exposing its military weakness, was to prove ultimately its own undoing.

The raid had taken place on the 19th of August, 1864. Six days afterwards the Government issued a proclamation which amounted to a declaration of war against the Prince of Chōshiū. It is given in the *Kinreikō*, a collection of Tokugawa enactments, published by the Department of Justice, the two first volumes of which appeared in 1894. It was addressed to all the feudal nobility, twenty-one of whom received it in Kiōto from the Shōgun's resident there.

The proclamation described the raid made by the Prince of Chōshiū, and said that circumstances showed that it was evidently part of a military plot. It ordered, therefore, the immediate punishment of the rebellious clan.

The official editors of the collection of enactments above mentioned give in a note what are called the military instructions which the Prince of Chōshiū and his son were accused in the proclamation of giving to one of the leaders of the raid. They show the proneness to minute detail so characteristic of the Tokugawa period. The leader to whom the instructions are addressed is told that the men of the various companies bound for Kiōto are placed under his charge, and

that he has authority in all matters. Stress is laid
on the necessity of harmony between the various
companies. Private feuds are strictly forbidden,
and dissipation of all kinds and all extravagance in
dress are condemned. Propriety of behaviour and
discretion in speech are enjoined ; and it is added
that any one offending against these orders is to
be tried by military law, and sentenced, if guilty,
to perform *harakiri*.

When every allowance has been made for the
situation, these sound rather singular orders for
troops on the point of starting for the capital
to make a raid on the palace of their sovereign.

Another interesting state-paper of this time,
coming from the opposite side, appears in the
collection of enactments already mentioned. It is
called ' A respectful inquiry from the Prince of
Chōshiū inviting the decision of the Government
after he and his retainers had been reprimanded ',
but whether this was the original title of the
document, or is simply that given by the official
editors, is not clear. However this may be, this
document, which is dated the 4th of September,
1864, was evidently the public reply of the Prince
of Chōshiū and his son to the Government's
impeachment. In spite of the deferential language
used, a note of defiance can be detected in the
communication. It stated that the prince and
his son had learnt with profound regret of the
conduct of certain runaway retainers, who, in
company with some *rōnin*, had, it appeared,

proceeded to the palace precincts, and, showing no reverence for the Court, had been guilty of riotous behaviour. The prince and his son had relied on the Chōshiū clansmen being restrained by their leaders, but the latter had apparently lost control of their men, and thus a disturbance had taken place. For this the two princes felt their responsibility, and they asked that judgement might be passed on them.

No notice was taken of this communication by the Government, but preparations for the campaign were rapidly made. The chief command of the expedition was given to the ex-Prince of Owari, the second in command being the ex-Prince of Échizen.

The expedition was successful, and early in the following year (1865) the Tokugawa forces returned to Ōsaka, their port of departure, having accomplished all that was desired. The rebellious clan had been ' chastised ' according to instructions, the five Court nobles who still remained in Chōshiū territory had been handed to the safe custody of other clans, and the three Chōshiū leaders of the raid had been executed.

The success of the Government was due, however, not to the overwhelming superiority of the Tokugawa troops, but to the co-operation of several of the leading clans, including that of Satsuma ; and to the fact that the Chōshiū clan was at the time divided into two parties. Of these one was eager and ambitious for the clan to play

a prominent part in the stirring times which were
beginning, and was as devoted to the Court as it
was hostile to the Shōgunate ; while the other,
nicknamed the Vulgar View Party, was in favour
of a cautious and moderate policy, and strongly
disapproved of the raid on Kiōto. Before the
advanced guard of the Tokugawa forces had
reached Chōshiū territory the latter party had
gained the ascendant, and, having imprisoned the
leaders of the raid, and many others concerned
in it, had gone so far as to lay hands on the prince
and his son, and confine them in a Buddhist
temple.

The return of the Tokugawa forces to Ōsaka
was generally interpreted as signifying that the
resistance of the clan was at an end, and the
Government were congratulating themselves on
the prompt suppression of a movement which at
one time had caused much anxiety, when the
aspect of things was suddenly changed by the
receipt of news that the anti-Shōgunate party
in Chōshiū, which had appeared to be crushed, had
again gained the upper hand, and that the whole
clan was once more in commotion.

The change was due to the efforts of a certain
Chōshiū clansman named Takasugi Shinsaku, to
whose initiative the raising of the irregular troops,
previously mentioned, had been due. He had
returned to Chōshiū as soon as the Government
forces had withdrawn, and, collecting a large
number of the men he had previously enrolled,

had attacked and defeated the adherents of the
Vulgar View Party, and gained control of the clan
territory. His proceedings had apparently the
sanction of the Prince of Chōshiū. To tell the
truth, however, neither this feudal chief nor his
son seem to have counted for much in the councils
of the clan. We have already heard of them as
having been confined in a temple before the arrival
of the Government troops. The same historian
now tells us :—

'Takasugi and his friends' (the quotation is
from Sir Ernest Satow's translation) 'carried off
the prince and his son to the town of Yamaguchi,
where extensive fortifications had been constructed
in the year when the expulsion of the barbarians
was first resolved upon. The two princes had been
originally removed to this stronghold, but after
the attack on Kiōto the "Vulgar View Party"
had placed them in a temple at Hagi, and they
were now carried back again.'

At this critical juncture, when the Chōshiū clan
were preparing for the fresh struggle with the
Tokugawa Government which could no longer be
avoided, their hands were unexpectedly strengthened by the action of the clan of Satsuma. In
the previous year the Chōshiū forts at Shimonséki
had fired upon and sunk a Satsuma steamer,
mistaking her for a foreign vessel. Several lives
had been lost on this occasion, and it was said at
the time of the Kiōto attack that the Satsuma
men who defended the palace against the Chōshiū
raiders still bore a grudge against them in connexion

with this incident. The wounded Chōshiū men, however, who fell into their hands on this occasion were kindly treated, and eventually sent back to Chōshiū ; and soon afterwards private overtures were made by the Satsuma clan for the establishment of a good understanding between the two clans. These were gladly accepted by the Chōshiū clansmen, and the arrangement had a great effect on the result of the campaign.

It seems also to have occurred to the clan, or to the party there in the ascendant at the time, after the affair of the Kiōto raid, that it might be advisable to make their position clearer to foreigners. Some such intention apparently underlay the letter addressed by the Prince of Chōshiū to the British admiral just after the bombardment of Shimonoséki in the autumn of 1864. In this the prince explained that when in the previous year, and subsequently, he had, in obedience to the commands of the court and the Shōgunate, fired on foreign vessels, he was surprised to learn that his conduct was regarded as violent and irregular, and contrary to the imperial commands. About this time he heard from two of his retainers who had returned to Chōshiū that they had been treated with kindness by the admiral. His son, the Prince of Nagato, had gone to Kiōto in order to ascertain definitely the wishes of the Emperor (in regard to foreigners), but on his way there the disturbances in Kiōto had taken place, and he was therefore unable to carry out his intention.

The prince had endeavoured on two occasions
to communicate with the admiral in order to explain
that there would be no interference with vessels
passing through the straits, but without success,
and then the Shimonoséki fighting had taken place.
He wished the admiral to understand that there
was no settled ill-will on his part, that he had no
wish to cause suffering to large numbers of people,
and that all he desired was peace.

A glance at the map will show that the two
provinces of Suwo and Nagato, forming the
territory of the Chōshiū clan, lie at the extreme
southern end of the main island, the former
bordering on the inland sea, and the latter
touching the same sea on the south, and the Sea
of Japan on the west. The Chōshiū territory
was accessible, therefore, both by land and sea.
The Tokugawa forces included contingents from
several clans, but their previous Satsuma allies
were conspicuous by their absence, the clan having
sent in a memorial protesting against the injustice
of the war, and declining to furnish its quota.

The Satsuma people were not alone in their
objection to the renewal by the Government of
hostilities with Chōshiū. The ex-Prince of Owari,
who had, as we have seen, held the chief command
on the previous occasion, remonstrated strongly
against this course being taken, pointing out that
' it was not right to take up arms without manifest
cause, that the Prince of Chōshiū had made
atonement by inflicting capital punishment on

his chief retainers, and that the Shōgunate, by taking this unjustifiable action, was imperilling the very existence of the Tokugawa family '. Another kinsman of the Shōgun, the ex-Prince of Échizen, spoke in the same sense. Similar advice was given by other councillors, but it was not taken, and at the end of May, 1865, an imperial decree announcing the impending chastisement of Chōshiū was issued, and it was arranged that this time the Shōgun would take the field in person at the head of all his vassals.

It seems reasonable to assume that for this decision to resume hostilities the young Shōgun, who was only nineteen years of age, was not responsible. His personal influence in the Government seems never to have been great, and so little relish had he for State affairs that he petitioned about this time to be allowed to retire from the position of Shōgun in favour of his cousin and ex-guardian, Prince Kéiki. Nor, although the Court had openly approved the original expedition against the clan, is it likely that its opinion would have been opposed on this point to that held in common by the Satsuma clan, the ex-Princes of Owari and Échizen, and other prominent personages, not to speak of the strong claim on its goodwill which the clan of Chōshiū had established before the raid took place. The Tokugawa statesmen who were responsible for the disastrous course which was followed may have been influenced by the fact that the previous proceedings against the clan had lacked the final conclusion in such cases, namely, the formal punishment of the Mōri family. When the Tokugawa forces were withdrawn on the previous occasion, this point was reserved for future decision. A difference of opinion had arisen subsequently, the Court being disposed not to proceed further in the matter, while the Shōgunate was inclined to impose humiliating conditions, which included the conveyance of the Prince of Chōshiū and his son to Yedo under arrest. The Government may have felt that in the circumstances their dignity had suffered, and that it was necessary to do something to reassert their waning authority.

Let us look for a moment at the military position of the Shōgunate. By a law passed in 1648, known as the Keian law from the name of the year-period in which it was issued, the feudal nobility were called on to furnish two men for military service in time of war for every hundred pounds sterling worth of annual produce which their lands were estimated to yield. This placed at the Shōgunate's disposal a force variously estimated at between 400,000 and 500,000 men. In 1861, a few years before the date at which we have now arrived, the contribution of men for £100 of revenue was reduced by one-half. Further changes were made at the same period by the introduction of the rule that money or rice might be substituted for men. Advantage was taken very generally of this permission. The military power

of the Shōgunate had, therefore, by this time been
reduced in two ways, the smaller contingents
furnished, and the commutations permitted. And
the testimony of many Japanese writers goes to
show that there was a great falling off also in
military efficiency. The Shōgunate troops included,
we are told, large numbers of needy adventurers,
and a large proportion was without cohesion or
proper military training. The fighting capacity, too,
of the *samurai* in many parts of the country had,
according to the same testimony, greatly deteriorated. The view generally expressed that the
value of the *samurai* lay in his fighting capacity,
and that when he no longer excelled as a fighting
man he was useless for all purposes, is one which
will be endorsed by all who had an opportunity
of making the acquaintance of Japanese troops
before the introduction of conscription on the
Western model.

In the summer of 1865 the Shōgun proceeded
to Ōsaka from Yedo, and for many weeks afterwards contingents from various clans were to be
seen pursuing their way from different parts of
the country to the same place, where preparations
for the forthcoming campaign were being made
on a large scale. But there was much delay.
Operations did not commence till more than
twelve months later. In the interval the Government continued to publish fierce denunciations
against Chōshiū, coupled with calls to arms
against the ' rebels ' as they were termed ; orders,

to which no attention was paid, were issued for the attendance of the two princes at Yedo; instructions, which were without practical result, were promulgated for the holding of a species of tribunal at Hiroshima; and notifications prohibiting the entry of persons, or goods, into Chōshiū by sea were sent to various parts of the country. Finally, with the nominal approval of the Throne, a decree was published removing from the Mōri family the stigma of 'rebels', but confiscating a large portion of their lands, ordering the abdication of the Prince and his son, and the appointment of a fitting successor, to be nominated by the Government, and notifying the extinction of the families of the three chief retainers concerned in the Kiōto raid. On the Chōshiū side communications of all kinds protesting against the action taken against the clan were addressed to the Court, to the Government, and to other clans.

In one of these documents—signed by the *karō*, or chief retainers, of the clan—complaint is made of the refusal of the Government to forward a petition of the clan to the Court, and of its neglect to answer repeated memorials from the clan. The Shōgunate is reminded of its weak and vacillating action; of its having asked the advice of the Court and of the nation on the policy of establishing foreign intercourse; of the fact that the 'Shimoda' Treaty [1] never received the sanction of the Throne beforehand; of its written promise,

[1] American Treaty of 1857.

to which all the members of the Council of State
set their seals, to expel all foreigners within five,
or, at the most, eight, years, and of its complete
failure to fulfil it ; of the Shōgun's visit to Kiōto,
and of the imperial vow taken before the gods
to drive away the barbarians ; and of the notifications which were accordingly circulated throughout
the country.

' The prince and his son have,' it is added, ' ever
since been troubled in their minds about the two
policies of opening or closing the country, but
it is clear that they have had no selfish motives,
but have been actuated solely by the desire to obey
the imperial wishes ; and now they are accused of
having, in their attempts to expel the barbarians,
committed an act of private and unauthorized
war. The offence of firing on foreign vessels at
Shimonoséki having been expiated, the troops
of the Government under the ex-Prince of Owari
were withdrawn. But now it is announced that
hostilities are to be reopened. The Shōgun is
to take the field in person, and commissioners
charged with the collection of information are
already at work in the neighbouring province.
Nothing remains,' it is said, ' but to die, but we
make a last appeal to the Government to stay
its hand, and, by exercising generosity and justice,
to give tranquillity to the spirits of the deceased
ancestors of the prince and his son, and happiness
to the people of the two provinces.'

Another of these state-papers is a memorial
issued in the name of the whole clan :—

' The reputation for loyalty to the Throne,'
says the memorial, ' which has distinguished our

two princes for many years has been lost in
a single morning. Not only has this happened,
but a national calamity has been brought about,
and no opportunity is given to them for removing
the stain of an unjust accusation, or for discharging
even a small portion of their obligations to the
Throne. We, who have stolen our lives, and
wasted our days, are overwhelmed with fear,
trembling with the perfect sincerity induced by
a sense of many crimes.'

And after protesting that no thought of irrever-
ence towards the Throne was ever in the minds
of the two princes, the memorial concludes with
the statement that the clansmen have come to
a common decision to defend their territory, and
refuse to obey the Government's commands.

A letter addressed about the same time, the
summer of 1865, by the two princes to the Geishiu
clan, whose territory, the province of Aki, or
Geishiu, formed the eastern frontier of Chōshiū,
is couched in the same defiant tone.

' We put ourselves to some trouble,' it says,
' to go to Kiōto by arrangement, and render
assistance to the Court, and we were under the
impression that some ease had thereby been
vouchsafed to the imperial mind. We told our
opinion freely, and without reserve, to the responsible officers of the Throne, but evil officials having
maligned us, we incurred the imperial censure,
and now the Shōgun is coming to chastise the
two provinces. We do not think the continuance
of our useless lives can benefit either the Empire
or the Government. We have, therefore, agreed
to give battle at once, and die fighting. It being

the practice of our House when we go to war to
announce the fact to the Emperor, we have the
honour to give you this notice.'

Another curious document, written evidently
on the eve of hostilities, is given in the *History of
Thirty Years*. The date is June, 1865. It bears
no signature nor address, but the author calls it
'a notice in writing sent to the House of Chōshiū',
—in other words the Mōri family. The internal
evidence points to its having been written by
some member of the Tokugawa Government who
was friendly to the Chōshiū Prince. It runs as
follows :—

'It is said that the Shōgun takes the field in
person. This being so, it will be a great happiness
if you atone for your fault by submission, and if
your submission is accepted. If you do not agree
to do this, war is inevitable, but I beg earnestly
that you will tender your submission. Then, if
it is not accepted, it cannot be helped, and you will
be prepared for the worst. I entreat you to
discharge your duty of loyalty even at the sacrifice
of life. Bear in mind that it is not to us only that
you owe loyalty, but also to your ancestors.'

The campaign commenced in July, 1866, the
town of Hiroshima, in Geishiū, close to the eastern
frontier of Chōshiū, which served a similar purpose
in Japan's two recent foreign wars, being chosen
as the base of operations. From the first the
Government troops were unable to make any
headway, although they had the advantage of
numbers, and could attack both by sea and land ;

and after some months of fruitless effort they were driven back to their base at Hiroshima.

In September of that year (1866) the young Shōgun Iyémochi died, being succeeded by his cousin Prince Kéiki,[1] and, in accordance with the etiquette of court mourning, orders for a temporary cessation of hostilities were issued. To these Chōshiū, distrusting the Government's intentions, seems to have demurred, and the war smouldered on in a fitful way.

The death of the Shōgun was followed shortly by that of the Emperor Kōmei, which took place in February, 1867. He was succeeded by his son the present Emperor. By this time it was apparent that no success could be looked for in the operations against Chōshiū. The country, which had never been in favour of the renewal of hostilities, was tired of war. The Government, financially embarrassed and crippled by the Shimonoséki and Kagoshima indemnities, and by the heavy and unaccustomed expenditure, which in one way and another foreign intercourse had entailed, were coming to the end of their resources, being already reduced to call for donations to the war fund from Buddhist and Shintō shrines. The issue therefore, in March, of a notification announcing a general disbandment of the troops on account

---

[1] The name of Kéiki was in reality only assumed by him on his accession as Shōgun. He was previously known by his surname of Hitotsubashi, but we have throughout spoken of him as Kéiki in order to prevent confusion.

of national mourning for the late Emperor was
welcomed on all sides.

Thus the war came to an end.   But one matter
still remained for settlement, as had occurred on
the previous occasion.   This was the question of
the punishment of the clan.   It was not till July
of the same year that this point was dealt with.
But the proclamation then issued settled nothing.
It merely suggested that lenient steps should be
taken, and added that the four clans which had
come to Kiōto and the Shōgun concurred in this
view.   But the two princes had already by decree
been deprived of their rank and titles, and the
withholding for the present of the formal restoration
of these was probably regarded as meeting the
case.[1]

During the stormy period beginning with the
Kiōto raid, and ending with this Proclamation of
July, 1867, the course of foreign relations is marked
by the conclusion of further treaties and arrangements.   The first which calls for notice is the
Shimonoséki Convention, concluded on the 22nd
of October, 1864.[2]   So much has been said and
written in condemnation of the conduct of the
four powers concerned, Great Britain, America,
France, and Holland, in exacting a pecuniary
indemnity for the act of what the convention
itself terms ' a rebellious prince ', that it may be
well to recall the fact that the agreement gave

---

[1] The two princes were formally pardoned in January, 1868,
after the Shōgun's resignation.   [2] Appendix 19.

to the Japanese Government the option of opening
the port of Shimonoséki in lieu of an indemnity,
and that the foreign powers would have much
preferred the former solution. The other important
agreement is the Tariff Convention of June 25,
1866,[1] to which Japan and the same four powers
who signed the Shimonoséki Convention were
parties. The effect of this Tariff Convention was
to substitute for the existing tariff of varying
rates averaging about 15 % *ad valorem* a simplified
tariff of one uniform duty of 5 % *ad valorem* on
all imports and exports ; to place on record the
right of a Japanese subject to go abroad on
obtaining a passport from his authorities ; to
make a beginning in the lighting of the Japanese
coasts and harbours ; and to take measures for
the establishment of a Government Mint, as a
first step in the reorganization of the Japanese
currency. Treaties were also entered into with
Belgium in 1866, and with Italy and Denmark
in 1867. Various arrangements were also made
regarding the foreign settlement at Yokohama and
other matters. The two questions, however, which,
perhaps, more than anything else occupied the
attention of the foreign representatives were
the ratification by the Emperor of the existing
treaties, and the opening of the port of Hiōgo.

In the diary of the first American representative
in Japan we notice not long after his arrival the
first dawning of a suspicion that the Shōgun, or

[1] Appendix 20.

Tycoon, was not the real sovereign of Japan. Mr. Harris, like others after him, felt that there was something in the background, a puzzle to be cleared up, though its solution was not possible then. At the time of which we are now speaking several years had elapsed since the negotiation of the Harris Treaty, and foreign Governments were well aware of the existence of a sovereign in seclusion, though the exact relations between Kiōto and Yedo were not fully understood. They were aware, moreover, that the Imperial Court was not well disposed towards foreigners, and foreign intercourse, for, in addition to the dangers attending residence in the Shōgun's capital, their representatives had been confronted with the unpleasant duty of rejecting official overtures, emanating from Kiōto, for the closing of the country, which meant the abandonment of all that had been gained in the course of several years by a combination of force and diplomacy. The representatives themselves, in the freshness of their knowledge, could not fail to be impressed by the growing influence of a Throne whose existence had only recently been realized. It was generally felt, therefore, that as an important step in the consolidation of good relations, the Emperor, who had given his formal approval to the earlier treaties, should be invited to ratify those which had taken their place. Accordingly a powerful combined squadron of foreign vessels assembled in the harbour of Hiōgo in the autumn of 1865 with the object of putting pressure on the Shōgunate, and indirectly on the Court at Kiōto, in regard to this matter. The demonstration had the desired effect. The Shōgun addressed a strong representation to the Court, pointing out the necessity of the imperial ratification, and the Court gave way, and granted the formal approval desired; attaching to it the condition, which was not communicated to the foreign representatives, that the port of Hiōgo was not to be opened.

This was the other question which proved so troublesome. It will be remembered that in 1862 the Treaty Powers had agreed to postpone for five years the date of opening the port of Hiōgo, our share in the matter being recorded in the London Protocol of that year. The objections in Court and feudal circles to the opening of Hiōgo rested on a double basis of sentiment and expediency. The peculiar position of the monarchy, standing as it had done for centuries above and apart from administrative activities, and equally removed until recent years from jealousies of faction or party, depended to some extent on the geographical situation of the capital. This was in the centre of the country, and remote from the outlying districts which would naturally serve as points of contact with the outside world. The security of the Court would, it was considered, be diminished by the establishment of foreigners so near the capital, and the proximity of an open port might, it was felt, interfere with the maintenance of

the exclusive traditions attaching to the place
of imperial residence, which, on the principle
of *quieta non movere*, there was a general reluctance to disturb.   The policy followed by the
Shōgunate in concealing from the Foreign Representatives the attitude assumed by the Court on
this point probably served in this instance, as in
so many others during the early days of foreign
intercourse, a useful purpose, by preventing for
the moment a serious collision of views.   Later
on, the political situation having in the meantime
changed, the opposition of the Court was withdrawn, and Hiōgo, and at the same time the city
of Ōsaka, were opened to trade on the 1st of
January, 1868, the date fixed by the London
Protocol.

In the autumn of the year 1867 occurred the event
which was the prelude to the rupture between the
Court and the Shōgunate.   This was the resignation
of the Shōgun.   To the student of those times it
seems as if the end of the system of dual government
must have been in sight for many years—as if
it must have suggested itself to all foreseeing
minds as a thing inevitable, which nothing short
of a miracle could prevent.   It has been pointed
out already in the course of these pages how ever
since Commodore Perry's first visit to Japan the
Shōgunate's influence began to decline.   When
on that occasion the Yedo Government renounced,
or forebore to exercise, its traditional right to
govern the country, and referred to the Throne

and the feudal nobility the question of foreign
intercourse, which by the law of the country it
ought to have settled itself, the thin end of the
wedge which broke the Tokugawa rule was inserted.
It was a confession of weakness of which advantage
was at once taken. Little by little the Court
recovered powers it had not wielded for centuries,
and what it regained the Shōgunaté, and no one
else, lost, until in 1863, as we have seen, Kiōto
and not Yedo was fast becoming the political
centre of the country. Then came the Chōshiū
affair, and the Kiōto raid, which, had the reins
been in more skilful hands, should have furnished
an opportunity for retrieving the situation. The
opportunity was lost through the blindness of the
Council of State, which, by its obstinate insistence
on disproportionate and vindictive conditions for
Chōshiū's submission, lost the confidence of the
country, and the support of its friends, driving
into the opposite camp even those, like Satsuma,
whose co-operation was indispensable. It had also
played the game of its enemies by suddenly, at
the very moment when its conduct was alienating
public opinion, and when those daimiōs who had
obeyed the call to arms against Chōshiū were
busy with warlike preparations, decreeing a return
to the system of the attendance of daimiōs in
Yedo in alternate years, which had been entirely
changed three years before (in 1862), and intimating the necessity of immediate compliance
with the order. The effect on the feudal nobility

M 2

of this rash attempt to reassert a position which it had abandoned was disastrous for the Tokugawa interests.   Finally the Yedo Government had been worsted in a campaign against a single clan. The Tokugawa power and prestige had alike disappeared.

Hitherto throughout this short sketch of events before the Restoration we have preferred to speak as far as possible of the Shōgunate, rather than of the Shōgun, as the moving power in the administration ; and this method has been alike convenient, and more in keeping with Japanese ideas.   This method will serve us no longer.   The Shōgun comes naturally now to the front of the stage as he did for a moment, as Tycoon, when the first treaties were signed—and the Shōgunate retires into the background.

The new Shōgun (Kéiki) had been formally installed in January, 1867.   Highly accomplished, but of an unassuming temperament and retiring disposition, it was with reluctance that he had accepted the dignity of Shōgun ; and after a few months' experience of the cares of the post, and of the difficulty of holding his own against the combination of western clans which was formed as soon as the Chōshiū campaign had ended, he announced his resignation in a manifesto addressed to the feudal nobility.

In this remarkable document, unique as was the occasion which produced it, the Shōgun alludes to the administrative power having passed in

early times from the hands of the Emperors to
those of the Ministers of State, to its subsequent
transfer in the Middle Ages to the military class,
and to the eventual assumption of ruling authority
by his Tokugawa ancestors.   He confesses to having failed to carry on the work of administration
in a satisfactory manner, and dwells on the desirability, in view of the gradual extension of relations
with foreign powers, of the Government being
directed from one central point.   ' If, therefore,'
he adds, ' the old order of things be changed, and
the administrative authority be restored to the
Imperial Court, if national deliberations be conducted on an extensive scale, and the imperial
decision then invited, and if the Empire be
protected with united hearts and combined effort,
our country will hold its own with all nations of
the world.   This is our one duty to our country,
but if any of you have other views on the subject,
you should state them without reserve.' [1]

In the adoption of this course the Shōgun was
probably influenced by a memorial received by
him from the ex-Prince of Tosa—countersigned,
it should be noted, by three leading retainers—
who pointed out the danger to which the country
was exposed by the discord existing between the
Court, the Shōgun, and the feudal nobility, and
advocated the discontinuance of the dual system
of administration, and a return to the ancient form
of government—the direct rule of the Mikado.

[1] Appendix 21.

Further light is thrown on the manifesto by
the personal letter addressed at the same time by
the Shōgun to the Hatomoto, a class of vassal
gentry specially created by the founder of the
Tokugawa line of Shōguns. In this he says :—

' The great change I have made by my own
unaided decision is due to what has been in my
mind from the first. It has caused you all great
grief for the sake of my family, and you are now
pressing me to return to Yedo. Your sincere
affection for my house has been shown for more
than 200 years, and it gives me profound satisfac-
tion. But I appeal to you. My feelings for my
family, the house of Tokugawa, are the same as
yours. This is only natural. But is there not good
reason for changing the great laws, and the mag-
nificent system handed down to us by our ancestors ? Of late years as a result of the progress of
the times, there have been two channels for the
exercise of administrative power. And in view
of the development of foreign relations it was
impossible for me, if things went on in this way,
to feel at ease with regard to the permanent repose
of the Empire, and the welfare of my family.
Grieving over this, I reflected deeply, and made
up my mind that if the supreme power were
concentrated in single hands, and the power of
the whole country combined by co-operation,
and joint deliberation, the great work by which
the Empire would take its place with all other
foreign nations would be achieved. Do you also
carefully consider your obligations to the Empire,
and to my family, and, fostering the feelings of
affectionate and devoted loyalty you have entertained for me, give now, I beseech you, your
whole energies unceasingly and without sloth to
the performance of your official duties. I have

for a long time been a guest in Kiōto, and I am
eager to go home, but I have been occupied
without any intermission ever since the autumn
of last year with business concerning the relations
between the Court nobility and the military class.
The desire to return to Yedo is with me night and
day, for there are things connected with the feelings
and conduct of the people of Kwantō which need
looking into, but there is much state work to be
done, and having received much kindness and
many favours from the Court, both during the
reign of the late Emperor and since, I am bound
by the feelings of a subject towards his sovereign,
and I cannot leave the vicinity of the imperial
palace. Truly I may say that I am tied here and
cannot get away. I wish you to understand that
I am exercising great patience, and am intent on
preserving my reputation, reverencing the Court,
and doing my duty to my ancestors, and that my
position is one of trouble and anxiety. Prosperity
and decay, success and failure, follow natural
laws. The great man when going a long journey
adapts himself to circumstances, and watches his
opportunity before giving full play to his energies
Foolish as I am, I desire not to discredit the lineage of my ancestor Tōshgōu (Iyéyasu), to carry on
the family succession, and to do my duty to the
country. Bear in mind that you are now in the
autumn of obligations for having been enabled
to live and eat in peace for more than two hundred
years ; strengthen your sense of patriotic duty ;
be diligent in your work, and, in rendering me your
assistance, be careful in all matters. I say this
to you all from the highest to the lowest official.'

The Shōgun's resignation was accepted ; and
it was notified to the foreign representatives in
a memorandum explaining the reasons for the

step.[1] But the Throne intimated its desire that
he should continue to remain responsible for the
direction of affairs until a council of the leading
daimiōs should have time to meet and deliberate
in the capital.

The ex-Shōgun, therefore, remained in Kiōto
after his resignation awaiting the meeting of the
Council, being in charge of the administration, as
before, and relying for support on a force which
consisted chiefly of Aidzu and Kuwana *samurai*.
His position there was, however, rendered un-
tenable by a sudden change in the situation.
Several of the western clans had been increasing
the number of their troops in the capital in
preparation for a concerted movement, and on
the 3rd of January, 1868, a Court order deprived
the Aidzu clan of the duty of guarding the palace
gates.   Other orders of an uncompromising character followed, abolishing the offices of Shōgun
and *Kwambaku*, and creating new offices and titles,
the recipients of which included no supporter of
the Shōgun.   A provisional Government, the real
power in which lay with the fifteen members
who represented the five clans of Satsuma, Tosa,
Geishiu, Owari, and Échizen, was formed ; a formal
pardon was granted to the Prince of Chōshiū and
his son ; and, the ban of expulsion having been
removed, a large Chōshiū force re-entered the
capital.   Four days later the ex-Shōgun addressed
a memorial to the Court protesting against these

[1] Appendix 22.

new measures, and retired to Ōsaka.[1] He was at first inclined to content himself with this protest, as appears from the statement made by him to the British and French Ministers on the same day after his arrival at Ōsaka, and also from his reply to the address presented by the foreign representatives on the 10th of January, but he was eventually persuaded by his more impetuous adherents to endeavour to reassert his authority. He therefore marched on Kiōto with the troops at his disposal at the end of January. Half-way to the capital he encountered the imperial forces, was defeated, and was forced to retire to Ōsaka, whence he reached Yedo by sea.

The prospect of a peaceful settlement of the crisis which had appeared so hopeful a short time before was thus interrupted by civil war. Hostilities were, however, of short duration. Except in the north-eastern provinces, where the Aidzu and Yonézawa troops made a final gallant stand, and in the northern island of Yezo, where a small remnant of Tokugawa sympathizers held out until the following year (1869), little resistance was encountered by the imperial forces; and by the spring of 1869 peace was re-established everywhere.

With the restoration of the direct rule of the Mikado the curtain falls on this period of Japanese history—a period separated by a wide gulf from the Japan of to-day. Whatever faults the dual

[1] Appendix 23.

system of government represented by the Tokugawa rule may have had, it secured to Japan the blessings of peace for more than 250 years, and in the course of that long period the seeds of much of what we admire in modern Japan were sown.

From this brief survey of the history of the few troubled years which ended with the fall of the Shōgunate we derive a sense of very definite progress having at last been achieved. Out of the political confusion and turmoil of those times certain outstanding features appear, showing clearly the direction which national tendencies are taking. We see, as regards the authorities, the end of the authorized anti-foreign crusade, and, on the part of the people, the first symptoms of an improved feeling towards foreigners. From the strife of civil war, and the misfortunes of foreign complications, Japan emerged with a clearer view both of the possibilities lying before her in the future, and of the duties and responsibilities she had deliberately, and also unconsciously, assumed.

CHAPTER VI

THE ABOLITION OF FEUDALISM

WHEN, as mentioned in the preceding chapter, the foreign representatives were informed by the ministers in Yedo of the Shōgun's resignation, an official explanation of the matter in writing was supplied at the same time. The version of this document given in the *Bakumatsu Gwaikō Dan*, ' Story of Foreign Relations in the last days of the Shōgunate,' bears no date. Allowing, however, for some variations in the text, and it is no secret that more than one version was prepared— the statement [1] is evidently the same as that communicated at Yedo to the British Minister about the 27th of November, 1867, by Ogasawara Iki no Kami, who was then Minister for Foreign Affairs.

' The Tycoon ', says this statement, ' has of his own free will decided to return to the Mikado the administrative authority handed down to him by his ancestors through a period of more than two hundred and fifty years. Fearing that at this moment of political change people's minds may be led astray by false rumours, we think it necessary to explain the circumstances of the case to all countries.'

Then follows a long summary of historical events showing how the dual system of government originated, and how the administrative authority

[1] Appendix 16, p. 289.

became eventually concentrated in the hands of the founder of the Tokugawa line of Shōguns, and with a brief allusion to the Christian troubles, and the closing of the country, the narrative is brought down to Perry's arrival, and the reopening of foreign intercourse. The statement then refers to the dissatisfaction caused throughout the country by the change of policy in regard to foreigners, and to the internal troubles and foreign complications which occurred, and ascribes to the ex-Shōgun the credit for the success achieved by the Government in having, in spite of all these difficulties, secured the observance of the stipulations of the treaties with foreign powers.

Allusion having been made to the friendliness manifested by the ex-Shōgun in his relations with the foreign representatives, the memorandum proceeds to explain that under the dual system of government peculiar to Japan, which was the natural result of circumstances, the tranquillity of the country was maintained, but that now that intercourse with the whole world has been established much inconvenience is caused by the name under which this intercourse is carried on ; and that the ex-Shogun's resignation is due to his appreciation of this fact, and of the necessity for a reform of the constitution. And it concludes by assuring the foreign representatives that there will be no change in the foreign policy of Japan, and asking them for their assistance and co-operation.

In addition to the official statement of the

Shōgun's resignation given by the Yedo authorities to the foreign representatives, an official announcement of the fact was also made to the latter by the Emperor. In this communication it was stated that in place of the title of Tycoon, which had hitherto been employed in the treaties, that of Emperor would be substituted, that officers would be appointed to conduct foreign affairs, and that in future the Emperor would exercise supreme authority both in the internal and external affairs of the country.

A point to which attention may now conveniently be drawn is the intimate connexion between the Shōgunate and the feudal system, of which, in one of its aspects, it formed a part. Japanese feudalism, in the form in which we find it towards the close of the Tokugawa régime, was largely a creation of the first and third Shōguns of the line. Its most distinctive features had been given to it by those two rulers, and by the effects of intermarriage [1] and adoption, and the use of a common surname, many of the chief feudal houses had become identified with the fortunes of the ruling family. Moreover, to how great an extent what has been described as the figure-head system of government prevailed in Japan has already been explained at some length. It has been pointed out how this system of make-believe had its origin in the structure of society, whence it permeated the whole political organization ; so that the position of the head of

[1] Matsudaira.

a family was reproduced in that of the *Karō* who governed a clan in the name of the daimiō, in that of the daimiō whose affairs were thus managed, in that of the Shōgun who presided over the Government, and in that of the sovereign who reigned but did not rule. This contradiction between appearance and reality, between theory and practice, was, as we have said, the common characteristic of all Japanese institutions; it constituted the tie which held them together; and in it lay the secret of their stability.[1] The Shōgunate and the feudal system must therefore be regarded as forming very closely knit together parts of a wider political organization, resting on a social basis peculiar to Japan, any portion of which it was difficult to disturb without danger to the rest of the structure. To the politician of those days it may have seemed a simple enough matter to do away with the Shōgunate, but the foregoing view of the situation, if correct, points to the conclusion that the downfall of the Shōgunate could only be the prelude to the abolition of feudalism.

With the disappearance of the Shōgunate its territorial revenues passed into the hands of the Crown. It may be interesting to note what these revenues were,[2] and to trace at the same time their distribution throughout the country, since

---

[1] See Stubbs's *Constitutional History*, vol. i, pp. 3 and 4.

[2] The revenues in question would, of course, only represent the portion derived from the land in the form of land-tax, and would not include other taxation.

it gives some idea of the territorial basis on which
the influence of the Tokugawa Government rested.
Out of the 68 provinces into which Japan at the
time of the Restoration was divided, no less a
number than 47, by reason of lands owned therein
by the Government, contributed directly towards
the Tokugawa Exchequer. The most notable
exceptions were the provinces of Satsuma and
Ōsumi in the southern island of Kiūshiū, which
constituted the territories of the Satsuma clan;
in the island of Shikoku the province of Tosa
belonging to the clan of that name; and in the
main island the provinces of Nagato and Suwo,
which were held by the clan of Chōshiū, and
the provinces of Owari and Kii, which were the
possessions of two of the three princely Tokugawa families known as the *Gosankė*. The
lands thus owned by the Government were remarkable, however, rather for the wide extent
of their distribution than for the actual area
comprised. The total annual assessed yield in
rice of all these lands amounted to a little
over 10,000,000 koku of rice, equivalent to
about £10,000,000. More than half of this sum
represented the yield of land in eleven provinces,
the average annual yield of the produce of lands
in the other 34 provinces amounting on an average
to less than £50,000. But on the recognized
principle of four parts to the feudal lord, or owner,
and six parts to the cultivator, which governed
the apportionment of the produce of the Shōgun's

territories in those days,[1] not more than £4,000,000 found its way into the Tokugawa Exchequer.

In the early years of the revival of foreign intercourse, when the Shōgunate was vainly endeavouring to recover some of the authority it had at a weak moment abandoned, when the Court at Kiōto was bestirring itself to turn the new spirit imported into the situation to its own profit, and the feudal nobles were occupied with intrigues against the Court, against the Shōgunate, and against each other, political opinion was represented mainly by three parties. There were, according to the author of *The Awakening of Japan*, the Federalists led by the Satsuma clan, whose aim was the overthrow of the Shōgunate, and the reorganization of the feudal system much on the lines which existed during the half-century preceding the Tokugawa domination. There were the Imperialists, represented by the Chōshiū clan, ' who sought their ideal further back, and desired the restitution of the imperial bureaucracy as it had existed before the establishment of the feudal system.' The third party consisted of what Mr. Okakura terms the Unionists, who, following the rather indefinite teaching of the famous scholar, Sakuma Shōzan, advocated administrative reform on Western lines. The vague aspirations

---

[1] Outside the Shōgun's dominions the proportion varied from three parts to the cultivator and seven to the landlord, to seven parts to the former and three to the latter. In some places the division was equal.

of this last-named group of politicians did not
survive the death of their leader, whose enthusiasm
for reform drew upon him the suspicion of a
Government too weak to tolerate any liberal pre-
tensions; and whatever ambitions the Satsuma clan
may originally have entertained, by the time
the Restoration took place the course of events
had led to their becoming merged, together with
the independent ambitions of other clans, in
a common programme of Imperialism. But it
was Imperialism resting on a feudal basis, and
with a strong leaven in it of the spirit of reform,
in imitation of the foreign institutions which had
so much impressed the minds of the young *samurai*
of progressive tendencies.

Among other reasons for adopting as the new
form of government the old bureaucratic system
of administration, which had existed before the
establishment of feudalism, there were two which
in themselves alone justified the selection. In
the first place, it was inadvisable, even had it
been possible, to attempt to retain the constitution
of the Shōgunate which had been just overthrown.
In the second place, it was necessary to take full
advantage of the current of popular feeling in favour
of the Restoration, and at the same time to work
as far as possible, while as yet the influence of
the rising men was still small, through men of
high rank in the class of *kugé*, or Court nobles,
who had administered this system in early days,
and through the feudal nobility.

The constitution of the new Government was briefly as follows :—

There were eight departments of state called *Kioku*. The first was the *Sōsaikioku*, or Department of Supreme Administration; the second had control of all matters connected with the Shintō religion. Of the other six, one dealt with legislation, while the remaining five corresponded in a general way to similar departments in Western countries.

The high position assigned to the Shintō religion will be noticed, Buddhism being as conspicuously ignored. In the reorganization which took place later in the same year (1868) still greater importance was given to Shintō, the department dealing with Shintō affairs ranking with, but after the Council of State (*Dajōkwan*), which replaced the *Sōsaikioku*, and not with the ordinary state departments. In 1871, however, Shintō, while retaining its privileged character as the Court religion, ceased to be recognized as the only state church, and the department regulating its affairs became simply the department of religion.

Feudal interests were represented in the new Government by a special class of councillors with deliberative functions, chosen from the various clans, the number furnished by each clan being regulated according to the annual assessed yield of its territory. The character of a deliberative assembly thus given to the new administration was in accordance with principles of reform subsequently enunciated

in the imperial oath.   From this representation,
however, seven clans were excluded on the ground
of their holding views opposed to the new order of
things.

A member of the imperial house, Prince Arisu-
gawa, was appointed president of the new administration, and two leading court nobles, Sanjō and
Iwakura, became the two Vice-Presidents.   Sanjō
was one of the seven *Kugé* who had incurred the
displeasure of the late Government by taking
refuge in Chōshiū territory shortly before that
clan's raid on Kiōto, while Iwakura became afterwards one of the foremost statesmen of the new
era.   Two other imperial princes and five Court
nobles were placed at the head of the remaining
seven departments, the second position in three
of these being given to the daimiōs of Échizen,
Geishiu, and Higo.   Among those who held office
under the new Government in minor capacities
were Ōkubō and Terashima of Satsuma, Kido of
Chōshiū, Gotō of Tosa, Itō and Inouyé, the two
young Chōshiū clansmen who on their return
from England in 1864 had tried unsuccessfully
to prevent the Shimonséki hostilities, and others
whose names will always be associated with the
great work of Japan's progress.

There was by this time a complete change of
attitude in regard to foreign intercourse on the
part of the leaders of the Restoration movement,
and we hear of the anti-foreign party as a party
no more.   Evidence of the altered state of feeling

is furnished by a memorial to the Throne presented about this time by five of the leading daimiōs.[1] The memorial refers to the recent resumption of administrative authority by the Emperor, and to the urgent necessity of placing the question of foreign intercourse on a clear basis. It gives a short sketch of foreign relations both before and after the conclusion of treaties with foreign powers, and concludes with an earnest exhortation to all officials in high positions to appreciate rightly the circumstances of the present foreign situation, to eschew the Chinese principles on which all ceremonies and functions had hitherto been modelled, and, abandoning the prejudiced and ignorant views prevailing for so long in regard to foreigners, to unite in establishing relations with foreign countries on a footing of cordiality and friendship.

On the 6th of April, 1868, in the Throne Room of the palace in Kiōto, took place the function which serves as a landmark in Japanese constitutional history, and occupies for the Japanese people a position similar to that of the granting of the Magna Charta with us. This was the ceremony in which the Emperor, in the presence of the Imperial Princes and high officials of state, took what is known as the Imperial Oath of Five Articles. It is not too much too say that this Imperial Oath was the foundation on which the whole structure of new Japan was raised. No

[1] Those of Échizen, Tosa, Chōshiū, Satsuma, Geishiū, and Higo.

apology, therefore, is needed for quoting it in full.[1] It runs as follows :—

' 1. Deliberative Assemblies shall be established on an extensive scale, and all measures of Government shall be decided by public opinion.

' 2. All classes, high and low, shall unite in vigorously carrying out the plan of government.

' 3. All classes of the people shall be allowed to fulfil their just aspirations, so that there may be no discontent.

' 4. Uncivilized customs of former times shall be abolished, and everything shall be based upon just and equitable principles of nature.

' 5. Knowledge shall be sought for throughout the world, so that the foundations of the Empire may be strengthened.

' Desiring to carry out a reform without parallel in the annals of our country, We Ourselves here take the initiative and swear to the Deities of Heaven and Earth to adopt these fundamental principles of national government, so as to establish thereby the security and prosperity of the people. We call upon you to make combined and strenuous efforts to carry them out.'

The general correspondence of the language of the Imperial Oath, with reference to the necessity of widening, and, in a sense, popularizing the basis of government, with that of the ex-Shōgun's manifesto, when he tendered his resignation in the autumn of the previous year, will be noticed. We are reminded, too, of what was said in memorials presented to the Government on this subject.

---

[1] The translation given in Baron D. Kikuchi's *Japanese Education* has in the main been followed.

This shows that the feeling in favour of reform was very widely entertained.   The Oath is not a declaration of rights, but a declaration of intentions, a statement of the principles on which it was resolved in future to conduct the Government, and as such it has always been regarded as of the highest value.   In introducing the principle of deliberation, or discussion, into the conduct of state business there was, of course, no intention of giving the masses a voice in the Government, or of establishing popular representative institutions at once.   Any such idea was at the time quite unthinkable, for the feudal system was still in existence, and the bulk of the population had no interest in public affairs.   But that it was intended to make a beginning in this direction—that representative institutions were the goal towards which men's thoughts were turning—there can be little doubt.   The crudeness of the attempt to give practical effect to the new theories of government by importing into the constitution a deliberative element, out of keeping with the otherwise bureaucratic character of the new administration, was due simply to inexperience, and a confusion of ideas not unnatural in the circumstances.

In June of the same year the constitution of the Government was reorganized, much of its original framework, including the deliberative features already described, being, however, retained.   In the decree announcing these changes the text of the Oath was quoted, and it was

THE ABOLITION OF FEUDALISM 199

also expressly stated that the object in view was to proceed with the work of administrative reform in the direction therein indicated. The administrative system was fated to undergo so many changes in succeeding years that a detailed examination of the constitution as elaborated by this decree is hardly necessary. It may be interesting, however, to mention a few of its main points.

The administrative authority was centred in one body called the *Dajokwan*, or Council of State, which was divided into seven departments :—

1. The deliberative chamber (*Sei-in*), which took over the duties of the former Legislative Department, consisting of an upper and a lower house, and including an office for the publication of the ' Official Gazette ' (the issue of which has continued uninterruptedly from that date).

2. The office of the Lords President of the Council, which had functions combining those of the former Department of Supreme Administration and Home Department, which it replaced.

The five other departments were, as before, those of the Shintō religion, Finance, War, Foreign Affairs, and Justice.

One important change made was the extension of the privilege of representation in the Government by means of deliberative councillors to the great cities of Yedo, Kiōto, and Ōsaka, and imperial territories, besides the clans to whom this right was originally limited.

How slowly the new Government was feeling

its way in the conduct of state affairs, and how curiously, and even incoherently, in its first creative efforts, the old and the new were blended, may be seen from the explanations given in the decree.

'The power and authority of the Council of State,' it says, 'is threefold, legislative, executive, and judicial.' This division was of course borrowed from the West. The Government also, as we have seen, contained a deliberative element.

'The reason,' we read in another place, 'why appointment to the highest rank in the various offices is limited to princes of the blood, the nobles of the Court, [kugé], and territorial nobles, is because due affection should be shown to the relations of the sovereign, and due respect to people of rank. The selection of other officials from the military class and the common people is in order that wisdom may be honoured.'

In another passage we are told that 'the object of establishing the system of a deliberative body is that open discussion and the opinion of the majority may be secured.'

The reason, we learn, that princes of the blood, kugé, and territorial nobles were, when out of doors, to be accompanied by only six two-sworded men and three lackeys, and persons of lower rank by only two two-sworded men and one lackey, is 'in order to do away with the appearance of pomp and grandeur, and to prevent the existence of a barrier between classes.'

The decree also established the rule, in imita-

tion probably of the precedent furnished by the
Government of the United States, that all officials
should be changed after four years' service. But
this rule is qualified by the practical proviso that
' such as cannot conveniently be dismissed, because
they have won general approval, must be retained
for a further period of years.'

In view of the slender financial resources at
the disposal of the new Government it is not
surprising to read of a forced contribution, to
which the term of 'tribute' is given, being levied
on all classes of the people, officials being called
upon to pay a tax amounting to one-thirtieth of
their salaries.

By the transfer of the Shōgunate territories to
the Crown the classification for purposes of local
administration had become rearranged into three
divisions. The large cities of the Empire, Yedo,
Kiōto, and Ōsaka, formed a group by themselves,
the territories of the clans, and the imperial
domains, constituting the two other administrative
areas. The decree provided that in each of these
separate areas local administration was to be conducted in accordance with the principles laid down
in the Imperial Oath, the separate and distinct
character of each being maintained. At the same
time, with a view to strengthening the imperial
authority, and counteracting any decentralizing
tendencies which had made the task of government
so difficult in the past, it was enacted that no rank
was to be bestowed, no money coined, and no

foreigners employed without special permission, and no alliances formed either between neighbouring clans, or between any clan and a foreign State.

It was not till April of the following year (1869) that full effect was given to the intentions announced in the Imperial Oath by the opening in Yedo of a deliberative assembly, or parliament, to which the name of *Kōgisho* was given. It consisted of 276 members, one for every clan.

The plan of convoking a parliament did not originate with the men who took the leading part in the Restoration. The idea of consulting public opinion was in the air long before then. It is true, as the British Minister, Sir Harry Parkes, reported to his Government at the time, that the establishment of such an institution formed one of the objects of the promoters of the revolution. But the idea did not originate with them. It was equally in the minds of the Shōgun's advisers. In a manifesto issued by the ex-Shōgun in February, 1868, he stated his intention ' to listen to the voice of the majority, and to establish a deliberative assembly '—(the very word *Kōgisho* being used) —' where any one who has an opinion to express may do so without fear of the consequences '.

Speaking at the time of this first attempt at parliamentary institutions, a foreign paper published in Yokohama observed :—

' It must be remembered that not only was the Assembly composed of nothing but two-sworded men, who, in order to render them eligible, were declared to rank as *karō*, but that the members were there as representatives of the clans alone. In this attempt at a Parliament there were no members from cities or towns, but only from clans ; the merchants and the people at large had no voice in the deliberations ; they could neither elect nor be elected. The House could not therefore lay claim to the appellation of a National Assembly ; it was a first attempt to introduce a liberal element into the new constitution, and to form a channel for the expression of public opinion. It should in fact be looked upon as a species of debating society, where opinions could be broached, and subjects discussed ; but it could pass no laws.'

Sir Harry Parkes puts the matter very clearly in a dispatch to Lord Clarendon when he says :—

' The object of the *Kōgisho* was to enable the Government to sound public opinion on the various topics of the day, and to obtain the assistance of the country in the work of legislation by ascertaining whether the projects of the Government were likely to be favourably received.'

Perhaps a little more was intended, for the ambitions of the reformers were much in advance of the times—but this is all that was done.

It would have been very surprising if this first attempt at representative institutions, made, it must not be forgetton, in the atmosphere of feudalism, had been attended with any marked success. The inexperience associated everywhere with all such early experiments showed itself as usual in many ways, chiefly perhaps in the bewildering variety of subjects introduced for debate. But the British Minister, in forwarding to the Foreign Office an account of one of the debates, the subject discussed being foreign trade, was able to say that, viewed as an illustration of the capacity of the members, and of the tone of the House on the question of foreign commerce, the debate appeared to him to possess considerable interest, and its result to be creditable to the discernment of the assembly.

The impression produced on foreign observers by the proceedings of the parliament was on the whole favourable, though it was noticed that conservative and reactionary tendencies showed themselves in the rejection of proposals for the abolition of *harakiri* and the wearing of swords, and in the contemptuous tone adopted by many members when speaking of foreigners. Public interest in the assembly did not survive the year of its institution, but the assembly lingered on, nevertheless, till the autumn of 1870, when it was amalgamated with the bureau created for the receipt of memorials, and it was not formally dissolved till 1873. But before its dissolution a discussion had taken place on the most important point of all the business which had occupied its attention. This was the momentous question of the surrender of their fiefs to the Crown by the feudal nobility—in other words, the abolition of feudalism.

The sentiments disclosed in memorials presented

by various daimiōs to the Throne at the time of
the Shōgun's resignation in the autumn of 1867
showed that there was a great conflict of opinion
in regard to the situation.   Some of the daimiōs,
notably those of the leading western clans, had
been loud in their denunciation of the Tokugawa
rule, and had dwelt on the necessity of putting
an end to the dual system of government.   Others,
like the Daimiō of Kii, and Makino of Mikawa,
had expressed themselves in favour of the continuance of the Tokugawa Shōgunate under somewhat
altered conditions ; while a third party, consisting
of the Shogun's staunchest supporters, had bluntly
recommended that his resignation should not be
accepted, and that things should go on as before.
A thing often said, too, at the time, though not in
memorials, was that the west [1] had never ruled
Japan, and it was doubtful if it ever could.   This
divergence of views points to the existence of
a very general feeling that the Shōgunate was an
integral part of the machinery of government,
and that its abolition would result in a serious
disturbance of the whole administrative system.
To the close connexion between the Shōgunate
and feudalism the first of the memorials on the
subject of the surrender of the fiefs bears eloquent
testimony ; and from the recognition of this fact
to a conviction of the necessity of a sweeping
change in the government of the country, even
if such change were to involve the disappearance

[1] The Western Provinces, see p. 125.

of the clans, was not after all a very great transition. This conviction had taken root in the minds of the leading reformers, of men like Kido, Iwakura, and Ōkubō. From them it spread to others, with the result that in March, 1869—a month before the opening of the Deliberative Assembly— memorials were presented by several daimiōs, the lead in this matter being taken by the chiefs of four of the western clans, those of Satsuma, Chōshiū, Hizen, and Tosa. These four stated their views in the well-known joint memorial.[1]

The points emphasized in the memorial were the necessity of one central body of Government, and one universal authority ; the fact that the combination of the name and reality of power in ancient days had resulted in the tranquillity and contentment of the people ; the circumstances which had led to the establishment of the dual form of government ; and the gradual usurpation of all authority by the Tokugawa Shōguns. And in proof of the sincerity of their statements, and of their conviction as to a complete change of government being the only remedy for the existing situation, the memorialists concluded by surrendering their territories and revenues to the Crown.

There seems to be no reason to question the correctness of the popular view which has assigned the authorship of this remarkable document to Kido. A curious feature about it is the vehement denunciation of the dual system of government

[1] Appendix 21.

in the face of the fact that the last of the Shōguns
had resigned eighteen months before, and that
nearly a year had elapsed since the short civil
war had come to an end. This supports the
suggestion, already made, that in the thoughts
of the nation feudalism and the Shōgunate were
inseparably associated.

The example of the four clans was at once
followed by others, including the president of the
Deliberative Assembly. Before many weeks had
elapsed similar memorials had come in from most
of the clans, and by the end of the year out of 276
feudatories there were only seventeen abstainers
from the movement, these being daimiōs of
eastern territories who had taken the Shōgun's
side in the civil war. One of the earliest and most
enthusiastic memorialists was the Daimiō of Kii,[1]
the Tokugawa prince who has already come under
our notice as an advocate in 1867 of the continuance
of the Shōgunate, and who had only succeeded to
the fief by the promotion of his relative, Prince
Kéiki, to be Shōgun. This change of attitude on
the part of a feudal prince of such commanding
position indicates the unsettled state of political
opinion, but it may also be interpreted as showing
how natural was the association of feudalism
with the Shōgunate in men's minds, and how
difficult for him, as for others, was the conception
of feudalism existing without a Shōgunate ; if

[1] Or Kishiū (not to be confused with Kiūshiū, the southernmost
of the islands constituting the Japanese Empire of that time).

the one was to go, so must the other, was the natural conclusion to be reached.

In dealing with the question raised by these memorials the Government proceeded cautiously. The answers given to the memorialists stated that the question would be submitted to the council of daimiōs about to assemble in Yedo. The matter was also referred, as we have seen, to the parliament. Whatever hesitation, however, existed related more to the method in which effect should be given to the proposal than to the spirit in which it should be met; and early in August a decree was issued stating that the Emperor, 'having submitted the matter freely to public discussion,' had been pleased to acquiesce in the proposal for the surrender of the clan fiefs, feeling that this course would consolidate the authority of the Government. Many details were left for arrangement afterwards, but, as a preliminary step, the administration of the clans was remodelled so as to bring them into harmony with the rest of the Empire, and the daimiōs convened to pronounce upon their own fate returned in the new capacity of governors (Chihanji) to the territories they had hitherto ruled.

A further step in the same direction was taken by the abolition of the distinction between court nobles and the feudal aristocracy, the two classes being thenceforth merged into one, to which the name of *kwazoku* (nobles) was given.

Two years later, the necessary arrangements

having by that time been completed, the matter was finally settled by the issue on August 29, 1871, of a decree singular in its brevity. ' The clans,' so it ran, ' are abolished and Prefectures are established in their place.' At the same time the officials administering the clans were ordered to continue to perform their duties till other arrangements had been made ; and an imperial message was addressed to the ex-daimiōs, who were, as we have seen, acting as governors of the clan territories, pointing out the unsatisfactory state of things resulting from the separation of theory from practice in matters generally, and the distribution of governing authority in several hands instead of one ; and mentioning, amongst other reasons for the change, the better opportunities that would be afforded for putting an end to the special evils indicated.

The ex-daimiōs received pensions amounting to one-tenth of their former revenues, and provision was made out of the latter for the support of the clan *samurai*. From this arrangement, however, the *samurai* of one or two clans, who had offered a protracted resistance to the imperial forces, were excluded, and much suffering and hardship resulted.

The surrender of the clan fiefs involved of course the rendition of the lands, varying greatly in extent, which were held by two large sections of the military class, the *hatamoto* and *gokénin,* who numbered several thousand, and formed the hereditary personal following of the Tokugawa

Shōguns.   Their pensions were regulated on a scale
similar to that adopted for other members of the
military class.

The question of the revenues acquired by the
Crown from the abolition of the feudal system
is a difficult problem.   In the Tokugawa law called
' The Hundred Articles ', but better known to
foreigners as ' The Legacy of Iyéyasu ', the total
assessed yield of the country is stated to be
28,190,000 *koku* of rice.[1]   Of this 20,000,000 *koku*
represented the produce of the territories of the
feudal nobility and gentry, and the balance the
yield of the Shōgun's estates.   This statement was
made in the early part of the seventeenth century,
that is to say, nearly 300 years before the Restoration, and it is natural to suppose that in the course
of this period the revenues of feudal territories
may, in spite of the unfavourable economic
conditions known to have existed in the century
preceding the opening of the country, have
increased with the general progress of the nation.
In the absence of exact data, we shall probably
be not far wrong if we estimate the gross revenue
which came into the possession of the Crown by
the abolition of the Shōgunate and the feudal
system as not much under 35,000,000 *koku* (or
£35,000,000).   From this had to be deducted the
portions due to the cultivators, which varied,
as we have explained, with the locality in question,

[1] Only a portion of this production was actually rice, but the
value of other produce was stated in terms of rice.

and out of the residue the pensions due to members of the military class had to be paid (until the commutations had been effected), so that the balance accruing to the imperial exchequer, in the first few years of the new administration, could not have been large.

It may be asked what effect the abolition of the feudal system had upon the peasantry throughout Japan. Unlike the *samurai* the farmer was a gainer by the change. His position under feudalism had been full of anomalies, and had varied according to the locality of his holding. But even in those parts of the country where the peasant was little better than a serf, and he was subject to grave disabilities and restrictions in the cultivation and disposal of his land, fixity of tenure was, as was explained in the opening chapter, virtually assured to him. It might perhaps have been expected that the Government would have taken advantage of the surrender of the fiefs to place the matter of land tenure on a clear footing. This, however, was not done. No decree affecting the broad issue raised for the farming class by the disappearance of the feudal landlords was promulgated, and it was only by degrees that the policy of the new Government was disclosed. One by one the various restrictions which had curtailed the rights of the cultivator were removed, until by the year 1872 it became clear that while retaining the theory that the ownership of all land was vested as of

right in the Crown, it was intended that, subject
to the obligation of paying land tax, the farmer
should become virtually the proprietor of his land.

' A more picturesque incident,' says Captain
Brinkley in his *History of Japan*, speaking of the
surrender of their fiefs by the daimiōs, ' could
scarcely be conceived, nor one less consistent
with the course that human experience would
have anticipated.' As a general statement this
may be accepted, but with the important qualifica-
tion that the situation was unique. The absence
of personal control was the hall-mark of clan
and Shōgunate administration, and long before
the Restoration took place the government of
the fiefs had passed out of the hands of the
nominal rulers. The state of things in the provinces
resembled that in Yedo. Both daimiō and *karō*
were, like the Shōgun, relegated to a position of
nonentity. Of this there is abundant evidence.
Confusion existed everywhere. We have seen
how completely at the time of Chōshiū's struggle
with the Shōgunate the prince and his son were
in the hands, not of the clan *karō*, but of lesser
men, whom the crisis had elevated to positions
of control ; how the policy of the other great
Western clan, Satsuma, was directed, not by its
hereditary chief, nor by his *karō*, but by his father,
Shimadzu Saburō, with whom were associated
clansmen of quite independent views ; and how
the authority of the daimiōs of Hizen and Tosa
was exercised by retainers in the names of their

masters. In the clan of Mito things were in a condition approaching anarchy. The rival parties in that territory were animated by feelings of hostility to each other fiercer perhaps than the rivalry which existed between the Court and the Shōgunate, or between the latter and the western clans ; and the increasing number of *rōnin* in all parts of the Empire afforded conclusive proof of the universal decadence of clan authority. If in the course of the period under review we come across instances of feudal chiefs who had some share of power and influence, these were exceptions to the general rule ; and the authority they wielded was brought to bear rather on the affairs of the state, than in the administration of their own territories.

Under circumstances such as these little opposition was to be looked for on the part of the daimiōs. Brought up in traditions of seclusion analogous to those which characterized the tenure of the throne and the Shōgunate, denied by custom all share in the management of clan affairs, the daimiōs had no reason to object to the abolition of feudalism. It involved no sacrifice on their part. Their material interests remained unaffected, and there was no authority to be relinquished, save in name. As a matter of state policy it was beyond their control. Personally the change meant for those who could appreciate it a release from irksome conditions of existence, and a wider scope for the exercise of individual energies, of which, in a few cases, brilliant use was made. Picturesque and dramatic as the incident of the surrender by the daimiōs of their fiefs may appear to the casual observer, a study of the facts reveals the simple truth that throughout all the negotiations for the surrender of their fiefs the feudal nobility counted for nothing, and were as a class only dimly conscious, if aware at all, of the importance of what was going on.

When the endeavour is made to explain the feelings with which the *samurai* class generally regarded the great change introduced, a more difficult task is encountered. It is only natural that they should view with great reluctance the abolition of a system centuries old under which they occupied a position of superiority in the social order, and its replacement by a new state of things which to them promised nothing. Moreover, shortly before the Restoration, the Tokugawa Government had been compelled, for reasons of economy, to reduce the establishments of several of the *hata-moto*, and the disbandment of many hundreds of *samurai*, which was the effect of this measure, must have served as an object-lesson to the *samurai* of each fief, intimating possibilities which might occur nearer home. There is probably no little truth in Captain Brinkley's suggestion that the lead given by the four Western clans was in harmony with the spirit of the Restoration, and with the self-sacrificing ideals in which the *samurai* had been trained. But there is more to be said. A wave of Imperialism had swept over the nation, of which the reforming statesmen took full advantage, and it must also be remembered that in spite of the effete character of clan administration there was everywhere a strong under-current of feudal loyalty, which showed itself in a spirit of implicit obedience to the decision of the feudal lord, no matter through what channel it might be conveyed, and survived years after the disappearance of the clans. Discontent, too, was rampant, induced by the impoverished condition of the *samurai*, and of the daimiōs on whom they depended for support. Then again, the spirit of change was abroad, and with it came an attraction for novelty, not unnatural in a nation shut off for so long from free contact with the outside world, which was stimulated by the study of Western literature, and an acquaintance with Western things gained through intercourse with foreigners. And there was the influence of the reformers, the leaders of public opinion, whose efforts to convince their countrymen of the necessity of great changes in the body politic never slackened till the work of reform was placed on a solid basis. From these men, the first to be affected by the impulse of the new imperialist tendencies, the first to be moved by the feeling of national exaltation common to times of great popular commotion, came the inspiration which guided the nation in this critical hour of its fortunes. Swept along by the movement of reform they had done so much to initiate, it was not given to them to see very far ahead, but they must have seen through the hollow artificiality of administration, whether of Shōgunate or clan, and recognized the sacrifice of substance to shadow so frequently condemned in the memorials and other writings of the time. Moreover, defective as their knowledge of Western countries might be, some at least knew enough to understand that feudalism was a stage of evolution through which most European countries had passed, and it is not assuming too much to suppose that in their eagerness to imitate the progress of other lands they very soon came to realize that the abolition of the dual system must entail the abolition of clan government, and that the continuance of feudalism, no less than that of the Shōgunate, was incompatible with the new extension given to foreign relations.

Finally there was the question of finance. As has been pointed out by more than one writer, the financial embarrassments of the Shōgunate had been one of the contributing causes of its downfall. Although the Crown had succeeded to the Shōgunate's revenues, these were manifestly insufficient to meet the increasing needs of the national exchequer,—more especially in view of the heavy expenditure entailed by the reorganization of the Government, and the various new calls on state revenue arising out of the development of foreign intercourse. Of this the leaders of the reform movement must have been fully aware.

In these considerations, to which may perhaps be added the influence of personal ambitions, may be found the key to the solution of the problem.

The Restoration had brought Japan to the parting of the ways. Thanks to the genius of her statesmen the decision to advance was carried out with no uncertain footsteps. With the abolition of feudalism the last strands which bound her to an antiquated past were severed, and the history of modern Japan begins. In great national changes the operation of two different agencies— revolution within, and pressure from outside—may often be traced. It was so in the case of Japan. Otherwise the success attending the efforts of the reformers would have been less conspicuous. On the one hand the presence of foreign troops, stationed in the country since 1864, and the fear of sharing China's fate; on the other the conviction of the urgent need of something to take the place of the worn-out fabric of administration —these two together constituted the driving power which urged Japan forward. Henceforth it was in a fresh spirit of unity that the nation prepared itself to meet the difficulties of the future which lay before it. This future was not without its checks and relapses, but the new instinct of co-operation, always latent in the people, prevailed, until in the end a higher form of patriotism, better suited to the needs of the country, was evolved than that represented by clan loyalty.

CHAPTER VII

CONCLUSION

In the preceding pages the progress of Japan
has been traced during eighteen eventful years.
The period opened with the reversal at foreign
instance of the policy of seclusion. It was distinguished throughout by sustained resentment
of foreign intrusion, by the conflict of opposing
factions, and by the gradual shifting of power from
Yedo to Kiōto. And when it ended, both Shōgunate
and feudalism had vanished. Two things were in
doubt during the greater part of that period, the
survival of the Shōgunate, and the permanence of
the newly-established foreign intercourse. There
was a close connexion between the two. Not only
did the Shōgunate from the first favour the conclusion of treaties, thus identifying itself with the
cause of the intruding foreigner, but the anti-foreign
party had deliberately joined in one programme
the two cries of ' honour the sovereign ' and ' drive
away the barbarian '. It seemed, therefore, certain
that if the anti-Shōgunate party gained the day,
the triumph of their cause would mean the expulsion of the foreigner. But this is just what
did not happen. The Court party triumphed,
and the Shōgunate came to an end, but foreign
intercourse, instead of sharing its fate, was recog-

nized as essential to the country, and received the formal sanction of the Throne.

Notwithstanding a general vagueness of agreement amongst Japanese writers as to the general trend of affairs at the time of the Restoration, there is some divergence of opinion in regard to the causes which brought it about. On the one hand it is suggested that the existence of the dual form of government was incompatible with the changed conditions which followed upon the establishment of foreign intercourse on the new basis ; that the Shōgun, while a subject of the Emperor, was claiming a position of equality with the sovereigns of other countries, which was clearly improper ; and that when once foreign Governments had understood the real state of the case, the continuance of the Shōgunate was impossible. It is also contended that the raising of the question of the Shōgun's real position in Japan caused confusion in the country, produced a conflict of authority between the Court and the Shōgunate, and created doubts as to the quarter where homage was due.

The other view is that there was no essential incompatibility between the dual form of government and the new foreign intercourse, and that the Restoration was the result of many causes, amongst which the complications arising out of the conclusion of foreign treaties had but a secondary place.

There is truth in both views. It is possible to

argue that the dual form of government was one
to which the nation had become thoroughly
accustomed, imperial princes having at one period
been Shōguns for nearly a century; that it was
not the first time, either as regards foreigners, or
Japanese, that the question of the Shōgun's position
had been raised; that the change back to direct
imperial rule was a leap in the dark; and that had
the Shōgunate retained its influence undiminished,
there would have been no discord between Kiōto
and Yedo, no conflict of authority, and no need
for the Shōgun's resignation. But there is no
getting away from the fact that the new foreign
relations were hardly in keeping with the existence
of a phantom court at the old capital; that the
changed conditions which were the result of the
opening of the country introduced new and per-
plexing problems; and that it was not possible
for the nation to adjust itself to these new
conditions without a degree of friction which
would probably have been fatal to the continuance
of dual government. This is admitted in the
Shōgun's manifesto itself, and in the official explanation of his resignation given by his Ministers.

Nor, on the other hand, is it likely that the
Shōgunate would have survived very long, even
if the country had not been opened. The view
that it carried within itself the seeds of its dissolution seems well-founded. Economic causes were
operating everywhere, in the territories ruled
directly from Yedo, as well as in those of the self-

governing clans, to the detriment of the two classes, the *samurai* and the farmer, which formed the backbone of the feudal system. The increase of population, in spite of famine and other adverse causes, without a corresponding growth of the national resources; the presence of a large un-productive class which became an ever-increasing burden to the country; over-production of rice to the exclusion of other uses of the land, uncertain and unjust taxation; defective communications, and careless management of state and clan revenues, had created widespread poverty amongst the military class and the farmers. And this general distress resulted in a gradual fusion of classes, leading to the loosening of feudal ties, and clan disorganization. With progress and expansion of all kinds hindered by the narrow spirit and routine of feudalism, with commercial and maritime enterprise rendered alike impossible by the closure of the country, it would have been strange indeed if the Shōgunate, itself the central government, and, at the same time, a part of the system it controlled, had not shown symptoms of weakness before ever foreigners came; and stranger still, perhaps, if this weakness had not been increased by the complications which arose out of their coming.

A failing cause is naturally at a disadvantage, inasmuch as attention is concentrated on its shortcomings. This was notably the case in the closing days of the Tokugawa administration. Its services to the country in the past in rescuing it from a condition of anarchy, and establishing the period of order and tranquillity known as The Great Peace, were forgotten, and its many excellences were lost sight of in the high tension of public feeling and the popular clamour which ushered in the Restoration. But its claims to the nation's gratitude for the encouragement given to education, to literature, and to art are now generally recognized, and have recently received special acknowledgement from one of Japan's most prominent statesmen in an educational work written for the youth of the nation.[1]

In thinking of Japan's long seclusion from the world one is apt to dwell only on one side of it, the shutting out of foreigners, and to overlook, what for Japan was the more important side, the confinement of the Japanese people to their own shores. In the one direction the seclusion was never, as we know, complete, for through the Dutch, if not the Chinese, the Japanese Government were kept informed of important events in Europe and elsewhere. They knew in this way of Perry's mission long before he arrived, and news of what was passing in China reached them through the same channels. But in the other direction the isolation was absolute. Their knowledge of the outside world was acquired only at second hand, it was influenced by the personal equation of the medium through which it came,

---

[1] The *Kokumin Tokuhon* ('National Reader'), by Count Okuma, 1910.

and it was limited to official circles. This explains
why the nation as a whole, up to the time at least
of the Kagoshima and Shimonoséki hostilities,
displayed such ignorance of the power of Western
countries. It also accounts for the vivid impression produced on the minds of Japanese, when
they did go abroad, by what they saw, for the
enthusiasm of the reformers, and for the haste
with which reforms were adopted.

A question which must occur to most readers of
Japanese history is, how it was possible for a people
which had already given proofs of unusual vitality
and enterprise to submit to being penned up within
its own shores by the edict of 1636. No explanation
seems quite satisfactory. It is possible that the
invasion of Corea, still fresh in the memories of
the people, may, by its exhaustion of national
energies, have taken the edge off the spirit of
enterprise which existed before. There is also
reason to think that the severity of the laws, to
which attention has been called in the opening
chapter, the fact that trade was largely a Government monopoly, the antagonism provoked by
religious strife, and the example of China's rigid
conservatism, may to some extent explain the
phenomenal acquiescence of a high-spirited people
in a situation so abnormal, and altogether without
precedent. Be this as it may, the effects of the
long-continued policy of isolation were visible
long after the country was opened. Neither the
Government which had imposed the restrictions,

nor the people which had submitted to them, were able readily to free themselves from the prejudice which attached to the free intercourse of Japanese with other nations, and a faint echo of the trammels of the past exists to this day.

And when we speak of the opening of Japan we must remember how small a fraction of the country it was after all to which foreigners were admitted by the earlier treaties. During the first twenty years of foreign intercourse foreign ships were permitted to visit only four places scattered at wide intervals along Japan's extensive seaboard. Foreign trade and residence were limited to these, and to two towns, Tōkiō and Ōsaka, from which foreign ships were excluded. One other port was opened subsequently without appreciable result, and of the four ports first opened commerce only really throve at two. At the places opened foreigners were restricted as regards trade and residence to the boundaries of the settlements, with the privilege of making excursions within an area of a few miles known as treaty limits. Some twenty years after the first treaty was signed the introduction of a passport system gave foreigners some liberty of travel in the interior, and although this system was extended somewhat in later years, it was not until after the operation of the revised treaties in 1899 that the real opening of the country can be said to have taken place.

We take leave of Japan at an interesting stage in her development. The old order of things had

crumbled away, and out of the wreck of the Shōgunate and feudal system she was piecing together
with not a little trouble a new kind of administration. The form of this new government was
borrowed, as we have seen, from an ancient model.
And it was the same with the principle it represented, that of direct imperial rule.   But here the
resemblance ended. Japan had entered on a new
departure. She was moving in the direction of
reform on Western lines. For China as pattern
was now substituted the West, and in this breaking
with tradition and precedent lay not the least
of her difficulties. In the long and laborious work
of reform, upon which she now embarked, she was
helped by two things; the large stock of national
energy stored up during her long seclusion from
the world, and the knowledge and advice of the
foreigner, against whose admission to intercourse
on a footing of equality she had rebelled as a
violation of the country's ancient laws.

APPENDIXES[1]

APPENDIX 1

AMERICAN TREATY, MARCH, 1854

*Signed at Kanagawa, March 31st, 1854. Ratified by the
President of the United States, July, 1854. Ratifications
exchanged at Simoda, February 21st, 1855.*

THE United States of America and the Empire of Japan,
desiring to establish firm, lasting, and sincere friendship'
between the two nations, have resolved to fix, in a manner
clear and positive, by means of a treaty or general convention of peace and amity, the rules which shall in future
be mutually observed in the intercourse of their respective
countries ; for which most desirable object the President
of the United States has conferred full powers on his
commissioner, Matthew Calbraith Perry, special embas-
sador of the United States to Japan, and the August
Sovereign of Japan has given similar full powers to his
commissioners, Hayashi, Dai-gaku-no-kami, Ido, prince of
Tsussima, Izawa, prince of Mimasaka, and Udono, member
of the Board of Revenue.   And the said commissioners,
after having exchanged their said full powers and duly considered the premises, have agreed to the following Articles:—

I. There shall be a perfect, permanent and universal
peace, and a sincere and cordial amity between the United
States of America on the one part, and the empire of
Japan on the other part, and between their people
respectively, without exception of persons or places.

II. The port of Simoda in the principality of Idzu, and
the port of Hakodade[2] in the principality of Matsmai, are
granted by the Japanese as ports for the reception of
American ships, where they can be supplied with wood,

---

[1] The translations of all documents, not treaties, which appear as
appendixes, are, except where otherwise stated, the author's.

[2] Hakodaté.

water, provisions, and coal, and other articles their necessities may require, as far as the Japanese have them. The time for opening the first named port is immediately on signing this treaty ; the last named port is to be opened immediately after the same day in the ensuing Japanese year.

[*Note.*—A tariff of prices shall be given by the Japanese officers of the things which they can furnish, payment for which shall be made in gold and silver coin.]

III. Whenever ships of the United States are thrown on the coast of Japan, the Japanese vessels will assist them, and carry their crews to Simoda or Hakodade, and hand them over to their countrymen appointed to receive them ; whatever articles the shipwrecked men may have preserved shall likewise be restored, and the expenses incurred in the rescue and support of Americans and Japanese who may thus be thrown upon the shores of either nation are not to be refunded.

IV. Those shipwrecked persons and other citizens of the United States shall be free as in other countries, and not subjected to confinement, but shall be amenable to just laws.

V. Shipwrecked men and other citizens of the United States, temporarily living at Simoda and Hakodade,[1] shall not be subject to such restrictions and confinement as the Dutch and Chinese are at Nagasaki, but shall be free at Simoda to go where they please within the limits of seven Japanese miles (or *ri*) from a small island in the harbour of Simoda, marked on the accompanying chart hereto appended ; and shall in like manner be free to go where they please at Hakodade, within limits to be defined after the visit of the United States squadron to that place.

VI. If there be any other sort of goods wanted, or any business which shall require to be arranged, there shall be careful deliberation between the parties in order to settle such matters.

VII. It is agreed that ships of the United States resort-

---

[1] Hakodaté.

ing to the ports open to them shall be permitted to exchange gold and silver coin and articles of goods for other articles of goods, under such regulations as shall be temporarily established by the Japanese government for that purpose. It is stipulated, however, that the ships of the United States shall be permitted to carry away whatever articles they are unwilling to exchange.

VIII. Wood, water, provisions, coal, and goods required, shall only be procured through the agency of Japanese officers appointed for that purpose, and in no other manner.

IX. It is agreed, that if at any future day the government of Japan shall grant to any other nation or nations privileges and advantages which are not herein granted to the United States and the citizens thereof, that these same privileges and advantages shall be granted likewise to the United States and to the citizens thereof, without any consultation or delay.

X. Ships of the United States shall be permitted to resort to no other ports in Japan but Shimoda and Hakodade, unless in distress or forced by stress of weather.

XI. There shall be appointed by the government of the United States consuls or agents to reside in Simoda, at any time after the expiration of eighteen months from the date of the signing of this treaty : provided that either of the two governments deem such arrangement necessary.

XII. The present convention having been concluded and duly signed, shall be obligatory and faithfully observed by the United States of America and Japan, and by the citizens and subjects of each respective power ; and it is to be ratified and approved by the President of the United States, by and with the advice and consent of the Senate thereof, and by the August Sovereign of Japan, and the ratifications shall be exchanged within eighteen months from the date of the signature thereof, or sooner if practicable.

In faith whereof, we, respective plenipotentiaries of the United States of America and the Empire of Japan aforesaid, have signed and sealed these presents.

Done at Kanagawa this thirty-first day of March, in the year of our Lord Jesus Christ one thousand eight hundred and fifty-four, and of Kayei, the seventh year, third month, and third day.

(L.S.) M. C. PERRY.[1]

APPENDIX 2

American Treaty, Additional Regulations

Agreed upon at Shimoda in September, 1854.

ARTICLE I. The imperial governors of Simoda will place watch-stations wherever they deem best, to designate the limits of their jurisdiction ; but Americans are at liberty to go through them, unrestricted, within the limits of seven Japanese *ri*, or miles (equal to sixteen English miles), and those who are found transgressing Japanese laws may be apprehended by the police and taken on board their ships.

ARTICLE II. Three landing-places shall be constructed for the boats of merchant ships and whale ships resorting to this port ; one at Simoda, one at Kakizaki, and the third at the brook lying south-east of Centre Island. The citizens of the United States will, of course, treat the Japanese officers with proper respect.

ARTICLE III. Americans, when on shore, are not allowed access to military establishments, or private houses, without leave ; but they can enter shops and visit temples as they please.

ARTICLE IV. Two temples, the Rioshen at Simoda, and the Yokushen at Kakizaki, are assigned as resting-places for persons in their walks, until public houses and inns are erected for their convenience.

ARTICLE V. Near the Temple Yokushen, at Kakizaki,

[1] The signatures of the Japanese Plenipotentiaries were appended to the Japanese text.

·a burial-ground has been set apart for Americans, where their graves and tombs shall not be molested.

ARTICLE VI. It is stipulated in the treaty of Kanagawa, that coal will be furnished at Hakodade [1]; but as it is very difficult for the Japanese to supply it at that port, Commodore Perry promises to mention this to his government, in order that the Japanese government may be relieved from the obligation of making that port a coal dépôt.

ARTICLE VII. It is agreed that henceforth the Chinese language shall not be employed in official communications between the two governments, except when there is no Dutch interpreter.

ARTICLE VIII. A harbour-master and three skilful pilots have been appointed for the port of Simoda.

ARTICLE IX. Whenever goods are selected in the shops, they shall be marked with the name of the purchaser and the price agreed upon, and then be sent to the Goyoshi,[2] or government office, where the money is to be paid to Japanese officers, and the articles delivered by them.

ARTICLE X. The shooting of birds and animals is generally forbidden in Japan, and this law is therefore to be observed by all Americans.

ARTICLE XI. It is hereby agreed that five Japanese ri, or miles, be the limit allowed to Americans at Hakodade, and the requirements contained in Article I of these regulations are hereby made also applicable to that port within that distance.

ARTICLE XII. His Majesty the Emperor of Japan is at liberty to appoint whoever he pleases to receive the ratification of the treaty of Kanagawa, and give an acknowledgment on his part.

It is agreed that nothing herein contained shall in any way affect or modify the stipulations of the treaty of Kanagawa, should that be found to be contrary to these regulations.

[1] Hakodaté. [2] Goyōsho.

APPENDIX 3

BRITISH CONVENTION, OCTOBER, 1854.

*Signed at Nagasaki, October 14th, 1854.   Ratified by Her
Britannic Majesty, January 23rd, 1855.   Ratifications
exchanged at Nagasaki, October 9th, 1855.*

IT is agreed between Sir James Stirling, Knight, Rear-
Admiral and Commander-in-chief of the ships and vessels
of Her Britannic Majesty in the East Indies and seas
adjacent, and Mizu-no[1] Chikugo-no Kami, Obugio[2] of
Nagasaki, and Nagai Iwa-no jio,[3] Ometske[4] of Nagasaki,
ordered by His Imperial Highness the Emperor of Japan
to act herein ; that—

I. The ports of Nagasaki (Hizen) and Hakodate
(Matsmai) shall be open to British ships for the purposes
of effecting repairs, and obtaining fresh water, provisions,
and other supplies of any sort they may absolutely want
for the use of the ships.

II. Nagasaki shall be open for the purposes aforesaid
from and after the present date ; and Hakodate from and
after the end of fifty days from the Admiral's departure
from this port.   The rules and regulations of each of
these ports are to be complied with.

III. Only ships in distress from weather or unmanageable will be permitted to enter other ports than those
specified in the foregoing Articles, without permission
from the Imperial Government.

IV. British ships in Japanese ports shall conform to the
laws of Japan.   If high officers or commanders of ships shall
break any such laws, it will lead to the ports being closed.
Should inferior persons break them, they are to be delivered
over to the Commanders of their ships for punishment.

V. In the ports of Japan either now open, or which

---

[1] Mizuno.   [2] Bugiō.   [3] Iwa-no-jō.
[4] Métsuké.   (This official was not an *Ōmétsuké*, the *o* in the word
being simply an honorific prefix.)

may hereafter be opened, to the ships or subjects of any foreign nation, British ships and subjects shall be entitled to admission and to the enjoyment of an equality of advantages with those of the most favoured nation, always excepting the advantages accruing to the Dutch and Chinese from their existing relations with Japan.

VI. This Convention shall be ratified, and the ratifications shall be exchanged at Nagasaki on behalf of Her Majesty the Queen of Great Britain, and on behalf of His Highness the Emperor of Japan, within twelve months from the present date.

VII. When this Convention shall be ratified, no high officer coming to Japan shall alter it.

In witness whereof we have signed the same, and have affixed our seals thereunto, at Nagasaki, this fourteenth day of October, 1854.

(L.S.) JS. STIRLING.[1]

APPENDIX 4

EXPOSITION OF THE ARTICLES OF THE CONVENTION OF NAGASAKI OF THE 14TH OCTOBER, 1854

Agreed to on the 18th October, 1855, by Their Excellencies the Rear Admiral Commanding in Chief and the Japanese Commissioners.

THE first Article of the Convention opens the ports of Nagasaki and Hakodade[2] to British ships for repairs and supplies. It opens the whole and every part of those ports ; but ships must be guided in anchoring by the directions of the local government. Safe and convenient places will be assigned where ships may be repaired. Workmen, materials, and supplies will be provided by the local government according to a tariff to be agreed upon, by which also the modes of payment will be regu-

---

[1] The signatures of the Japanese Plenipotentiaries were appended to the Japanese text.   [2] Hakodaté.

lated. All official communications will hereafter, when Japanese shall have time to learn English, be made in that language. A British burial-ground shall be set apart on Medsume Sima, fenced in by a stone wall, and properly protected.

The second Article provides that, at each of the ports of Nagasaki and Hakodade [1] the Port Regulations shall be obeyed ; but the Japanese Government will take care that they shall not be of a nature to create embarrassment, nor to contradict in any other way the general tenour and intent of the Treaty, the main object of which is to promote a friendly intercourse between Great Britain and Japan.

The third Article declares that only ships in distress from weather, or unmanageable, shall enter other parts than Nagasaki and Hakodade [1] without permission from the Imperial Government ; but ships of war have a general right to enter the ports of friendly Powers in the unavoidable performance of public duties, which right can neither be waived nor restricted ; but Her Majesty's ships will not enter any other than open ports without necessity, or without offering proper explanations to the Imperial authorities.

The fourth Article provides that British ships and subjects in Japanese ports shall conform to the laws of Japan ; and that if any subordinate British subjects commit offences against the laws, they shall be handed over to their own officers for punishment ; and that if high officers or commanders of ships shall break the laws, it will lead to the closing of the ports specified. All this is as it should be ; but it is not intended by this Article that any acts of individuals, whether high or low, previously unauthorized or subsequently disapproved of by Her Majesty the Queen of Great Britain, can set aside the Convention entered into with Her Majesty alone by His Imperial Highness the Emperor of Japan.

The fifth Article secures in the fullest sense to British

[1] Hakodaté.

ships and subjects in every part of Japan, either now open or hereafter to be opened, an equality in point of advantage and accommodation with the ships and subjects or citizens of any other foreign nation, excepting any peculiar privilege hitherto conceded to the Dutch and Chinese in the port of Nagasaki. If, therefore, any other nation or people be now or hereafter permitted to enter other ports than Nagasaki and Hakodadi,[1] or to appoint Consuls, or to open trade, or to enjoy any advantage or privilege whatever, British ships and subjects shall, as of right, enter upon the enjoyment of the same.

APPENDIX 5

TRAITÉ DE COMMERCE, DE NAVIGATION, ET DE DÉLIMITATION, ENTRE LA RUSSIE ET LE JAPON

Signé à Simoda, le $\frac{26\ Janvier,}{7\ Février,}$ 1855. [Ratifications échangées à Simoda, le $\frac{25\ Novembre,}{7\ Décembre,}$ 1856.]

LES Plénipotentiaires de Sa Majesté l'Empereur de Toutes les Russies, l'Aide-de-Camp-Général Vice-Amiral Euphème Poutiatine ; et de Sa Majesté le Grand Souverain du Japon, Tsoutsouï-Khizenno-Kami[2] et Kavadzi-Saié-monno-Dzio,[3] ont arrêté et conclu, dans la ville de Simoda, le 26 Janvier, 1855 (ou le 21e jour du 12ème mois de la première année Ansey), un Traité et des Articles explicatifs qui contiennent ce qui suit :

Voulant assurer la paix et l'amitié entre la Russie et le Japon, et les consolider par un Traité, Sa Majesté l'Empereur de Toutes les Russies a nommé pour son Plénipotentiaire son Aide-de-camp et Vice-Amiral Euphème Poutiatine, et Sa Majesté le Grand Souverain du Japon a nommé de son côté pour ses Plénipotentiaires ses illustres sujets Tsoutsouï-Khizenno-Kami et Kavadzi-Saïemonno-Dzio.

---

[1] Hakodaté. [2] Tsutsui Hizen no Kami. [3] Kawaji Sayemon-no jō.

Lesquels Plénipotentiaires ont arrêté les Articles suivants :

ART. I. Il y aura à l'avenir paix et amitié sincère entre la Russie et le Japon. Les Russes et les Japonais jouiront dans les possessions des deux États de toute protection et assistance, tant pour leur sûreté personnelle que par rapport à l'inviolabilité de leurs propriétés.

II. La frontière entre la Russie et le Japon passera désormais entre les îles Itouroup et Ouroup. L'île Itouroup appartient tout entière au Japon, et l'île Ouroup, ainsi que les autres îles Kouriles situées au nord de cette île, appartiennent à la Russie. Quant à l'île Krafto (Sakhaline ou Saghalien), elle reste, comme par le passé, indivise entre la Russie et le Japon.

III. Le Gouvernement du Japon ouvre 3 ports aux navires russes, savoir : Simoda, dans la Principauté de Idzou ; Hakodadi, dans la Province de Hakodadi ; et Nagasaki, dans la Principauté de Khisen. Dans ces 3 ports, les navires russes pourront réparer leurs avaries, s'approvisionner d'eau, de bois de chauffage, d'aliments et autres objets néçessaires, de charbon de terre même, là où il s'en trouverait ; ils paieront tous ces objets en monnaie d'or ou d'argent, ou à défaut d'espèces, en marchandises de leur chargement.

A l'exception desdits ports, les navires russes ne visiteront aucun autre port, sauf les cas de nécessité absolue, lorsqu'ils seront dans l'impossibilité de continuer leur route. Les dépenses faites dans ce cas seront remboursées dans un des ports ouverts aux navires.

IV. Toute assistance sera prêtée dans les deux États aux navires naufragés et à leurs équipages ; ces derniers seront expédiés dans un des ports ouverts ; pendant toute la durée de leur séjour sur le territoire étranger, ils jouiront de la liberté en se soumettant aux lois équitables du pays.

V. Les Russes ont la faculté de faire dans les deux premiers des ports ouverts (Simoda et Hakodadi) l'échange des marchandises, objets et monnaies qu'ils auront apportés, contre les marchandises et les objets qu'ils désireraient acquérir.

VI. Le Gouvernement russe nommera, lorsqu'il le jugera nécessaire, un Consul dans l'un des deux premiers ports susnommés.

VII. Chaque fois qu'une question ou une affaire quelconque aura été jugée ou décidée, elle le sera scrupuleusement par le Gouvernement du Japon.

VIII. Tout Russe au Japon, et tout Japonais en Russie, jouira toujours d'une liberté complète et ne sera soumis à aucune vexation. Tout individu qui aurait commis un crime peut être arrêté, mais il ne peut être jugé que selon les lois de son pays.

IX. En considération du voisinage des deux États, les sujets russes participeront de plein droit à tous les droits et privilèges que le Gouvernement du Japon a déjà accordés ou accordera par la suite aux sujets des autres nations.

Le présent Traité sera ratifié par Sa Majesté l'Empereur de Toutes les Russies et par Sa Majesté le Grand Souverain du Japon, ou par leurs Plénipotentiaires, ainsi que cela est mentionné dans les Articles Séparés annexés au présent Traité, et les ratifications en seront échangées à Simoda dans un délai de 10 mois au moins ou à toute autre époque favorable.

Présentement, on échangera des copies du Traité, revêtues des signatures et des sceaux des Plénipotentiaires des deux Puissances ; les dispositions du Traité entreront en vigueur dès le jour de sa signature et seront fidèlement et inviolablement observées par les Parties Contractantes.

Fait et signé à Simoda le 26 Janvier, 1855, ou le $2^{\text{ème}}$ jour du $12^{\text{ème}}$ mois de la première année Ansey.

(L.S.) C. E. POUTIATINE.
(L.S.) TSOUTSOUI-KHIZENNO-KAMI.
(L.S.) KAVADZI-SAIEMONNO-DZIO.

APPENDIX 6

ARTICLES EXPLICATIFS DU TRAITÉ, CONFIRMÉS PAR LES PLÉNIPOTENTIAIRES RUSSES ET JAPONAIS

AD. ART. III (*a*). Dans les deux premiers ports désignés dans le Traité, les Russes pourront librement circuler dans la ville de Simoda et ses environs dans un rayon de 7 milles japonais, en partant de l'Île Inoubassiri ; à Hakodadi[1] dans un rayon de 5 lieues japonaises. Il leur est permis de visiter les boutiques, les temples, et de se reposer dans les maisons provisoirement désignées à cet effet en attendant la construction d'auberges spéciales ; ils n'entreront dans les maisons des particuliers que lorsqu'ils y auront été invités. A Nagasaki ils se conformeront à ce qui sera statué par la suite pour les autres nations.

(*b*) Pour la sépulture des morts, il sera réservé dans chacun des ports un terrain spécial, qui sera inviolablement protégé.

AD. ART. V. L'expédition des marchandises se fera dans un bâtiment désigné à cet effet pour le Gouvernement ; les marchandises et la monnaie d'or et d'argent apportées par les Russes y seront déposées. Les Russes, après, avoir choisi dans les boutiques les marchandises et objets qui leur conviennent et être convenus de leur prix avec les vendeurs, effectueront le paiement ou l'échange des marchandises dans ledit entrepôt par l'entremise des employés japonais.

AD. ART. VI (*a*). Les Consuls russes seront nommés dès l'année 1856.

(*b*) Les édifices et le terrain nécessaires pour l'installation du Consulat seront désignés par le Gouvernement du Japon. Les Russes y demeureront d'après leurs lois et coutumes.

AD. ART. IX. Les droits et privilèges qui seront reconnus aux autres nations, quelle que soit d'ailleurs leur nature, s'étendront par ce fait même sur les sujets russes,

---

[1] Hakodaté.

ainsi qu'il est dit dans l'Article IX, sans qu'on ait besoin de recourir à de nouvelles négociations.

Les présents Articles explicatifs ont la même force que le Traité et sont également obligatoires pour les deux Parties Contractantes. En foi de quoi ils ont été signés par les Plénipotentiaires des deux Puissances, et revêtus de leurs sceaux.

> (L.S.) C. E. POUTIATINE.
> (L.S.) TSOUTSOUI-KHIZENNO-KAMI.[1]
> (L.S.) KAVADZI-SAIEMONNO-DZIO.[2]

APPENDIX 7

SUPPLEMENTARY TREATY OF COMMERCE AND NAVIGATION BETWEEN RUSSIA AND JAPAN

Signed at Nagasaki, October $\frac{12}{24}$, 1857.

(Translation.)

IN addition to the Treaty concluded between Russia and Japan at Simoda, on the 26th January, 1855, or of Ansey the first year, 21st day of the 12th month, the undersigned Count Euphinicus Poutiatine, Vice-Admiral and Aide-de-Camp, General of His Majesty the Emperor of all the Russias, and their Excellencies Midzno-Tsikogono-Kami,[3] Controller and First Governor of Nagasaki, Alao-Iwamino-Kami,[4] Second Governor of Nagasaki, and Twase-Igano-Kami,[5] Imperial Commissioner, came to an agreement, and have stipulated the following Articles :

ART. I. In order to establish commerce and friendly intercourse between Russia and Japan on a more solid foundation, new regulations are hereby enacted for the guidance of the Russians and Japanese in the ports of Hakodate and Nagasaki.

As to the Port of Simoda, it being an unsafe harbour,

[1] Tsutsui Hizen no Kami.
[2] Kawaji Sayemon-no-jō.
[3] Mizuno Chikugo no Kami.
[4] Arao Iwami no Kami.
[5] Iwasé Iga no Kami.

the former stipulations alone will there remain in force. The new regulations will then be applicable, when it is finally decided that Simoda, or some safer port, is to be opened for foreign trade.

II. In future the number of ships, or the amount of money employed in trade will not be limited, and all commercial transactions will be done by the mutual consent of both parties.

III. When a Russian merchant vessel arrives in one of the above-mentioned ports, the captain and supercargo is bound to present through the Russian Consul, or where there is not one, to deliver himself to the local authorities, a declaration comprising the name of the ship, its tonnage, the name of the captain or supercargo, as well as the sort and quantity of goods brought by him, such declaration is to be made during the first day or not later than 48 hours; in that space the captain is bound to pay anchorage money, consisting of 5 mace or 42 copecks for each ton, if the vessel is above 150 tons, and 1 mace or 9 copecks for every ton, if the vessel is 150 tons, or of a smaller size.

The anchorage money is to be paid even when a vessel has entered the port not for the purposes of trade, but has been staying in it longer than 48 hours.

No anchorage money is levied from a vessel coming for repairs except its cargo, or a part of it, has been discharged on land, or into another ship.

The Custom-House having received the anchorage money is bound to give a receipt, and to allow at the same time the unloading of the ship.

IV. If the captain of a merchantman does not present a declaration during the first 48 hours after his arrival in port, he will have to pay a penalty of 65 roubles 50 copecks for each day, which is not to exceed 266 roubles.

In case of a false declaration, the captain will be fined 655 roubles, and for unloading the cargo without licence, besides the aforesaid penalty, his goods will be confiscated.

V. Russian vessels having paid the anchorage money on their arrival in the first Japanese port, can go into other ports, without further payment, if they only produce the receipt given them at the first port.

It is understood that this rule does not apply to vessels, which during their voyage enter and take new cargoes in ports of other nations.

VI. Boats employed in towing vessels, loading, or discharging goods, and all sorts of workmen are to be hired from the number appointed for that purpose by the local Japanese authorities. These boats, as well as all others, are to land at fixed places and wharfs.

VII. The goods purchased by Japanese from Russian merchant vessels, as well as those that are sent in return, are to be transmitted through the Custom-House. Besides this transmission the Custom-House is not to interfere in any commercial transaction between Japanese and Russian merchants.

VIII. In default of Japanese goods to be exchanged in return for a Russian cargo sold in Japan, the Custom-House will pay for it in silver, or gold foreign coin, according to the fixed rate of exchange.

IX. The existing duty of 35 per cent. will be levied on the sums realized for goods sold by public sale or private transactions, till a tariff shall be enacted. For this purpose the Consul, or the captain of the merchant vessel is bound to signify at the Custom-House the payments agreed for the purchase of the Russian goods.

The above-mentioned duty does not apply to the goods purchased by the Custom-House.

The exposition of the goods and the public sale may be repeated as often as the Russian merchant desires, and the Custom-House cannot limit the number of Japanese merchants coming to that sale.

X. If the goods are sold at the public sale the Custom-House is answerable for their payment. In private transactions it does not take the responsibility on itself, but will examine and decide any complaints which may arise, together with the Consul.

After the goods have been once delivered, neither party can complain about the quality or value of the purchased goods.

XI. Goods bought by Russians in Japanese ships will be paid in paper money, delivered by the Custom-House, for which it is bound to give real coin to the Japanese merchants immediately on the presentation of the paper money. The Russians will make payment in the same way for the hiring boats, purchasing provisions and other objects, but the pay in Russian or foreign coin is only to be made through the Custom-House.

XII. In settling accounts for purchased goods and all sorts of objects, the value of the money will be defined by the comparative weight and quality of the Russian or foreign gold and silver, with the Japanese gold and silver itsebous, viz., gold with gold, and silver with silver, and after an exact appreciation of their value, a further sum of 6 per cent. will be allowed for the expenses of recoinage. The settlement of accounts may also be done by reckoning 1 Spanish dollar equal to $2\frac{1}{2}$ Dutch florins, or 1 rouble 33 copecks, or 1 Mexican dollar to 2 Dutch florins 55 cents, or 1 rouble 35 copecks.

The weights, the measures of capacity and length will be compared and fixed in each of the opened ports by persons appointed for this purpose by both Governments.

XIII. All articles of war are not to be sold to private persons, but to the Government alone.

If in future the Japanese Government finds it necessary to stop the sale into private hands of some imported goods unknown to it, they will be purchased then on account of the Custom-House.

XIV. In case Russian vessels shall import opium in Japan, their cargoes will be confiscated and the guilty will be dealt with according to the Russian laws, strictly forbidding that pernicious trade.

XV. The exportation from Japan of gold and silver in coin or bars is prohibited, except gilt objects or gold and silver manufactured wares.

Copper, all sorts of arms, harness, silk stuff, under the name of 'Pamatonisiki',[1] can only be exchanged for objects purchased or ordered by the Japanese Government.

XVI. Rice, barley, wheat, red and white beans, coals, writing paper called ' Mino ' and ' Hanci ',[2] books, charts, and copper wares, can only be obtained by purchase from the Custom-House ; but this prohibition does not apply to persons buying these objects for their own use, with the exception of prohibited books and charts.

In case of scarcity, the exportation of articles of food, vegetable wax, and paper may be stopped for a time.

XVII. To prevent smuggling, guard-boats may be stationed about merchant vessels by the local authorities, but the expenses on that account are not to be levied on Russian trade.

XVIII. For the above-mentioned reason the crew of a merchantman and boats loaded with merchandise may be searched at the Custom-House, or at the place appointed as a dépôt for goods.

XIX. If any loss of goods or other objects belonging to the Russians shall ensue during the transportation in hired boats, a strict examination will be made and all means taken to recover what was lost, but in this case, as in all similar difficulties, the Custom-House, besides making inquiries, will not be responsible for any losses.

XX. The transhipment of goods from one Russian vessel to another or a foreign one, cannot be done without previous declaration to the Custom-House by the Consul or the captain of the vessel. The declaration must contain the sort and quantity of merchandise intended for the transhipment, and in such cases the Custom-House can send an officer on board to insure that no contraband should take place during the dischargement.

[1] Yamato-nishiki.   [2] Hanshi.

If the transhipment is done without licence, the Custom-House will make it known to the Consul, and where there is not one, will itself stop and seize the transhipped goods.

XXI. When any Russian merchantman is found smuggling in open ports, the goods alone will be confiscated, but if in other places of Japan, the vessel also will be seized.

This, however, must not be done before a previous examination and decision of the case shall be made by the Japanese authorities, together with the Russian Consul.

XXII. If a merchantman or any one belonging to the vessel, desire to make a present to a Japanese, they are to deliver with the donations a note certifying its being made by them.

XXIII. During the stay of a vessel in port, all the ship's papers are to be kept at the Russian Consulate, and where there is none they are to be delivered to the local authorities.

The Consul or the authorities at the departure of the vessel will not give up the ship's papers till all accounts are settled with the Custom-House and the Japanese merchants.

XXIV. Russians desiring to study the Japanese language or any of the Japanese arts, are bound to make their wishes known through the Consul or Captain to the local authorities, and proper persons will be appointed for the desired instruction.

XXV. All communications of the Russian Government with the Japanese, will be done through the highest person representing Russian authority in Japan, and by him transmitted to the local Governor. If from some circumstances, the communication or the letter is brought to a port where there is no Consul resident, it will be presented by the person to whom it was intrusted to the Governor of the place, and immediately sent by him to its destination. The answer may be forwarded to the port where the letter was delivered, if the vessel is awaiting it there, or may be sent through the Consul to forward it by the first opportunity to Russia.

XXVI. The rights of neutrals, acknowledged by all

civilized nations, oblige two belligerent States not to attack the ships of their adversaries in neutral ports, it is understood that in case of war between Russia and another nation, the Russian ships will not attack their enemies lying in Japanese ports.

XXVII. Russians residing constantly or temporarily in Japan, have a right to bring their wives and families to live in that country.

XXVIII. If in future it may be found necessary to alter or add any Articles to this Treaty, each of the Governments has a right to demand a revision of it.

The ratification of this Supplementary Treaty will be exchanged in 8 months, or as circumstances will allow. The copies in Russian, Japanese, Dutch, and Chinese languages, signed and sealed by those who have concluded this Treaty, will be now exchanged, and all the Articles are binding from the date of the signature and will be observed by the Contracting Parties faithfully and inviolably.

Done and signed at Nagasaki the $\frac{12}{24}$th October, in the year of our Lord, 1857, and the 3rd of the reign of His Majesty Alexander II, Emperor of All the Russias, or of Ansey, the 4th year, 7th day of the 9th moon.

(L.S.) C. E. POUTIATINE.
(L.S.) MIDYNO-TSIKOGONO-KAMI.[1]
(L.S.) ALAO-TWAMINO-KAMI.[2]
(L.S.) TWASE-IGANO-KAMI.[3]

APPENDIX 8

PRELIMINARY CONVENTION OF COMMERCE BETWEEN THE NETHERLANDS AND JAPAN.

Signed at Nagasaki, November 9, 1855.

(*Translation.*)

CONVENTION between Mr. Jan Hendrik Donker Curtius, Netherlands Commissioner in Japan, Knight of the Order of the Netherlands Lion, and Plenipotentiary Extra-

[1][2][3] See p. 239.

ordinary of His Majesty the King of the Netherlands, and Arawo Iwamino Kami,[1] and Kawa Moera Tsoesimano Kami,[2] Governors of Nagasaki, and Asano Ihkakf,[3] Imperial Superintendent at Nagasaki, entered into at the Government House in that town on the 9th of November, 1855.

ART. I. From the 1st December, 1855, the Netherlanders shall enjoy full personal freedom, and may therefore leave Desima at all times without an escort, just as they are allowed to do now, upon leave, with an escort.

II. If a Netherlander should at any time transgress any Japanese law, information thereof shall be given to the highest Netherlands officer stationed at Desima, and through his interposition the transgressor shall be punished by the Netherlands Government according to the Netherlands laws.

III. In case any Netherlander should be improperly treated by a Japanese, the matter shall, on complaint by the Netherlands Commissioner in Japan, be inquired into by the Japanese magistrates, and the Japanese shall be punished according to the Japanese law.

IV. In case one or more other ports of the Japanese empire may be opened now or hereafter to one or more other nations, exactly the same privileges shall be immediately granted to the Netherlands.

V. Whenever an officer or other seaman belonging to one of the ships-of-war of His Majesty the King of the Netherlands, or any person belonging to the Netherlands land forces, may die in Japan, his funeral shall take place with the military ceremonies used by the Netherlands land and sea forces, and hitherto observed. Salutes may also be fired from small arms at the burial-place, as well as on board the Netherlands ships-of-war, even with great guns.

VI. The Netherlands merchant-ships coming to the port of Nagasaki shall, upon nearing the coast, show a private signal-flag in addition to the national flag, as has been the custom hitherto. The ships-of-war have no private signal flag.

[1] [2] [3] See p. 239.

VII. When the two flags are seen by the watch on the Island of Iwo Sima, the Netherlands flag shall be exhibited from the flag-staff there, in token of recognition, just as is usual now also for the ships-of-war.

VIII. The Netherlands ships-of-war and merchant vessels shall come to anchor behind the Papenberg, as has been the custom hitherto.

IX. So soon as the Governor of Nagasaki shall have satisfied himself of the nationality of the vessels, by sending off for that purpose an officer of the guard accompanied by one of the officers from the Netherlands factory at Desima, the ships shall be at liberty to sail or steam into the harbour, or to have themselves towed therein by Japanese vessels, as has been the custom hitherto, but without giving hostages.

X. The crews of the ships shall be at liberty to use the ships' boats for communication with the other Netherlands ships and with the Island of Desima, or in rowing round the bay for their health, with this understanding, that the sailors of the Netherlands merchant ships may only enjoy this privilege when a captain or mate is with them in the boat or boats. They shall, of course, land nowhere else than at the water-gate of Desima, and they must have no intercourse with the crews of Japanese vessels. The boats shall bear the Netherlands flag for the purpose of recognition.

XI. There shall be no landing from the boats at any other place than the water-gate of Desima.

XII. Except the outer wall, the guard-houses, and public buildings of Desima, all the dwellings and warehouses shall be sold, through the intervention of the Governors of Nagasaki, to the Netherlands factory, and the ground of Desima let. They shall be under the direction of the highest Netherlands officer dwelling there, and be maintained at the cost of the Netherlands factory.

XIII. For the performance of the necessary repairs, the building or pulling down of warehouses or dwellings, or for making alterations and improvements therein, the Netherlands factory shall be at liberty to employ Japanese tradesmen and to buy Japanese materials, for which payment shall be made in ' kambang ' money. Previous notice of these operations shall be given to the Governor of Nagasaki.

XIV. The Netherlanders residing at Desima are at liberty to go round the bay in Netherlands or Japanese vessels, but without landing anywhere. They may fish from these vessels in the bay for recreation. These vessels shall bear the Netherlands flag for the purpose of recognition.

XV. The keys of the water-gate are in the exclusive keeping of the highest Netherlands officer at Desima.

XVI. The keys of the land-gate are in the keeping of the Japanese officer on guard there.

XVII. But the sailors belonging to the Netherlands merchant ships are, except the commanders, subject to personal search, as has been the custom hitherto, when they go by the land-gate of Desima to Nagasaki and when they return from thence. At the water-gate and on board the Netherlands ships no search takes place.

XVIII. The examination of goods only takes place when they are introduced into Japan from Desima, or when they are brought from Japan to Desima, as has been the custom hitherto, and not at the delivery from the ships into Desima, or at the delivery from Desima on board the ships. The strongest precautions shall be taken against smuggling.

XIX. During the presence of Netherlands merchant-ships in the port of Nagasaki, while works are going on there, a Japanese officer shall be stationed at Desima to keep order amongst the Japanese coolies in general who are then to be found there, as has been the custom hitherto.

XX. The management of mercantile affairs remains for the rest on the present footing. The keys of the ware-houses are always in the keeping of the highest Nether-lands officer residing at Desima, whenever Netherlands goods are deposited therein. No Japanese seals are placed upon the warehouses.

XXI. All Japanese who have the necessary permission according to the Japanese laws, are to be admitted into Desima.

XXII. At all meetings that take place at Nagasaki, the compliments and the reception by the Japanese are to be according to the Japanese forms, and by the Netherlanders according to the Netherlands forms.

XXIII. Whenever opportunities may occur, the Netherlanders residing at Desima shall be at liberty to send letters by the Chinese junks as well as by the ships of other nations.

XXIV. The Netherlanders shall be at liberty to have free correspondence by letters with the commanders of ships or squadrons of foreign nations at peace with Japan, who are stopping in the bay of Nagasaki.

XXV. Musterings are to take place only on board the Netherlands merchant ships, on their arrival and departure, and not at Desima.

XXVI. The Netherlands merchant-ships shall retain their gunpowder and arms, including their great guns.

XXVII. The customary presents for His Majesty the Emperor and other great personages, and the annual 'fassak',[1] are regulated on the present footing. No alteration is to be introduced in the manner in which the trade with the factory is carried on. If any alteration therein should be hereafter desired, either on the part of the Japanese or the Netherlanders, it shall be agreed upon and regulated by the Governor of Nagasaki and the Netherlands Commissioner in Japan.

● XXVIII. In case it should appear that any matter requires further regulation, it shall be taken into careful consideration by the Governor of Nagasaki and the Netherlands Commissioner in Japan, and all restrictions which are now found to be burthensome by the Netherlanders shall be removed as far as possible.

XXIX. So soon as a Treaty shall have been entered

[1] Hassaku.

into between the Netherlands and Japan, this Convention shall become void. In case such a Treaty should not be entered into soon, this Convention shall, nevertheless, remain in force, but subject to the ratification both of His Majesty the King of the Netherlands and of His Majesty the Emperor of Japan, and the ratifications signed by high officers empowered thereto on both sides, shall be exchanged at Nagasaki within the space of two years from the date hereof.

All the stipulations of this Convention come into immediate operation with the exception of the following Articles :

ART. I. The freedom therein granted comes into operation on the 1st December, 1855, and Articles IX, XII, XIII, XIV, XVIII, XX, and XXVI, come into operation on the 1st January, 1856.

In witness whereof we, Mr. J. H. Donker Curtius, Netherlands Commissioner in Japan, Knight of the Order of the Netherlands Lion, and Plenipotentiary Extraordinary of His Majesty the King of the Netherlands; and Arawo Iwamino Kami,[1] Kawa Moera Tsoesimano Kami,[2] Governors of Nagasaki, and Asano Ikkakf,[3] Imperial Superintendent at Nagasaki, have signed this Convention, and set our seals hereto.

Done in duplicate, in the town of Nagasaki, on the 9th November, in the year of our Lord, 1855.

(L.S.) J. H. DONKER CURTIUS.

APPENDIX 9

TREATY OF COMMERCE BETWEEN THE NETHERLANDS AND JAPAN.

Signed at Nagasaki, January 30, 1856. [Ratifications exchanged at Nagasaki, October 16, 1857.]

THEIR Majesties the King of the Netherlands, Prince of Orange-Nassau, Grand Duke of Luxemburg, &c., and the Emperor of Great Japan (Dai Nipon) desiring to confirm

[1] [2] [3] See p. 239.

the ancient relations between the inhabitants of the two empires, and considering the period favourable for making the privileges granted to the Netherlanders more in accordance with the tenor of those bestowed upon them by the Emperor's illustrious predecessors, have appointed for their respective Plenipotentiaries, that is to say, His Majesty the King of the Netherlands, Master Jan Hendrik Donker Curtius, Knight of the Order of the Netherlands Lion ; and His Majesty the Emperor of Japan, Arawo Iwamino Kami,[1] and Kawa Moera Tsoesimano Kami,[2] Governors of Nagasaki, and Nagai Iwamodsio[3] and Asano Ikkakf,[4] Imperial Superintendents ; who have agreed as follows :

Art. I. The Netherlanders have full personal freedom, and may therefore leave Desima at all times without an escort, just as they are allowed to do now, upon leave, with an escort.

II. If a Netherlander should at any time transgress any Japanese law, information thereof shall be given to the highest Netherlands officer stationed at Desima, and through his interposition the transgressor shall be punished by the Netherlands Government according to the Netherlands laws.

III. In case any Netherlander should be improperly treated by a Japanese, the matter shall, on complaint by the Netherlands Commissioner in Japan, be inquired into by the Japanese magistrates, and the Japanese shall be punished according to the Japanese law.

IV. In case one or more other ports of the Japanese empire are, or shall be, opened to one or more other nations, exactly the same privileges shall be immediately granted to the Netherlands.

V. Whenever an officer, or other seaman belonging to one of His Majesty the King of the Netherlands ships of war, or any person belonging to the Netherlands land forces, may die in Japan, his funeral shall take place with

[1][2][4] See p. 239.   [3] Nagai Iwa-no-jō.

the military ceremonies used by the Netherlands land and sea forces, and hitherto observed. Volleys may also be fired from small arms at the burial place, as well as on board the Netherlands ships of war, even with great guns.

VI. The Netherlands merchant-ships coming to the port of Nagasaki shall, upon nearing the coast, show a private signal flag in addition to the national flag, as has been the custom hitherto. The ships of war have no private signal flag.

VII. When the two flags are seen by the watch on the Island of Iwo Sima, the Netherlands flag shall be exhibited from the flag-staff there, in token of recognition, just as is usual now also for the ships of war.

VIII. The Netherlands ships of war and merchant vessels shall come to anchor behind the Papenberg, as has been the custom hitherto.

IX. So soon as the Governor of Nagasaki shall have satisfied himself of the nationality of the vessels, by sending off for that purpose, an officer of the guard accompanied by one of the officers from the Netherlands factory at Desima, the ships shall be at liberty to sail or steam into the harbour, or to have themselves towed therein by Japanese vessels, as has been the custom hitherto, but without giving hostages.

X. The crews of the ships shall be at liberty to use the ships' boats for communication with the other Netherlands ships and with the Island of Desima, or in rowing round the bay for recreation ; with this understanding, that the sailors of the Netherlands merchant ships may only make use of this privilege when a captain or mate is with them in the boats. They shall of course land nowhere else than at the water-gate of Desima, and they must have no inter-course with the crews of Japanese vessels. The boats shall bear the Netherlands flag for the purpose of recognition.

XI. There shall be no landing from the boats at any other place than the water-gate of Desima.

XII. The existing dwellings and warehouses remain

upon the old footing. They may, however, be repaired and altered by the Netherlands factory at its own cost, for which previous notice shall be given to the Governor of Nagasaki, and when he has given permission thereto, the materials purchased, and the workmen's wages shall be paid for in ' kambang ' money ; in like manner for new dwellings and warehouses to be built.

XIII. The Netherlanders residing at Desima are at liberty to go round the bay in Netherlands or Japanese vessels, but without landing anywhere. They may fish from these vessels in the bay for recreation. These vessels shall bear the Netherlands flag for the purpose of recognition.

XIV. The keys of the water-gate are in the exclusive keeping of the highest Netherlands officer at Desima. Notice of the opening and shutting of this gate shall be given to one of the Japanese officers at Desima, who shall take care that no Japanese go into Desima by the water-gate unless they have permission to do so.

XV. The keys of the land-gate are in the keeping of the Japanese officer on guard there.

XVI. But the sailors belonging to the Netherlands merchant-ships are, except the commanders, subject to personal search, as has been the custom hitherto, when they go by the land-gate of Desima to Nagasaki, and when they return from thence. At the water-gate and on board the Netherlands ships no search takes place.

XVII. The examination of goods only takes place when they are introduced into Japan from Desima, or when they are brought from Japan to Desima, as has been the custom hitherto, and not at the delivery from the ships to Desima or at the delivery from Desima on board the ships. The strongest precautions shall be taken against smuggling.

XVIII. During the presence of Netherlands merchant-ships in the port of Nagasaki, while works are going on there, a Japanese officer shall be stationed at Desima, as has been the custom hitherto,

XIX. The management of mercantile affairs remains for the rest on the present footing. The keys of the warehouses are always in the keeping of the highest Netherlands officer residing at Desima, whenever Netherlands goods are deposited therein. No Japanese seals are placed upon the warehouses.

XX. All Japanese who have the necessary permission according to the Japanese laws may come to Desima.

XXI. At all meetings that take place at Nagasaki the compliments and the reception by the Japanese are to be according to the Japanese forms, and by the Netherlanders according to the Netherlands forms.

XXII. Whenever opportunities may occur, the Netherlanders residing at Desima shall be at liberty to send letters by the Chinese junks, as well as by the ships of other nations.

XXIII. The Netherlanders shall be at liberty to have free correspondence by letters with the commanders of ships or squadrons of foreign nations at peace with Japan, who are stopping in the bay of Nagasaki.

XXIV. Musterings are to take place only on board the Netherlands merchant-ships on their arrival and departure, and not at Desima.

XXV. The Netherlands merchant-ships shall retain their gunpowder and arms, including their great guns.

XXVI. The customary presents for His Majesty the Emperor and other great personages, and the annual ' fassak ', are regulated on the present footing. No alteration is to be introduced in the manner in which the trade with the factory is carried on. In case any alteration therein should be hereafter desired, either on the part of the Japanese or the Netherlanders, it shall be agreed upon and regulated by the Governor of Nagasaki and the Netherlands Commissioner in Japan.

XXVII. In case it should appear that any matter requires another regulation, it shall be taken into careful consideration by the Governor of Nagasaki and the

Netherlands Commissioner in Japan, and all restrictions which are now found to be burdensome or needless by the Netherlanders or the Japanese shall be removed as far as possible.

XXVIII. This Treaty shall be subject to the ratification, both of His Majesty the King of the Netherlands and of His Majesty the Emperor of Japan, and the ratifications signed by high officers empowered thereto on both sides shall be exchanged at Nagasaki within the space of two years from the date hereof.

All the stipulations of this Convention come meanwhile into immediate operation.

In witness whereof we, Master Jan Hendrik Donker Curtius, Netherlands Commissioner in Japan, Knight of the Order of the Netherlands Lion, and Plenipotentiary Extraordinary of His Majesty the King of the Netherlands, and Arawo Iwamino Kami,[1] and Kawa Moera Tsoesimano Kami,[2] Governors of Nagasaki, and Nagai Iwamodsio[3] and Asano Ikkakf,[4] Imperial Superintendents at Nagasaki, have signed these presents and set our seals hereto, with the exception of the first-named of the Japanese Plenipotentiaries, who has been prevented from doing so by his departure for Jeddo.

Done in duplicate in the town of Nagasaki on the 30th of January, in the year of our Lord 1856.

(L.S.)   J. H. DONKER CURTIUS.

APPENDIX 10

ADDITIONAL ARTICLES TO THE TREATY OF COMMERCE CONCLUDED JANUARY 30, 1856, BETWEEN THE NETHERLANDS AND JAPAN.

Signed at Nagasaki, October 16, 1857.

ADDITIONAL ARTICLES agreed upon between the Netherlands and the Japanese Plenipotentiaries :

Master Jan Hendrik Donker Curtius, Netherlands Com-

[1] [2] [3] [4] See pp. 239 and 251.

missioner in Japan ; and Midsoeno Tsikoegono Kami,[1] Financial Governor and Governor of Nagasaki, Alao Iwamino Kami,[2] Governor of Nagasaki, Iwase Igano Kami,[3] Imperial Superintendent ;

In order to form part of the Treaty concluded between the Netherlands and Japan, at Nagasaki, on the 30th January, 1856.

ART. I. Trading shall be allowed from henceforth in the ports of Nagasaki and Hakodate.

Trading at Hakodate shall begin 10 months from the date hereof.

II. Tonnage dues calculated at Sp. m. 0.5 (5 maas), or f. 0.80 (80 cents.) Netherlands currency per ton, shall be paid within two days after arriving.

For ships of less than 150 tons burden Sp. m. 0.1 (1 maas) or f. 0.16 (16 cents.) Netherlands currency is to be paid per ton.

Ships of war pay no tonnage dues, but they pay pilot dues, and the hire of towing vessels.

In case the tonnage dues have been once paid at Nagasaki, and the ships depart from thence direct for Hakodate, the tonnage dues are not to be paid a second time. For this effect a receipt shall be given at Nagasaki, on the manifest for the tonnage dues paid, and *vice versa*, in like manner on departing from Nagasaki for Hakodate. After having visited a foreign port a manifest must again be produced, and tonnage dues paid whenever new articles are brought.

In case vessels are hired for unloading, loading or towing, coolies are to be employed who are registered as such. No coolies shall be employed who are not provided with a certificate of registration.

III. Merchant ships which do not trade, but remain longer than twice 24 hours in a port pay tonnage dues.

Merchant ships which run in for repairs, from distress, &c., without trading or transhipping, pay no tonnage

[1][2][3] See p. 239.

dues. In case the cargo disembarked before the repairs should be sold, tonnage dues must be paid.

❀ IV. Within 48 hours after the arrival of a merchant-ship at Nagasaki the name of the ship and of its commander shall be sent in by the highest Netherlands officer at Desima, accompanied by the manifest and the burden of the ship in tons, on pain of punishment for the commander, as provided in Article XXII. At Hakodate the same shall be done by the commander within 24 hours. At Nagasaki the unloading can take place at once during the day ; but at Hakodate the unloading must be after the manifest is presented, and in presence of Japanese officers appointed for the purpose. If a place for the examination of imported or exported goods should be provided also at Nagasaki, negotiations shall take place thereon, and the necessary regulations shall be established.

V. The number of merchant ships is unlimited. There is no limitation of the trade to a certain sum of money. In case goods brought in are not bought by the Japanese, or that there is deficiency of goods for return, then they remain unsold. In case the goods brought in are bought, but there is a deficiency of goods for return, then payment shall be made in foreign gold and silver coin, whenever there is any in the Treasury, more or less in quantity.

VI. A duty of 35 per cent. shall be levied on the produce of all merchandize sold at public sale, or by private contract ; but this levy is not applicable in regard to goods which are disposed of to the Treasury. Duties upon importation, transit, and exportation shall be fixed by negotiation from time to time. Until then, the present levy continues.

VII. After inspection of the goods for sale, the sales take place at the Treasury, which receives and takes care of the purchase money unless goods are received in payment by the sellers. If the buyers who have purchased at the public sales fail to pay the purchase money, it shall be made good by the Treasury. But if the purchase

1247   R

money of goods sold privately, be not paid, it is not made good by the Treasury. The Netherlands merchants shall be at liberty to have such public sales held as often as they think fit, without limitation of the number of merchants who are admitted thereto.

VIII. Whenever any goods are brought for sale, but remain unsold, and these are kept at Desima, to be again offered for sale, the proceedings shall be always according to the foregoing Article. The goods may also be sold privately.

But all articles bought privately by the Japanese must be paid for in hard cash at the Treasury. Direct returns must not be given for them by the Japanese buyers. In case a list of goods privately sold to the Japanese, be presented through the highest Netherlands officer at Desima, to the Treasury with a statement of the purchase money, then the goods shall be delivered to the buyers, upon production of a proof of payment at the Treasury.

IX. Not only the appointed purveyors, but all merchants may come to Desima to treat concerning the buying and selling of goods. At Hakodate a place (commercial house or bazaar) shall be appointed for the purpose.

X. In case the Japanese merchants have bought goods privately, and these have been delivered by the Netherlands merchant before the purchase money has been paid at the Treasury, and thereupon difficulties arise ; if the goods should have disappeared or the buyers have fled, or also, if agreements for commission cause difficulties, the matter shall be inquired into as far as possible ; but the Treasury shall not be answerable for the damage. After the delivery and reception of goods, complaint can no longer be made respecting the quality, the weight, and the measure of the goods bought or sold.

XI. If a Netherlander buy goods of a Japanese he shall pay for them in notes which are to be issued by the Treasury. These notes shall be immediately paid by the Treasury to the Japanese holders in Japanese coin. All the expenses of Desima, the hire of towing vessels, &c., shall be paid for with money kept by the Treasury.

XII. The Netherlanders may also pay in foreign gold and silver coin. In case the Japanese should wish to receive foreign gold and silver coin, they shall arrange thereupon with the Netherlanders. All foreign gold and silver coin must, however, be taken only to the Treasury.

The silver Spanish dollar, or pillar dollar, is reckoned at the value of $f.$ 2.50 (2 guldens 50 cents). The silver Mexican dollar at the value of $f.$ 2.55 (2 guldens 55 cents).

XIII. Munitions of war in general may be delivered to the Japanese Government, but not to the merchants.

If amongst goods brought to Japan for the first time, articles should be found, which the merchants are forbidden to deliver in Japan, the matter shall be officially arranged.

XIV. The introduction of opium into Japan is forbidden.

XV. Gold and silver must not be bought by the Netherlanders, but this does not apply to gilt articles, nor to manufactured gold and silver. Japanese coin must not be exported. If there should be any other articles, the exportation of which cannot be allowed, official communications and decisions shall take place thereon in each case.

XVI. Rice, barley, wheat, ' daitz ',[1] ' schoods ',[2] coals, paper-' mino ' and paper-' hansi ', books, maps, brasswork, shall only be delivered by the Treasury. But this restriction has no application to articles bought for personal use of the purveyors or in the town. Books and maps which have been printed, or written, or sold without the permission of the Japanese Government, must not be exported.

XVII. Copper, sabres and appurtenances, ' Jamato nisiki '[3] (a certain silk stuff), armour, fire-arms, bows with appurtenances, harness and other warlike apparatus, must not be delivered by the Japanese merchants. But upon a contract for the delivery of goods to the Japanese Government, it may be agreed to make them serve in part payment. If there should be other forbidden articles,

[1] daidzu.   [2] shōdzu.   [3] Yamato-nishiki.

they shall be treated in the same way, according to official arrangement.

XVIII. All the goods sold by the Japanese are to be delivered at prices agreed upon in each case, and not at fixed prices.

On the failure of the harvest, the Japanese Government shall have the power of forbidding, for a time, the exportation of any provisions. The exportation of wax and paper may also be temporarily forbidden upon occasion of any disaster.

XIX. During the stay of the merchant-ships at Hakodate, all ships' papers shall be delivered into the keeping of the Government there. At Nagasaki they are to be given into the keeping of the highest Netherlands officer at Desima. In both ports Japanese guard-ships shall be placed near the merchant vessels, to prevent smuggling. The number of these vessels may be increased or diminished, according to circumstances. The Netherlanders pay nothing for these.

XX. As the boats for loading and unloading are hired privately, the goods which may be lost thereby are not to be made good by the Treasury. But the matter shall be inquired into, as far as possible, on the Japanese side.

XXI. If on the arrival of a merchant-ship a false manifest should be delivered, the highest Netherlands officer shall inquire into the matter, and impose a penalty on the commander to the amount of 500 silver dollars for the Treasury.

XXII. If on the arrival at Hakodate no manifest is delivered within 24 hours, the commander shall pay to the Treasury a penalty of 50 silver dollars for every day's neglect ; but in no case shall this penalty amount to more than 200 silver dollars. If unloading take place at Hakodate before the manifest has been delivered, the goods unloaded shall be declared forfeited, and the commander shall pay a penalty of 500 silver dollars to the Treasury.

XXIII. Nothing belonging to the cargo shall be transferred from one ship to another lying in the port, whether the ships be native or foreign, without the previous permission of the Government and in the presence of the appointed Japanese officers. Cargo transferred from ship to ship without this permission shall be declared forfeited to the Treasury.

XXIV. If smuggling should be carried on in the open ports, the Japanese smugglers shall be punished according to the Japanese law. The Netherlands smugglers shall be subject to the forfeiture of the goods smuggled in or out when legally seized. If smuggling should be carried on along the Japanese coasts, the boat and the cargo shall be declared forfeited. The highest Netherlands officer residing in Japan shall, after examination, make no difficulty in regard to these matters.

XXV. No Japanese may stay on board a Netherlands ship without the knowledge of the Government. If a Japanese goes on board a Netherlands ship of his own accord, or without consent, he shall be taken up and delivered to the Japanese officers.

XXVI. The highest Netherlands officer at Desima shall not allow any Netherlands merchant-ship to depart before all accounts are settled. At Hakodate, the goods bought there by the Netherlanders must not be all loaded before they have been entirely paid for, or goods have been delivered for them.

XXVII. Goods smuggled in or out through the landgate of Desima (not agreeing with the permit) shall, when legally seized, be declared forfeited.

XXVIII. Goods for private use, given by a Netherlander to a Japanese, can only be taken out at the gate, on a permit granted by the highest Netherlands officer at Desima.

XXIX. On the arrival of ships of any nation which has already entered into a Treaty with Japan, there shall be free personal intercourse between the Netherlanders and the persons coming on board such ships, both in the ships and at Desima. Due care shall be taken herein, that it may appear to the officer on guard, upon examination, to what nation the ships belong.

XXX. The Netherlanders shall not, unless invited to do so, enter batteries, Government buildings, houses or other places having a door. Temples, tea and resting houses, &c., are excepted. The prohibition of this Article is not applicable when the highest Netherlands officer residing in Japan wishes to visit the Government respecting matters of business.

XXXI. For payments in resting or tea houses and in temples, and for what is bought in the shops for private use, and for carriage hire, payment shall be made in notes to be issued by the Treasury.

XXXII. The boundaries for the excursions of the Netherlanders at Nagasaki are shown upon the accompanying map. At Hakodate the boundary is fixed at five Japanese miles. If a Netherlander has exceeded these bounds without the consent of the Government, upon receiving notice from those present, he shall go back. If he does not attend to such a notice, he shall, without respect of person, be taken up and delivered to the highest Netherlands officer.

• XXXIII. The Netherlanders are at liberty to practise their own or the Christian religion within their buildings and at the burying-places appointed for them.

XXXIV. Letters from the Netherlands Government to that of Japan shall be delivered by the highest Netherlands officer to the Governor of Nagasaki, or in his absence to the highest Japanese officer present there, in order that they may be sent on.

Vice versa letters from the Japanese Government to that of the Netherlands shall be delivered by the Governor of Nagasaki to the highest Netherlands officer at Desima in order to be sent on. Autograph letters from His Majesty the King of the Netherlands to His Majesty the Emperor of Japan, or from His Majesty the Emperor of

Japan to His Majesty the King of the Netherlands shall be transmitted in the same way.

XXXV. In case Netherlanders should wish to learn the Japanese language or other Japanese sciences and arts, then, at the request of the highest Netherlands officer at Desima, teachers shall be chosen and sent by the Japanese Government to give instructions therein at Desima in the day time.

XXXVI. In case disputes or disagreements should arise between the foreigners who arrive, they shall be settled without the interference of the Japanese Government.

XXXVII. If such should be the case between Netherlanders and Japanese, or if fighting, wounding, robbery, incendiarism, should take place between them, the matters shall be examined into, and if possible settled by officers on both sides.   And such occurrences shall not of themselves interfere with the mutual friendship of the two States.

XXXVIII. All matters on the part of the Netherlands shall, in the absence of the highest Netherlands officer at Desima, be managed by the Netherlands officer immediately next to him in rank.

XXXIX. All rights that are or shall be granted to other foreign nations shall at the same time be immediately extended to the Netherlands.   As for the rest, the local regulations shall be observed.

XL. The stipulations of the Treaty which are not altered hereby, and all other stipulations not annulled hereby, remain as at present.   At Hakodate, things shall be managed as nearly as possible in the manner provided in these Articles.

If any alteration or explanation should appear to be necessary in regard to some stipulations or subjects, they shall be settled by negotiation.

The foregoing Articles shall be looked upon as forming part of the above-mentioned Treaty between the Netherlands and Japan of the 30th January, 1856, and they shall have the same force as if they had been inserted word for word therein.

These Additional Articles shall be submitted for the ratification of His Majesty the King of the Netherlands and of His Majesty the Emperor of Japan, and the ratifications drawn up according to the provisions of Article XXVIII of the Treaty, shall be exchanged at Nagasaki within one year from the date hereof.

In witness whereof we, the Plenipotentiaries on both sides, Master Jan Hendrik Donker Curtius, Netherlands Commissioner in Japan, Knight, &c. ; and Midsoeno Tsikoegono Kami,[1] Finance Governor and Governor of Nagasaki, Alao Iwamino Kami,[2] Governor of Nagasaki, Iwase Igano Kami,[3] Imperial Superintendent, have signed these presents and set our seals hereto.

Done in duplicate in the town of Nagasaki on the 16th October, 1857.

(L.S.)   J. H. DONKER CURTIUS.

SUPPLEMENT TO THE ADDITIONAL ARTICLES AGREED UPON BETWEEN THE NETHERLANDS AND JAPANESE PLENIPOTENTIARIES.

ART. I. Considering that the Company trade (*kompshandel*) ceases from henceforth, and no copper may be exported, except by the Imperial Government alone, in payment of goods required, the presents and the ' fassak '[4] mentioned in Art. XXVI of the Treaty are hereby abolished.

II. The stipulations of Articles VI, VIII, IX, and XXIV of the Treaty are annulled. The Netherlands ships shall, therefore, for the future come to anchor immediately before the town, in the usual place.

In witness whereof, we, the Plenipotentiaries on each side, Master Jan Hendrik Donker Curtius, Netherlands Commissioner in Japan, Knight, &c. ; and Midsoeno Tsikoegono Kami, Finance Governor and Governor of

[1][2][3] See p. 239.   [4] Hassaku.

Nagasaki, Alao Iwamino Kami, Governor of Nagasaki, Iwase Igano Kami, Imperial Superintendent, have signed these presents and set our seals hereto.

Done in duplicate in the town of Nagasaki, on the 16th October, 1857.

(L.S.)   J. H. DONKER CURTIUS.

(*Translation.*)

To the Netherlands Commissioner in Japan.

NEGOTIATIONS shall take place respecting the manner in which the highest Netherlands officer shall travel to have audience with His Majesty the Emperor, after the local regulations of each place on the route shall have been examined.

The Netherlanders are not prevented from having their wives and children with them within the open ports of Japan.

Negotiations for the exportation of Japanese coins are still going on.

The manner of trading at Hakodate and Nagasaki has been agreed to for the Netherlanders.

Other nations who shall hereafter conclude treaties, shall not, therefore, be prevented from trading in the same manner in the said two ports.

So long as the duties levied by the treasury are not sufficient for the various disbursements, it will still carry on trade with some imported and exported goods.

The month Hatsigoeats,[1] of the 4th year of Ansei.

MIDSOENO TSIKOEGONO KAMI.
ALAO IWAMINO KAMI.
IWASE IGANO KAMI.

(*Translation.*)

To the Netherlands Commissioner in Japan.

THERE is nothing to prevent our answering the request, that, in accordance with the especial communication,

---

[1] Hachigwatsu (8th month).

there is, so far as concerns all nations on the Japanese side, no idea of concluding a treaty of friendship and commerce with the Kingdom of Portugal, like that with the Netherlands, in case such a treaty should be desired by that Kingdom.

The month Hatsigoeats, of the 4th year of Ansei.

MIDSOENO TSIKOEGONO KAMI.
ALAO IWAMINO KAMI.
IWASE IGANO KAMI.

(*Translation.*)

To the Netherlands Commissioner in Japan.

THE trampling on images is abolished from henceforth ; but the introduction of the Christian worship and the importation of the Christian and other foreign religious books, prints and images, are not allowed in Japan.

The month Hatsigoeats, of the 4th year of Ansei.

MIDSOENO TSIKOEGONO KAMI.
ALAO IWAMINO KAMI.
IWASE IGANO KAMI.

(*Translation.*)

To the Netherlands Envoy in Japan.

A QUESTION is asked respecting the port of Simoda.

They are busy inquiring about it and no communication can now be made.

The month Hatsigoeats, of the 4th year of Ansei.

MIDSOENO TSIKOEGONO KAMI.
ALAO IWAMINO KAMI.
IWASE IGANO KAMI.

APPENDIX 11.

AMERICAN CONVENTION, JUNE, 1857.

Concluded at Simoda, June 17th, 1857.

FOR the purpose of further regulating the intercourse of American citizens within the Empire of Japan, and after due deliberation, his excellency Townsend Harris,

consul-general of the United States of America for the
Empire of Japan, and their excellencies Ino-oo-ye [1], prince
of Sinano, and Nakamura, prince of Dewa, governors of
Simoda, all having full powers from their respective
governments, have agreed on the following articles, to
wit :—

I. The port of Nangasaki, in the principality of Hizen,
shall be open to American vessels, where they may
repair damages, procure water, fuel, provisions, and
other necessary articles, even coals, where they are
obtainable.

II. It being known that American ships coming to the
ports of Simoda and Hakodate cannot have their wants
supplied by the Japanese, it is agreed that American
citizens may permanently reside at Simoda and Hakodate,
and the government of the United States may appoint
a vice-consul to reside at Hakodate.

This article to go into effect on the fourth day of July,
eighteen hundred and fifty-eight.

III. In settlement of accounts the value of the money
brought by the Americans shall be ascertained by weigh-
ing it with Japanese coin (gold and silver itsebues),
that is, gold with gold, and silver with silver, or weights
representing Japanese coin may be used, after such
weights have been carefully examined and found to
be correct. The value of the money of the Americans
having been thus ascertained, the sum of six per cent. shall
be allowed to the Japanese for the expense of recoinage.

IV. Americans committing offences in Japan shall be
tried by the American consul-general or consul, and shall
be punished according to American laws. Japanese committing offences against Americans shall be tried by the
Japanese authorities, and punished according to Japanese
laws.

V. American ships which may resort to the ports of
Simoda, Hakodate, or Nangasaki, for the purpose of

[1] Inouyé.

obtaining necessary supplies, or to repair damages, shall pay for them in gold or silver coin, and if they have no money, goods shall be taken in exchange.

VI. The government of Japan admits the right of his excellency the consul-general of the United States to go beyond the limits of seven ri, but has asked him to delay the use of that right, except in cases of emergency, shipwreck, &c., to which he has assented.

VII. Purchases for his excellency the consul-general, or his family, may be made by him only, or by some member of his family, and payment made to the seller for the same without the intervention of any Japanese official, and for this purpose Japanese silver and copper coin shall be supplied to his excellency the consul-general.

VIII. As his excellency the consul-general of the United States of America has no knowledge of the Japanese language, nor their excellencies the governors of Simoda a knowledge of the English language, it is agreed that the true meaning shall be found in the Dutch version of the articles.

IX. All the foregoing articles shall go into effect from the date hereof, except article two, which shall go into effect on the date indicated in it.

Done in quintuplicate (each copy being in English, Japanese, and Dutch), at the Goyoso of Simoda, on the seventeenth day of June, in the year of the Christian era eighteen hundred and fifty-seven, and of the Independence of the United States of America the eighty-first, corresponding to the fourth Japanese year of Ansei, Mi, the fifth month, the twenty-sixth day ; the English version being signed by his excellency the consul-general of the United States of America, and the Japanese version by their excellencies the governors of Simoda.

Townsend Harris. [L.S.'

APPENDIX 12

ARTICLE 2 OF CONSTITUTION (OR ARRANGEMENT) OF SEP-
TEMBER 7, 1615, DEFINING AUTHORITY OF SHŌGUN.

Taken from *Tokugawa Kinreikō* (Collection of Tokugawa Enactments).

(*Translation.*)

THE Shōgun of the *Kwantō*, Chancellor of the two
Colleges, having been entrusted with the government of
the country, has complete authority over the three
Imperial Princes, the five *Sekké* [1] families, the court
nobles, and the feudal nobility. He will notify all appointments made in the service of the state, and in the matter
of administration no reference to the Throne is necessary.
If the country within the four seas is not kept tranquil,
the fault will lie with the Shōgun.

APPENDIX 13

TREATY OF AMITY AND COMMERCE, BETWEEN THE
UNITED STATES AND JAPAN

Signed at Yedo, July 29, 1858. [2] [*Ratifications exchanged at
Washington, May 22, 1860.*]

THE President of the United States of America and His
Majesty the Ty-Coon of Japan, desiring to establish on
firm and lasting foundations the relations of peace and
friendship now happily existing between the two countries,
and to secure the best interest of their respective citizens
and subjects by encouraging, facilitating, and regulating
their industry and trade, have resolved to conclude
a Treaty of Amity and Commerce for this purpose, and
have, therefore, named as their Plenipotentiaries, that is
to say : the President of The United States ; his Excellency Townsend Harris, Consul-General of the United
States of America for the Empire of Japan ; and His

[1] See Glossary.
[2] Signed also in the Japanese and Dutch languages.

Majesty the Ty-Coon of Japan, their Excellencies Ino-oo-ye,[1] Prince of Sinano, and Iwasay,[2] Prince of Hego [3] ; who, after having communicated to each other their respective full powers, and found them to be in good and due form, have agreed upon and concluded the following Articles :

ART. I. There shall henceforward be perpetual peace and friendship between the United States of America and His Majesty the Ty-Coon of Japan and his successors.

The President of The United States may appoint a Diplomatic Agent to reside at the city of Yedo, and Consuls or Consular Agents to reside at any or all of the ports in Japan which are opened for American commerce by this Treaty. The Diplomatic Agent and Consul-General of The United States shall have the right to travel freely in any part of the empire of Japan from the time they enter on the discharge of their official duties.

The Government of Japan may appoint a Diplomatic Agent to reside at Washington, and Consuls or Consular Agents for any or all of the ports of The United States. The Diplomatic Agent and Consul-General of Japan may travel freely in any part of The United States from the time they arrive in the country.

II. The President of The United States, at the request of the Japanese Government, will act as a friendly mediator in such matters of difference as may arise between the Government of Japan and any European Power.

The ships of war of The United States shall render friendly aid and assistance to such Japanese vessels as they may meet on the high seas, so far as can be done without a breach of neutrality ; and all American Consuls residing at ports visited by Japanese vessels shall also give them such friendly aid as may be permitted by the laws of the respective countries in which they reside.

III. In addition to the ports of Simoda and Hakodade, the following ports and towns shall be opened on the dates respectively appended to them, that is to say :

[1] Inouyé.   [2] Iwasé.   [3] Higo.

Kanagawa, on the 4th of July, 1859; Nagasaki, on the 4th of July, 1859; Nee-e-gata, on the 1st of January, 1860; Hiogo, on the 1st of January, 1863.

If Nee-e-gata is found to be unsuitable as a harbour, another port on the west coast of Nipon shall be selected by the two Governments in lieu thereof. Six months after the opening of Kanagawa the port of Simoda shall be closed as a place of residence and trade for American citizens. In all the foregoing ports and towns American citizens may permanently reside; they shall have the right to lease ground, and purchase the buildings thereon, and may erect dwellings and warehouses. But no fortification or place of military strength shall be erected under pretence of building dwelling or warehouses; and to see that this Article is observed, the Japanese authorities shall have the right to inspect, from time to time, any buildings which are being erected, altered, or repaired. The place which the Americans shall occupy for their buildings, and the harbour regulations, shall be arranged by the American Consul and the authorities of each place, and if they cannot agree, the matter shall be referred to and settled by the American Diplomatic Agent and the Japanese Government.

No wall, fence, or gate shall be erected by the Japanese around the place of residence of the Americans, or anything done which may prevent a free egress and ingress to the same.

From the 1st of January, 1862, Americans shall be allowed to reside in the city of Yedo; and from the 1st of January, 1863, in the city of Osaca, for the purposes of trade only. In each of these two cities a suitable place within which they may hire houses, and the distance they may go, shall be arranged by the American Diplomatic Agent and the Government of Japan. Americans may freely buy from Japanese and sell to them any articles that either may have for sale, without the intervention of any Japanese officers in such purchase or sale, or in making or receiving payment for the same ; and all classes of Japanese may purchase, sell, keep, or use any articles sold to them by the Americans.

The Japanese Government will cause this clause to be made public in every part of the empire as soon as the ratifications of this Treaty shall be exchanged.

Munitions of war shall only be sold to the Japanese Government and foreigners.

No rice or wheat shall be exported from Japan as cargo, but all Americans resident in Japan, and ships, for their crews and passengers, shall be furnished with sufficient supplies of the same. The Japanese Government will sell, from time to time at public auction, any surplus quantity of copper that may be produced. Americans residing in Japan shall have the right to employ Japanese as servants or in any other capacity.

IV. Duties shall be paid to the Government of Japan on all goods landed in the country, and on all articles of Japanese production that are exported as cargo, according to the tariff hereunto appended.

If the Japanese Custom-House officers are dissatisfied with the value placed on any goods by the owner, they may place a value thereon, and offer to take the goods at that valuation. If the owner refuses to accept the offer, he shall pay duty on such valuation. If the offer be accepted by the owner, the purchase-money shall be paid to him without delay, and without any abatement or discount.

Supplies for the use of The United States navy may be landed at Kanagawa, Hakodade, and Nagasaki, and stored in warehouses, in the custody of an officer of the American Government, without the payment of any duty. But, if any such supplies are sold in Japan, the purchaser shall pay the proper duty to the Japanese authorities.

The importation of opium is prohibited, and any American vessel coming to Japan for the purposes of trade, having more than three catties (four pounds avoirdupois) weight of opium on board, such surplus quantity shall be seized and destroyed by the Japanese authorities.   All goods imported into Japan, and which have paid the duty fixed by this Treaty, may be transported by the Japanese into any part of the empire without the payment of any tax, excise, or transit duty whatever.

No higher duties shall be paid by Americans on goods imported into Japan than are fixed by this Treaty, nor shall any higher duties be paid by Americans than are levied on the same description of goods if imported in Japanese vessels, or the vessels of any other nation.

V. All foreign coin shall be current in Japan and pass for its corresponding weight of Japanese coin of the same description.   Americans and Japanese may freely use foreign or Japanese coin in making payments to each other.

As some time will elapse before the Japanese will be acquainted with the value of foreign coin, the Japanese Government will, for the period of one year after the opening of each harbour, furnish the Americans with Japanese coin, in exchange for theirs, equal weights being given and no discount taken for re-coinage.   Coins of all description (with the exception of Japanese copper coin), may be exported from Japan, and foreign gold and silver uncoined.

VI. Americans committing offences against Japanese shall be tried in American Consular courts, and when guilty shall be punished according to American law. Japanese committing offences against Americans shall be tried by the Japanese authorities and punished according to Japanese law.   The Consular courts shall be open to Japanese creditors, to enable them to recover their just claims against American citizens, and the Japanese courts shall in like manner be open to American citizens for the recovery of their just claims against Japanese.

All claims for forfeitures or penalties for violations of this Treaty, or of the Articles regulating trade which are appended hereunto, shall be sued for in the Consular courts, and all recoveries shall be delivered to the Japanese authorities.

Neither the American or Japanese Governments are to be held responsible for the payment of any debts contracted by their respective citizens or subjects.

VII. In the opened harbours of Japan, Americans shall be free to go where they please, within the following limits :

At Kanagawa, the River Logo [1] (which empties into the Bay of Yedo between Kawasaki and Sinagawa), and 10 ri in any other direction.

At Hakodade, 10 ri in any direction.

At Hiogo, 10 ri in any direction, that of Kioto excepted, which city shall not be approached nearer than 10 ri. The crews of vessels resorting to Hiogo shall not cross the River Enagawa, which empties into the Bay between Hiogo and Osaca. The distance shall be measured inland from Goyoso,[2] or town hall, of each of the foregoing harbours, the ri being equal to 4,275 yards American measure.

At Nagasaki, Americans may go into any part of the Imperial domain in its vicinity. The boundaries of Nee-e-gata, or the place that may be substituted for it, shall be settled by the American Diplomatic Agent and the Government of Japan. Americans who have been convicted of felony, or twice convicted of misdemeanours, shall not go more than one Japanese ri inland from the places of their respective residences, and all persons so convicted shall lose their right of permanent residence in Japan, and the Japanese authorities may require them to leave the country.

A reasonable time shall be allowed to all such persons to settle their affairs, and the American Consular authority shall, after an examination into the circumstances of each case, determine the time to be allowed, but such time shall not in any case exceed one year, to be calculated from the time the person shall be free to attend to his affairs.

[1] Rokugo.   [2] Goyōsho.

VIII. Americans in Japan shall be allowed the free exercise of their religion, and for this purpose shall have the right to erect suitable places of worship. No injury shall be done to such buildings, nor any insult be offered to the religious worship of the Americans. American citizens shall not injure any Japanese temple or mia, or offer any insult or injury to Japanese religious ceremonies, or to the objects of their worship.

The Americans and Japanese shall not do anything that may be calculated to excite religious animosity. The Government of Japan has already abolished the practice of trampling on religious emblems.

IX. When requested by the American Consul, the Japanese authorities will cause the arrest of all deserters and fugitives from justice, receive in jail all persons held as prisoners by the Consul, and give to the Consul such assistance as may be required to enable him to enforce the observance of the laws by the Americans who are on land, and to maintain order among the shipping. For all such service, and for the support of prisoners kept in confinement, the Consul shall in all cases pay a just compensation.

X. The Japanese Government may purchase or construct, in the United States, ships of war, steamers, merchant ships, whale ships, cannon, munitions of war, and arms of all kinds, and any other things it may require. It shall have the right to engage in the United States, scientific, naval and military men, artisans of all kinds, and mariners to enter into its service. All purchases made for the Government of Japan may be exported from the United States, and all persons engaged for its service may freely depart from the United States : provided that no articles that are contraband of war shall be exported, nor any persons engaged to act in a naval or military capacity, while Japan shall be at war with any Power in amity with the United States.

XI. The Articles for the regulation of trade, which are appended to this Treaty, shall be considered as forming a part of the same, and shall be equally binding on both the Contracting Parties to this Treaty, and on their citizens and subjects.

XII. Such of the provisions of the Treaty made by Commodore Perry, and signed at Kanagawa, on the 31st of March, 1854, as conflict with the provisions of this Treaty are hereby revoked ; and as all the provisions of a Convention executed by the Consul-General of the United States and the Governors of Simoda, on the 17th of June, 1857, are incorporated in this Treaty, that Convention is also revoked.

The person charged with the diplomatic relations of the United States in Japan, in conjunction with such person or persons as may be appointed for that purpose by the Japanese Government, shall have power to make such rules and regulations as may be required to carry into full and complete effect the provisions of this Treaty, and the provisions of the Articles regulating trade appended thereunto.

XIII. After the 4th of July, 1872, upon the desire of either the American or Japanese Governments, and on one year's notice given by either party, this Treaty, and such portions of the Treaty of Kanagawa as remain unrevoked by this Treaty, together with the regulations of trade hereunto annexed, or those that may be hereafter introduced, shall be subject to revision by commissioners appointed on both sides for this purpose, who will be empowered to decide on, and insert therein, such amendments as experience shall prove to be desirable.

XIV. This Treaty shall go into effect on the 4th of July, 1859, on or before which day the ratifications of the same shall be exchanged at the city of Washington ; but if, from any unforeseen cause, the ratifications cannot be exchanged by that time, the Treaty shall still go into effect at the date above mentioned.

The act of ratification on the part of the United States shall be verified by the signature of the President of the

United States, countersigned by the Secretary of State, and sealed with the seal of the United States.

The act of ratification on the part of Japan shall be verified by the name and seal of His Majesty the Ty-Coon, and by the seals and signatures of such of his high officers as he may direct.

This Treaty is executed in quadruplicate, each copy being written in the English, Japanese, and Dutch languages, all the versions having the same meaning and intention, but the Dutch version shall be considered as being the original.

In witness whereof, the above-named Plenipotentiaries have hereunto set their hands and seals, at the city of Yedo, this 29th day of July, in the year of our Lord 1858, and of the Independence of the United States of America the 83rd, corresponding to the Japanese era, the 19th day of the 6th month of the 5th year of Ansei Mma.[1]

(L.S.)   TOWNSEND HARRIS.

Regulations under which American Trade is to be conducted in Japan.

REGULATION 1. Within 48 hours (Sundays excepted) after the arrival of an American ship in a Japanese port, the captain or commander shall exhibit to the Japanese Custom-House authorities the receipt of the American Consul, showing that he has deposited the ship's register and other papers, as required by the laws of the United States, at the American Consulate, and he shall then make an entry of his ship, by giving a written paper, stating the name of the ship, and the name of the port from which she comes, her tonnage, the name of her captain or commander, the names of her passengers (if any), and the number of her crew, which paper shall be certified by the captain or commander to be a true statement, and shall be signed by him ; he shall at the same time deposit a written

[1] For *5th year of Ansei Mma* read *5th year (or year of the horse), of Ansei.*

manifest of his cargo, setting forth the marks and numbers
of the packages and their contents, as they are described
in his bills of lading with the names of the person or persons
to whom they are consigned.   A list of the stores of the
ship shall be added to the manifest.   The captain or commander shall certify the manifest to be a true account
of all the cargo and stores on board the ship, and shall
sign his name to the same.   If any error is discovered in
the manifest, it may be corrected within 24 hours (Sundays
excepted) without the payment of any fee ; but for any
alteration or post entry to the manifest made after that
time, a fee of 15 dollars shall be paid.   All goods not entered
on the manifest shall pay double duties on being landed.
Any captain or commander that shall neglect to enter his
vessel at the Japanese Custom-House within the time
prescribed by this regulation shall pay a penalty of 60
dollars for each day that he shall so neglect to enter his
ship.

REGULATION 2. The Japanese Government shall have
the right to place Custom-House officers on board of any
ship in their ports (men-of-war excepted).   All Custom-
House officers shall be treated with civility, and such
reasonable accommodation shall be allotted to them as the
ship affords.   No goods shall be unladen from any ship
between the hours of sunset and sunrise, except by special
permission of the Custom-House authorities, and the
hatches, and all other places of entrance into that part
of the ship where the cargo is stowed, may be secured by
Japanese officers, between the hours of sunset and sunrise,
by affixing seals, locks, or other fastenings ; and if any
person shall, without due permission, open any entrance
that has been so secured, or shall break or remove any
seal, lock, or other fastening that has been affixed by the
Japanese Custom-House officers, every person so offending
shall pay a fine of 60 dollars for each offence.   Any goods
that shall be discharged or attempted to be discharged
from any ship, without having been duly entered at the

Japanese Custom-House, as hereinafter provided, shall be liable to seizure and confiscation.

Packages of goods made up with an attempt to defraud the revenue of Japan, by concealing therein articles of value which are not set forth in the invoice, shall be forfeited. American ships that shall smuggle, or attempt to smuggle, goods in any of the non-opened harbours of Japan, all such goods shall be forfeited to the Japanese Government, and the ship shall pay a fine of 1,000 dollars for each offence. Vessels needing repairs may land their cargo for that purpose without the payment of duty. All goods so landed shall remain in charge of the Japanese authorities, and all just charges for storage, labour, and supervision shall be paid thereon. But if any portion of such cargo be sold, the regular duties shall be paid on the portion so disposed of. Cargo may be transhipped to another vessel in the same harbour without the payment of duty ; but all transhipments shall be made under the supervision of Japanese officers, and after satisfactory proof has been given to the Custom-House authorities of the *bona fide* nature of the transaction, and also under a permit to be granted for that purpose by such authorities. The importation of opium being prohibited, if any person or persons shall smuggle or attempt to smuggle, any opium, he or they shall pay a fine of 15 dollars for each catty of opium so smuggled or attempted to be smuggled ; and if more than one person shall be engaged in the offence, they shall collectively be held responsible for the payment of the foregoing penalty.

REGULATION 3. The owner or consignee of any goods, who desires to land them, shall make an entry of the same at the Japanese Custom-House. The entry shall be in writing, and shall set forth the name of the person making the entry, and the name of the ship in which the goods were imported, and the marks, numbers, packages, and contents thereof, with the value of each package extended separately in one amount, and at the bottom of the entry shall be placed the aggregate value of all the goods contained in the entry. On each entry the owner or consignee shall certify, in writing, that the entry then presented exhibits the actual cost of the goods, and that nothing has been concealed whereby the Customs of Japan would be defrauded ; and the owner or consignee shall sign his name to such certificate.

The original invoice or invoices of the goods so entered shall be presented to the Custom-House authorities, and shall remain in their possession until they have examined the goods contained in the entry.

The Japanese officers may examine any or all of the packages so entered, and for this purpose may take them to the Custom-House, but such examination shall be without expense to the importer or injury to the goods, and after examination, the Japanese shall restore the goods to their original condition in the packages (so far as may be practicable), and which examination shall be made without any unreasonable delay.

If any owner or importer discovers that his goods have been damaged on the voyage of importation before such goods have been delivered to him, he may notify the Custom-House authorities of such damage, and he may have the damaged goods appraised by two or more competent and disinterested persons, who, after due examination shall make a certificate setting forth the amount per cent. of damage on each separate package, describing it by its mark and number, which certificates shall be signed by the appraisers in presence of the Custom-House authorities, and the importer may attach the certificate to his entry, and make a corresponding deduction from it. But this shall not prevent the Custom-House authorities from appraising the goods in the manner provided in Article IV of the Treaty, to which these regulations are appended.

After the duties have been paid, the owner shall receive

a permit authorizing the delivery to him of the goods, whether the same are at the Custom-House or on ship-board. All goods intended to be exported shall be entered at the Japanese Custom-House before they are placed on ship-board. The entry shall be in writing, and shall state the name of the ship by which the goods are to be exported, with the marks and numbers of the packages, and the quantity, description, and value of their contents. The exporter shall certify in writing that the entry is a true account of all the goods contained therein, and shall sign his name thereto. Any goods that are put on board of a ship for exportation before they have been entered at the Custom-House, and all packages which contain prohibited articles, shall be forfeited to the Japanese Government.

No entry at the Custom-House shall be required for supplies for the use of ships, their crews, and passengers, nor for the clothing, &c., of passengers.

REGULATION 4. Ships wishing to clear shall give 24 hours' notice at the Custom-House, and at the end of that time they shall be entitled to their clearance ; but if it be refused, the Custom-House authorities shall immediately inform the captain or consignee of the ship of the reasons why the clearance is refused, and they shall also give the same notice to the American Consul.

Ships of war of the United States shall not be required to enter or clear at the Custom-House, nor shall they be visited by Japanese Custom-House or police officers. Steamers carrying the mails of the United States may enter and clear on the same day, and they shall not be required to make a manifest, except for such passengers and goods as are to be landed in Japan. But such steamers shall, in all cases, enter and clear at the Custom-House.

Whale ships touching for supplies, or ships in distress, shall not be required to make a manifest of their cargo ; but if they subsequently wish to trade, they shall then deposit a manifest, as required in Regulation 1.

The word ship, wherever it occurs in these Regulations, or in the Treaty to which they are attached, is to be held as meaning ship, barque, brig, schooner, sloop, or steamer.

REGULATION 5. Any person signing a false declaration or certificate with the intent to defraud the revenue of Japan, shall pay a fine of 125 dollars for each offence.

REGULATION 6. No tonnage duties shall be levied on American ships in the ports of Japan, but the following fees shall be paid to the Japanese Custom-House authorities : for the entry of a ship, 15 dollars ; for the clearance of a ship, 7 dollars ; for each permit, $1\frac{1}{2}$ dollars ; for each bill of health, $1\frac{1}{2}$ dollars ; for any other document, $1\frac{1}{2}$ dollars.

REGULATION 7. Duties shall be paid to the Japanese Government on all goods landed in the country according to the following tariff :

Class 1. All articles in this class shall be free of duty.

Gold and silver, coined or uncoined.

Wearing apparel in actual use.

Household furniture and printed books not intended for sale, but the property of persons who come to reside in Japan.

Class 2. A duty of 5 per cent. shall be paid on the following articles :

All articles used for the purpose of building, rigging, repairing, or fitting out of ships.

Whaling gear of all kinds.

Timber for building houses.

Rice.

Paddy.

Steam machinery.

Salted provisions of all kinds.

Bread and breadstuffs.

Living animals of all kinds.

Coals.

Zinc.

Lead.

Tin.

Raw silk.

Class 3. A duty of 35 per cent. shall be paid on all intoxicating liquors, whether prepared by distillation, fermentation, or in any other manner.

Class 4.   All goods not included in any of the preceding classes shall pay a duty of 20 per cent.

All articles of Japanese production, which are exported as cargo, shall pay a duty of 5 per cent., with the exception of gold and silver coin and copper in bars.   Five years after the opening of Kanagawa the import and export duties shall be subject to revision if the Japanese Government desires it.

(L.S.)   TOWNSEND HARRIS.

APPENDIX 14

NOTES ON TREATIES OF 1858

ALTHOUGH the five treaties all followed the same general lines, there were differences of arrangement and other minor divergencies, reflecting, in some cases, the special circumstances under which the negotiation took place.   Thus, for instance, four out of the five treaties provided for free trade between the subjects and citizens of the contracting parties, *without the intervention of any Japanese officers*.   But this stipulation does not occur in the Russian treaty, and the American and Dutch treaties contain an additional clause which provides that this stipulation *is to be made public in every part of the Japanese Empire*.   The American, Dutch, and Russian treaties, moreover, revoked, in whole or in part, previous agreements : it was arranged that the American treaty should go into effect at the appointed time, even in the absence of an exchange of ratifications.   In the American, Russian, and French treaties the point of trampling on, or otherwise insulting, Christian emblems is mentioned ; the two other treaties are silent on the subject.   The British and French treaties are remarkable for the clearness with which the question of jurisdiction is treated, and they are also the only treaties which deal with the language of official communications, and with the hire of pilots, a very important matter in the days when Japanese waters were not fully surveyed. The American treaty, moreover, contained the singular provision that the President of the United States would at the request of the Japanese Government act as a friendly mediator in such matters of difference as might arise between the Governments of Japan and any European power.

The prohibition of the importation of opium, which occurs in all the treaties, is evidently taken from the Dutch supplementary treaty of 1857.

All the treaties agreed in making the Dutch version the authentic text, the French treaty containing an additional provision to the effect that the Dutch version was to be regarded as not differing in any respect *au fond* from the Dutch versions of the American, Russian, and British treaties.

In all these treaties, as in the earlier ones, the Mikado is not mentioned either in the foreign or Japanese texts. And in the way in which the Tycoon is spoken of there are differences between the earlier agreements and those of 1858, and between the foreign and the Japanese texts. In the foreign texts of all the earlier treaties the Tycoon is spoken of as the Emperor or Sovereign of Japan. In the corresponding Japanese texts he is called the ' Tycoon ', or the ' Tycoon of Japan ', except in the American Treaty of 1854, where he is described also as *Nihon Kunshiu*, ' the sovereign or ruler of Japan,' and the Dutch Treaty of 1856, which in the final article speaks of *Riōkoku-Kun*, the *Kun* of both countries, a term apparently invented for the occasion. In the foreign versions of the American, British, and Dutch Treaties of 1858 the Tycoon is called ' His Majesty the Tycoon of Japan ', whilst in the other two, the Russian and the French, he is still termed ' Emperor '. In the corresponding Japanese texts of all five treaties he is called ' Teikoku Dai Nihon no Taikun ', or ' Nihon Taikun ', and never ' Kunshiu ' (' sovereign or ruler ').

APPENDIX 15

MEMORIAL ON FOREIGN INTERCOURSE PRESENTED TO THE
SHŌGUNATE BY ĪI KAMON NO KAMI (AFTERWARDS KNOWN
AS THE REGENT ĪI), IN 1853.

(Extract from *Kaikoku Shimatsu*, 'The Affair of the Opening of
the Country'.)

(*Translation.*)

BEFORE the year 1636 there were nine government
vessels (of war), but at that date, owing to the prohibition
of Christianity during the rule of Iyémitsu, these vessels
were stopped from making voyages, and a law was passed
closing the seas to navigation, and shutting up the
country, trade being permitted only with the Chinese
and Dutch. Looking carefully at the circumstances of
to-day, distinguished and far-seeing scholars, who are
solicitous for the country's welfare, are discussing the
question eagerly. Should a crisis occur now, I do not
think that the peace of the country and the safety of the
State can be assured by simply maintaining the old laws
closing the seas to the navigation of our vessels, and in
any case some time must elapse before measures for
defence are complete. Since the destruction of all war
vessels of 500 *koku* and over, we have no war-ships which
could use heavy guns in a fight with foreigners. If they
were to obtain a foothold by seizing the Hachijō Islands
or Ōshima (Vries Island), we could not let the matter
rest there, but without war-ships I feel uneasy with regard
to any scheme for pursuing and attacking them. There
is a saying handed down from the past that if the bridge
of a besieged castle be taken away it cannot hold out for
ever ; that if two armies are fighting with a river between
them the one that crosses and attacks the other will win.
It is an old axiom that the advantage is with the side
which attacks, and not with that which defends. Our
ancestors passed a law closing the ocean to navigation

by our ships, but they left a Chinese and Dutch bridge. This bridge will now be convenient to the government in carrying out its foreign policy. If we postpone hostilities for the present, a scheme to obtain certain victory and complete security may be devised. Coal, which America desires, is said to be abundant in Kiūshiū, and although it has been stated, for reasons of policy, that it is required for use in Japan, if the Americans need it at sea in a sudden emergency, they will come to Nagasaki and ask for it. And if there is a surplus (not wanted by us), it should be given them ; firewood and water, too, are things which we should not grudge. With regard to provisions, there are plentiful and scarce years in all countries (and in the former stores ought to be accumulated to provide for the latter), but these ought to be given to shipwrecked people. Moreover, with regard to castaways, these should be cared for, and restored to their homes, as has been done of late years ; there is no necessity to examine especially into these cases ; communications with regard to all such matters can be made through the Dutch. Again, with regard to trade, there is a national prohibition, but there is a difference between the past and the present ; to exchange what one has for what one has not is the law of the universe.

After informing the spirits of our ancestors (of our intentions) we should send merchant vessels from Japan to the trading emporium of the Dutch Company in Java, and selling things to the Americans and Russians carry on trade with them through the medium of the Dutch. It is said that the building of big vessels for navigating the ocean will of course take one or two years. If the Government deals with them (the Americans and Russians) on the same general lines on which it has dealt with the Dutch, they will in this way be taken by surprise. Then we must restore the Government vessels which existed in and before the period of Kwanyei (1624–44). Orders should be given to the rich merchants of Ōsaka, Hiŏgo, or

Sakai, and, shares being given them in the enterprise, strong and big men-of-war and steamers should be built. (In these latter) goods not wanted by Japan should be loaded; Dutchmen should, for a time, be engaged as captains and sailors, honest and capable men should be placed on board, and they should be made to learn how to work the guns, how to navigate the vessel, and how to manage the compass. The vessels should be professedly merchant ships, but in reality no effort should be spared to obtain efficiency in naval drill; the number of these ships should be gradually increased, and at the same time naval training should gradually be perfected, so that Japanese might eventually navigate the high seas independently and, no longer needing the secret information supplied by the Dutch, see directly for themselves the condition of foreign countries; later on, complete naval preparations might be made, and the panic and apprehensions which have hitherto prevailed would be dispelled, the evil of luxury and extravagance be put an end to, and the internal condition of the country as regards military preparation being entirely satisfactory, we should be in a condition to display our martial vigour abroad. Thus no longer should we remain excluded from the world, but, being completely equipped at home and abroad, the Imperial land (Empire) would be secure. This is my view. Let us go forward (to meet difficulties—not wait for them to come to us) and set to work at once. Having done this, the Government can, in accordance with circumstances, at any time prohibit intercourse as in the Kwanyei period and prevent foreigners from coming to Japan. This is, I think, a good plan. Again with regard to the prohibition of the strange teaching, this should be maintained with the utmost strictness. I understand that it is only of recent years that the Americans and Russians have become fully skilled in the art of navigation. Japanese are naturally skilful and quick, and if they are from this time forward trained, they will surpass foreigners. If, consideration being given to the condition of the country, and the circumstances of the times, the state be guarded securely for ever without danger to the Empire from foreign barbarians, even if some alterations be made in the country's ancient laws, the gods will, I think, not disapprove. The point of first importance in the action now to be taken by the Government is, in my opinion, that truth and righteousness should be secured internally. Therefore I am of opinion that in the first place, a communication should be made to the Court, and Imperial messengers being sent to (the shrines at) Isé, Kiomidzu (Kiōto) and Kagoshima, and a Shōgun's representative to Nikkō, an announcement should be made of the decision to be arrived at by the Government for the tranquillity of the country and the security of the state, and the matter left to the will of the gods, and that in this way measures should be taken to bring into agreement the ancient laws of the country of the gods and the wishes of the people.

It is now by no means an easy matter by means of military dispositions in the seas adjacent to the seat of Government to arrange for everything to be in readiness to meet a sudden and unexpected crisis. There should, therefore, not be an instant's delay. However many rings of iron walls may be erected, if foreign complications occur, national harmony cannot be maintained. In any case what is now of pressing importance is that the Government should arrive at a decision for tranquillizing the whole country, and that the necessary orders should be issued to those concerned.

The above views being contrary to the august prohibition, I feel alarmed at putting them forward, but I offer this opinion because we are asked to speak fully, and place our plans, if we have any, before the Government.

(Sd.) ÏI KAMON NO KAMI.

APPENDIX 16

EXTRACT FROM THE *BAKUMATSU GWAIKŌDAN*, 'THE STORY
OF FOREIGN RELATIONS IN THE LAST DAYS OF THE
SHŌGUNATE ' (p. 53), WITH REFERENCE TO THE CON-
SULTATION, EARLY IN 1858, OF THE DAIMIŌS BY THE
GOVERNMENT IN REGARD TO THE CONCLUSION OF THE
AMERICAN TREATY OF THAT YEAR, AND THE ACTION
TAKEN BY THE COURT IN CONSEQUENCE.

(*Translation.*)

WHEN it had been decided in the *Bakufu* councils to
open the country, consent was given to the American
official's coming to Yedo (which he did on January 15,
1858) and having an audience of the Shōgun (which took
place on the 23rd of the same month). Five days later
Harris gave a lecture at the Yashiki of Hotta Bitchiū no
Kami on the conditions of the world. His eloquence was
like a rushing torrent, and must have made a great
impression on the officials present, and converted them
(to his way of thinking).

It was therefore decided to conclude a treaty, and on
the one hand plenipotentiaries were appointed to negotiate,
while on the other hand the daimiōs were informed of
what was to be reported to the throne, and asked for their
opinions. . . . We only possess the replies of sixty-four or
sixty-five of the clans. It is not possible, therefore, to give
a complete summary of the views of the feudal nobility.
There were, however, only two daimiōs who were dis-
tinctly and positively in favour of refusing to have intercourse with foreigners. These were Matsudaira Yamato
no Kami and Arima Nakatsukasa-taiyū. Some suggested
that an experimental permission for foreign intercourse
should be given ; others, that intercourse ought to be
restricted ; others again temporized and said they had
no opinion to offer. Two, however, were very decidedly

in favour of foreign intercourse. These were Matsudaira Mikawa no Kami and Tachibana Hida no Kami. The views of Matsudaira Échizen no Kami were the most valuable, and showed that he understood the conditions of the times. On the occasion of Perry's first visit the memorial presented by that noble had been entirely in favour of foreigners being driven away. His change of views was due, it is said, to the advice of a retainer named Hashimoto Sanai, who must have been a man of far-seeing views. Some of those consulted spoke of the Shōgun being charged with the duty of driving away barbarians by virtue of his office, while others laid stress on the importance of taking such action as might produce harmony in the nation. Both of these opinions might be taken to mean that foreign intercourse was undesirable, but this was not actually said. . . .

In consequence of the views expressed by the daimiōs the following decree was issued by the Court in the twelfth month (January or February, 1858) :

The Council of State in Yedo have reported as follows :

The letter sent from America and the statements of the envoy are difficult matters. Careful consideration is therefore being given to them by the Government. Commerce has been permitted. With regard to the matter of a minister being appointed to reside in Japan, the harmony of the public mind must be considered, and it will be necessary to make communications regarding rules for the date of residence (of the minister) and the place of residence, &c. With regard also to (trading) ports, permission has been given for Shimoda to be closed, and for another port to be opened instead. With regard to the place where the port shall be, this will be determined subsequently after negotiation. This has been decided. With regard to details a communication will be made later on. We will inform the two persons (Harris and his interpreter Heusken) that the above is to be laid before the throne at once.

Accordingly the matter has been communicated to the Kwambaku and Taikō, and brought to the notice of the throne. The Imperial mind is much distressed by these difficult things. With regard to the place of residence of the Minister, and the place to be chosen as a port in substitution (for Shimoda), no decision has been come to yet. The present Imperial residence is different from what it was in old days. If the matter be treated without due consideration by the Government, the Imperial mind will not be at ease. The five home provinces, and the other provinces near the capital, must be made an exception (namely, excluded from the operation of treaties), the national honour must not be endangered, and the security of the four classes of the people must be assured. This is the desire of the throne.

Let this be communicated to the Kwantō.[1]

APPENDIX 17

London Protocol, June, 1862

Signed by Earl Russell and the Japanese Envoys, June 6, 1862.

It has been represented to Her Britannic Majesty's Minister in Japan by the Ministers of the Tycoon, and to Her Majesty's Government by the Envoys who have been sent to England by the Tycoon, that difficulties are experienced by the Tycoon and his Ministers in giving effect to their engagements with foreign Powers having Treaties with Japan, in consequence of the opposition offered by a party in Japan which is hostile to all intercourse with foreigners.

Her Majesty's Government having taken those representations into consideration, are prepared, on the conditions hereinafter specified, to consent to defer for a period of five years, to commence from the 1st of

[1] See Glossary.

T 2

January, 1863, the fulfilment of those portions of the IIIrd Article of the Treaty between Great Britain and Japan of the 26th of August, 1858, which provide for the opening to British subjects of the port of Ni-igata or some other convenient port on the West Coast of Nipon on the 1st day of January, 1860, and of the port of Hiogo on the 1st day of January, 1863, and for the residence of British subjects in the city of Yedo from the 1st day of January, 1862, and in the city of Osaka from the 1st day of January, 1863.

Her Majesty's Government, in order to give to the Japanese Ministers the time those Ministers consider necessary to enable them to overcome the opposition now existing, are willing to make these large concessions of their rights under Treaty ; but they expect that the Tycoon and his Ministers will in all other respects strictly execute at the ports of Nagasaki, Hakodate, and Kanagawa, all the other stipulations of the Treaty ; that they will publicly revoke the old law outlawing foreigners ; and that they will specifically abolish and do away with—

1.—All restrictions, whether as regards quantity or price, on the sale by Japanese to foreigners of all kinds of merchandise according to Article XIV of the Treaty of the 26th of August, 1858.

2.—All restrictions on labour, and more particularly on the hire of carpenters, boatmen, boats, and coolies, teachers, and servants of whatever denomination.

3.—All restrictions whereby Daimios are prevented from sending their produce to market, and from selling the same directly by their own agents.

4.—All restrictions resulting from attempts on the part of the Custom-house authorities and other officials to obtain fees.

5.—All restriction limiting the classes of persons who shall be allowed to trade with foreigners at the ports of Nagasaki, Hakodate, and Kanagawa.

6. All restrictions imposed on free intercourse of a social kind between foreigners and the people of Japan.

In default of the strict fulfilment by the Tycoon and his Ministers of these conditions, which, indeed, are no other than those which they are already bound by Treaty to fulfil, Her Majesty's Government will, at any time within the aforesaid period of five years, commencing from the 1st of January, 1863, be entitled to withdraw the concessions in regard to the ports and cities made by this Memorandum, and to call upon the Tycoon and his Ministers to carry out, without delay, the whole of the provisions of the Treaty of August 26th, 1858, and specifically to open the aforesaid ports and cities for the trade and residence of British subjects.

The Envoys of the Tycoon accredited to Her Britannic Majesty announce their intention, on their return to Japan, to submit to the Tycoon and his Ministers the policy and expediency of opening to foreign commerce the port of Tsushima in Japan, as a measure by which the interests of Japan will be materially promoted ; and they engage to suggest to the Tycoon and his Ministers to evince their goodwill to the nations of Europe, and their desire to extend commerce between Japan and Europe, by reducing the duties on wines and spirits imported into Japan, and by permitting glass-ware to be inserted in the list of articles on which an import duty of 5 per cent. is levied, and thereby remedying an omission inadvertently made on the conclusion of the Treaty ; and they further engage to recommend to the Tycoon and his Ministers to make arrangements for the establishment at Yokohama and Nagasaki of warehouses in which goods coming from abroad may be deposited, under the control of Japanese officers, without payment of duties, until such time as the importers shall obtain purchasers for such goods, and be prepared to remove them on payment of the import duties.

Her Britannic Majesty's Principal Secretary of State for Foreign Affairs and the Envoys of the Tycoon have accordingly signed this Memorandum, which will be transmitted by the former to Her Majesty's Representative in Japan, and by the latter to the Tycoon and his Ministers, as an evidence of the arrangement made between them on this 6th day of June, 1862.

(Signed)   EARL RUSSELL.
TAKENOUCHI SHIMOTSUKE NO KAMI.
MATSUDAIRA YEWAMI NO KAMI.
KIOGOKU NOTO NO KAMI.

APPENDIX 18

CONVENTION OF PARIS, JUNE 20, 1864

L'arrangement suivant a été conclu entre le Ministre des Affaires Étrangères et les Ambassadeurs du Japon :

Sa Majesté l'Empereur des Français et Sa Majesté l'Empereur du Japon, désirant consolider par des témoignages d'une mutuelle confiance les relations d'amitié et de commerce qui existent entre les deux pays, ont résolu de régler, d'un commun accord et par arrangement spécial, les difficultés qui se sont élevées entre leurs Gouvernements depuis l'année 1862.

En conséquence, son Excellence M. Drouyn de Lhuys, Ministre Secrétaire d'État au Département des Affaires Étrangères de Sa Majesté l'Empereur des Français ; et leurs Excellences Ikeda Tsikougo no Kami, Kawatsou Idzou no Kami, Kawada Sagami no Kami, Ambassadeurs de Sa Majesté le Taïcoun, dûment autorisés à cet effet, sont convenus des Articles suivants :—

I. En réparation de l'acte d'hostilité commis, au mois de Juillet 1863, contre le bâtiment de la marine impériale le ' Kien Cheng,' sur lequel des coups de canon ont été tirés, dans la Province de Nagato, le Gouvernement japonais s'engage à verser entre les mains du Ministre de Sa Majesté l'Empereur des Français à Yedo, trois mois après le retour de leurs Excellences les Ambassadeurs du Taïcoun au Japon, une indemnité de 140,000 piastres mexicaines, dont 100,000 piastres seront payées par le Gouvernement lui-même, et 40,000 piastres par l'Autorité de la Province de Nagato.

II. Le Gouvernement japonais s'engage également à faire cesser, dans les trois mois qui suivront le retour de leurs Excellences les Ambassadeurs du Taïcoun au Japon, les empêchements que rencontrent en ce moment les navires français qui veulent passer le Détroit de Simonoseki, et à maintenir ce passage libre en tout temps, en recourant, si cela est nécessaire, à l'emploi de la force, et, au besoin, en agissant de concert avec le Commandant de la division navale française.

III. Il est convenu entre les deux Gouvernements que, pour favoriser le développement régulier des échanges commerciaux entre la France et le Japon, les réductions de tarifs accordées en dernier lieu par le Gouvernement de Sa Majesté le Taïcoun au commerce étranger seront maintenues en faveur des articles importés par des commerçants français, ou sous pavillon français, pendant toute la durée du Traité conclu à Yedo entre les deux pays le 9 Octobre, 1858.

En conséquence, tant que ce Traité demeurera en vigueur, la douane japonaise admettra en franchise les articles suivants destinés à la préparation et à l'emballage des thés—plomb en feuilles, soudures de plomb, nattes, rotins, huiles pour peinture, indigo, gypse, bassines et paniers. Elle percevra seulement un droit de 5 pour cent. de la valeur à l'entrée des vins et spiritueux, sucre blanc, fer et fer-blanc, machines et pièces détachées de machines, tissus de lin, horlogerie, montres et chaînes de montres, verreries, médicaments, et un droit de 6 pour cent. sur les glaces et miroirs, porcelaines, bijouterie, parfumerie, savons, armes, coutellerie, livres, papiers, gravures et dessins.

IV. Cet arrangement sera considéré comme faisant partie intégrante du Traité du 9 Octobre, 1858, entre la France et le Japon, et il sera immédiatement mis à exécution, sans qu'il soit nécessaire de le soumettre à la ratification des Souverains respectifs.

En foi de quoi, les Plénipotentiaires ci-dessus nommés ont signé le présent arrangement et y ont apposé le sceau de leurs armes.

Fait à Paris, en double original, le vingtième jour du mois de Juin de l'an mil huit cent soixante-quatre.

(Signé) DROUYN DE LHUYS.
IKEDA TSIKOUGO NO KAMI.
KAWATSOU IDZOU NO KAMI.
KAWADA SAGAMI NO KAMI.

APPENDIX 19

SHIMONOSEKI CONVENTION, OCTOBER, 1864.

Signed at Yokohama, 22nd October, 1864.

THE Representatives of Great Britain, France, the United States, and the Netherlands, in view of the hostile acts of Mori Daizen, Prince of Nagato and Suwo, which were assuming such formidable proportions as to make it difficult for the Tycoon faithfully to observe the Treaties, having been obliged to send their combined forces to the Straits of Shimonoseki, in order to destroy the batteries erected by that Daimio for the destruction of foreign vessels and the stoppage of trade ; and the Government of the Tycoon, on whom devolved the duty of chastising this rebellious Prince, being held responsible for any damage resulting to the interests of Treaty Powers, as well as the expenses occasioned by the expedition ;

The Undersigned Representatives of Treaty Powers, and Sakai Hida no Kami, a member of the Second Council, invested with plenipotentiary powers by the Tycoon of Japan, animated with the desire to put an end to all reclamations concerning the acts of aggression and hostility committed by the said Mori Daizen, since the first of these acts, in June, 1863, against the flags of divers Treaty Powers, and at the same time to regulate definitely the question of indemnities of war, of whatever kind, in respect to the allied expedition to Shimonoseki, have agreed and determined upon the four Articles following :—

I. The amount payable to the four Powers is fixed at 3,000,000 dollars. This sum to include all claims, of whatever nature, for past aggressions on the part of the Prince of Nagato, whether indemnities, ransom for Shimonoseki, or expenses entailed by the operations of the allied squadrons.

II. The whole sum to be payable quarterly in instalments of one-sixth, or 500,000 dollars, to begin from the date when the Representatives of said Powers shall make known to the Tycoon's Government the ratification of this Convention and the instructions of their respective Governments.

III. Inasmuch as the receipt of money has never been the object of the said Powers, but the establishment of better relations with Japan, and the desire to place these on a more satisfactory and mutually advantageous footing is still the leading object in view, therefore, if His Majesty the Tycoon wishes to offer in lieu of payment of the sum claimed, and as a material compensation for loss and injury sustained, the opening of Shimonoseki, or some other eligible port in the Inland Sea, it shall be at the option of the said foreign Governments to accept the same, or insist on the payment of the indemnity in money under the conditions above stipulated.

IV. This Convention to be formally ratified by the Tycoon's Government within fifteen days from the date thereof.

In token of which the respective Plenipotentiaries have signed and sealed this Convention in quintuplicate, with English and Japanese versions, whereof the English shall be considered the original.

Done at Yokohama this 22nd day of October, 1864,

corresponding to the twenty-second day of the ninth month of the first Year of Genji.

The Japanese character for :

(Signed)

SAKAI HIDA NO KAMI.

RUTHERFORD ALCOCK, *Her Britannic Majesty's Envoy Extraordinary and Minister Plenipotentiary in Japan.*

LÉON ROCHES, *Ministre Plénipotentiaire de Sa Majesté l'Empereur des Français au Japon.*

ROBT. H. PRUYN, *Ministre Resident of the United States in Japan.*

D. DE GRAEFF VAN POLSBROEK, *His Netherlands Majesty's Consul-General and Political Agent in Japan.*

APPENDIX 20

TARIFF CONVENTION, JUNE, 1866.

Signed at Yedo in the English, French, Dutch, and Japanese languages, on the 25th day of June, 1866.

THE Representatives of Great Britain, France, of the United States of America and Holland, having received from their respective Governments identical instructions for the modification of the Tariff of Import and Export Duties contained in the Trade Regulations annexed to the Treaties concluded by the aforesaid Powers with the Japanese Government in 1858, which modification is provided for by the VIIth of those Regulations ;—

And the Japanese Government having given the said Representatives, during their visit to Osaka in November, 1865, a written engagement to proceed immediately to the Revision of the Tariff in question, on the general basis of a duty of five per cent. on the value of all articles Imported or Exported ;—

And the Government of Japan being desirous of affording

a fresh proof of their wish to promote trade and to cement the friendly relations which exist between their country and foreign nations ;—

His Excellency Midzuno Idzumi no Kami, a Member of the Gorojiu and a Minister of Foreign Affairs has been furnished by the Government of Japan, with the necessary powers to conclude with the Representatives of the above-named four Powers, that is to say ;

Of Great Britain,

Sir Harry S. Parkes, Knight Commander of the Most Honourable Order of the Bath, Her Britannic Majesty's Envoy Extraordinary and Minister Plenipotentiary in Japan ;

Of France,

Monsieur Léon Roches, Commander of the Imperial Order of the Legion of Honour, Minister Plenipotentiary of His Majesty the Emperor of the French in Japan ;

Of the United States of America,

A. L. C. Portman, Esquire, Chargé d'Affaires ad interim ;

And of Holland,

Monsieur Dirk de Graeff van Polsbroek, Knight of the Order of the Netherlands Lion, Political Agent and Consul General of His Majesty the King of the Netherlands ;

The following Convention, comprising Twelve Articles.

I. The contracting Parties declare in the names of their respective Governments that they accept, and they hereby do formally accept as binding upon the subjects of their respective Sovereigns, and the citizens of their respective countries, the Tariff hereby established and annexed to the present Convention.

This tariff is substituted not only for the original Tariff attached to the Treaties concluded with the above-named four Powers, but also for the special Conventions and arrangements relative to the same Tariff, which have been entered into at different dates up to this time between the

Governments of Great Britain, France, and the United States on one side, and the Japanese Government on the other.

The New Tariff shall come into effect in the Port of Kanagawa (Yokohama) on the first day of July next, and in the ports of Nagasaki and Hakodate on the first day of the following month.

II. The Tariff attached to this Convention being incorporated from the date of its signature in the Treaties concluded between Japan and the above-named four Powers, is subject to revision on the first day of July, 1872.

Two years, however, after the signing of the present Convention, any of the contracting parties on giving six months' notice to the others, may claim a re-adjustment of the duties on Tea and Silk on the basis of five per cent. on the average value of these articles, during the three years last preceding. On the demand also of any of the contracting parties, the duty on timber may be changed from an *ad valorem* to a specific rate six months after the signature of this Convention.

III. The Permit fee hitherto levied under the VIth Regulation attached to the above-named Treaties, is hereby abolished. Permits for the landing or shipment of cargo will be required as formerly, but will hereafter be issued free of charge.

IV. On and from the first day of July next at the port of Kanagawa (Yokohama), and on and from the first day of October next at the Ports of Nagasaki and Hakodate, the Japanese Government will be prepared to warehouse imported goods on the application of the importer or owner, without payment of duty. The Japanese Government will be responsible for the safe custody of the goods, so long as they remain in their charge, and will adopt all the precautions necessary to render them insurable against fire. When the importer or the owner wishes to remove the goods from the warehouse, he must pay the duties fixed by the Tariff, but if he should wish to re-export them he may do so without payment of duty. Storage charges will in either case be paid on delivery of the goods. The amount of these charges, together with the regulations necessary for the management of the said Warehouses will be established by the common consent of the contracting parties.

V. All articles of Japanese production may be conveyed from any place in Japan to any of the Ports open to foreign trade, free of any tax or transit duty other than the usual tolls levied equally on all traffic for the maintenance of roads or navigation.

VI. In conformity with those articles of the Treaties concluded between Japan and Foreign Powers which stipulate for the circulation of foreign coin at its corresponding weight in native coin of the same description, dollars have hitherto been received at the Japanese Custom-house in payment of duties at their weight in Boos (commonly called Ichiboos), that is to say, at a rate of Three Hundred and Eleven Boos per Hundred dollars. The Japanese Government being, however, desirous to alter this practice and to abstain from all interference in the exchange of native for foreign coin, and being also anxious to meet the wants both of native and foreign commerce by securing an adequate issue of native coin, have already determined to enlarge the Japanese Mint so as to admit of the Japanese Government exchanging into native coin of the same intrinsic value, less only the cost of coinage, at the places named for this purpose, all foreign coin or bullion in gold or silver that may at any time be tendered to them by foreigners or Japanese. It being essential, however, to the execution of this measure, that the various Powers with whom Japan has concluded Treaties should first consent to modify the stipulations in those Treaties which relate to the currency, the Japanese Government will at once propose to those Powers the adoption of the necessary modification in the said stipulations, and on receiving their concurrence will be prepared from the first of January, 1868, to carry the above measure into effect.

The rates to be charged as the cost of coinage shall be determined hereafter by the common consent of the contracting parties.

VII. In order to put a stop to certain abuses and inconveniences complained of at the open Ports, relative to the transaction of business at the Custom-house, the landing and shipping of cargoes and the hiring of boats, coolies, servants, &c., the contracting parties have agreed that the Governor at each open port shall at once enter into negotiations with the foreign Consuls with a view to the establishment, by mutual consent, of such regulations as shall effectually put an end to these abuses and inconveniences and afford all possible facility and security both to the operations of trade and to the transactions of individuals.

It is hereby stipulated that in order to protect merchandise from exposure to weather, these regulations shall include the covering in at each port of one or more of the landing places used by foreigners for landing or shipping cargo.

VIII. Any Japanese subject shall be free to purchase either in the open Ports of Japan or abroad, every description of sailing or steam-vessel intended to carry either passengers or cargo ; but ships of war may only be obtained under the authorization of the Japanese Government.

All foreign vessels purchased by Japanese subjects shall be registered as Japanese vessels on payment of a fixed duty of three Boos per ton for steamers and one Boo per ton for sailing vessels. The tonnage of each vessel shall be proved by the Foreign Register of the ship, which shall be exhibited through the Consul of the party interested on the demand of the Japanese Authorities, and shall be certified by the Consul as authentic.

IX. In conformity with the Treaties concluded between Japan and the aforesaid Powers, and with the special arrangements made by the Envoys of the Japanese Government in their note to the British Government of the sixth of June, 1862, and in their note to the French Government of the sixth of October of the same year, all the restrictions on trade and intercourse between foreigners and Japanese alluded to in the said notes, have been entirely removed, and proclamations to this effect have already been published by the Government of Japan.

The latter, however, do not hesitate to declare that Japanese merchants, and traders of all classes are at liberty to trade directly, and without the interference of Government officers, with foreign merchants, not only at the open Ports of Japan, but also in all foreign countries, on being authorized to leave their country in the manner provided for in Article X of the present Convention, without being subject to higher taxation by the Japanese Government than levied on the native trading classes of Japan in their ordinary transactions with each other.

And they further declare that all Daimios or persons in the employ of Daimios are free to visit on the same conditions, any foreign country, as well as all the open Ports of Japan, and to trade there with foreigners as they please, without the interference of any Japanese officer, provided always they submit to the existing Police regulations and to the payment of the established duties.

X. All Japanese subjects may ship goods to or from any open Port in Japan, or to and from the Ports of any Foreign Power, either in vessels owned by Japanese or in the vessels of any nation having a Treaty with Japan. Furthermore, on being provided with Passports through the proper Department of the Government, in the manner specified in the Proclamation of the Japanese Government dated the twenty-third day of May, 1866, all Japanese subjects may travel to any foreign country for purposes of study or trade. They may also accept employment in any capacity on board the vessels of any nation having a Treaty with Japan.

Japanese in the employ of foreigners may obtain Government passports to go abroad on application to the Governor of any open Port.

XI. The Government of Japan will provide all the Ports open to foreign trade with such lights, buoys or beacons as may be necessary to render secure the navigation of the approaches to the said Ports.

XII. The Undersigned being of opinion that it is unnecessary that this Convention should be submitted to their respective Governments, for ratification, before it comes into operation, it will take effect on and from the first day of July, one thousand eight hundred and sixty-six.

Each of the Contracting Parties having obtained the approval of his Government to this Convention, shall make known the same to the others, and the communication in writing of this approval shall take the place of a formal exchange of Ratifications.

IN WITNESS WHEREOF the above-named Plenipotentiaries have signed the present Convention, and have affixed thereto their seals.

Done at Yedo in the English, French, Dutch, and Japanese languages this twenty-fifth day of June, one thousand eight hundred and sixty-six.

[L.S.] HARRY S. PARKES,
> *Her Britannic Majesty's Envoy Extraordinary and Minister Plenipotentiary in Japan.*

[L.S.] LÉON ROCHES,
> *Ministre Plénipotentiaire de S. M. L'Empereur des Français au Japon.*

[L.S.] A. L. C. PORTMAN,
> *Chargé d'Affaires a. i. of the United States, in Japan.*

[L.S.] D. DE GRAEFF VAN POLSBROEK, *Politiek Agent en Consul Generaal der Nederlanden, in Japan.*

[L.S.] MIDZUNO IDZUMI NO KAMI.

APPENDIX 21

MANIFESTO ANNOUNCING SHŌGUN'S RESIGNATION,
NOVEMBER 8, 1867.

(Extract from *Kaikoku Kigen*, 'The Beginning of the Opening of the
Country,' p. 2930.)

(Translation.)

LOOKING at the various changes through which the
Empire has passed, we see that when the monarchical
authority became weakened, the power was seized by
the Ministers of State, and that afterwards, owing to the
civil wars of the periods Hōgen (1156–9) and Heiji (1159–
60), it passed into the hands of the military class. Later
on again my ancestor received special favour from the
throne (by being appointed Shōgun), and his descendants
have succeeded him for over 200 years. Though I fill the
same office, the laws are often improperly administered,
and I confess with shame that the condition of affairs
to-day shows my incapacity. Now that foreign intercourse becomes daily more extensive, unless the Government is directed from one central point, the basis of
administration will fall to pieces. If, therefore, the old
order of things be changed, and the administrative
authority be restored to the Imperial Court, if national
deliberations be conducted on an extensive scale, and the
Imperial decision then invited, and if the Empire be
protected with united hearts and combined effort, our
country will hold its own with all nations of the world.
This is our one duty to our country, but if any persons
have other views on the subject they should be stated
without reserve.

APPENDIX 22

STATEMENT OF REASONS FOR SHŌGUN'S RESIGNATION
PRESENTED BY JAPANESE MINISTERS IN YEDO TO
FOREIGN REPRESENTATIVES IN NOVEMBER, 1867.

(Extract from *Bakumatsu Gwaikōdan,* ' The Story of Foreign Relations
in the last days of the Shōgunate,' pp. 524 *et seq.*)

(Translation.)

THE Tycoon of Japan has of his own free will decided
to return to the Mikado the administrative authority
which has been handed down to him by his ancestors
through a period of more than 250 years.   Fearing that
at this moment of political change people's minds may
be led astray by false rumours and idle reports, we think
it necessary to make the following explanation of the
circumstances of the case to all countries.

More than two thousand years ago, when the ancestors
of the Royal House came down from heaven they governed
the country by personal rule, and so did their descendants
after them.   They were then actually (as well as in name)
the sovereigns of Japan, and were known to foreign
countries by the name of Mikados.

After a time the condition of the country deteriorated,
and the governing power fell into the hands of a distant
branch of the Imperial House,—the family of Fujiwara,
the Mikados reigning, but taking no part in the administration.   After this family had assumed power, its members
gave themselves up to luxury and effeminacy, and though
the Court was supposed to be composed of officers combining civil and military duties, this state of things existed
only in name, and military power was in the hands of
hereditary military officials.   Whenever there was trouble
in the country, the Government were unable to cope with
it.   So when there were rebels, the Government relied on
these hereditary military officials to carry out their

chastisement. These hereditary military officials were grouped under two chief houses, the Minamoto and Taira. They divided the country between them, the Minamoto having authority in the east, and the Taira in the west. Then there was a quarrel regarding the Imperial succession, and the whole country ranged itself under the rival banners, even the house of Fujiwara taking sides. At first the Taira were victorious, and they succeeded to the position of the Fujiwara, and ruled the country for twenty years. But they acted arrogantly, and wrongly made use of the Imperial name to cloak their arbitrary designs. The Mikado thereupon called the Minamoto to his assistance, and caused them to destroy the house of Taira. The Minamoto destroyed their ancient enemies, and preserved the Imperial House. The latter, in reward for the services rendered, entrusted the whole country to the military authority of the Minamoto. The military class thus, as a result of the events of several years, came to the front everywhere, and, the power of the Court being unable to restrain it, in all parts of the country military chieftains rose to the head of affairs. None had any influence in the administration save members of the military class, and they gained it by service to the Throne, by lineage, and by gaining the confidence of the nation. In the end all power became concentrated in the military class. This was about A. D. 1200, according to Western reckoning. The political change thus introduced was very great. The official title (of the new administrator) was Sei-i-tai Shōgun. His position was conferred upon him by the Court, but his rule extended over the whole country. This is how the Tycoon came to preside over the Government under the Emperor of Japan.

Afterwards, any one disputing administrative authority in the country at once assailed the position of the Shōgun, civil war continued for nearly 400 years; great chieftains established themselves in all parts of the land, and fought with one another; both Mikado and Shōgun were non-

entities, and the condition of the Empire became more
disturbed than ever.

This was the state of affairs when Tōshōgu,[1] the ancestor
of our Tycoon, stepped on the scene, and by immense
exertions put an end to this disorder.

The Mikado of that day highly appreciating his great
services, appointed him to be Shōgun, and entrusted to
him all the administrative affairs of the country, both
civil and military. The ancestor of the ruler who became
known to foreign countries as our Tycoon, far surpassed
all previous Shōguns in regard to services rendered. His
authority also exceeded that of any other Shōgun who
had preceded him. Consequently he caused the various
feudal chieftains throughout the country who had previously established themselves by force of arms in various
places, and had enjoyed independent power, to assemble
in Yedo, his own place of residence, and take an oath of
fealty to him. He also acquired the right of investing
these feudal lords with their territories, or depriving
them of them, and this investiture was conferred by
special written grant. Yashikis were also established in
Yedo, and the system of attendance there every year, or
every alternate year, was introduced. All daimiōs, both
great and small, throughout the Empire, accepted these
laws, and submitted to them, and there was not one
dissentient voice.

The descendants of this ancestor have succeeded one
another for several generations, and have continued to
govern the country in this way for over 200 years with
the approval of the Court, the feudal nobility submitting
thereto and the people pursuing their avocations in tranquillity and enjoying the blessings of a long peace.

At the beginning of the long period (we have described)
foreign ships came to Japan, and Japanese vessels traded
abroad, and there was no hindrance to foreign commerce.
But from a certain foreign country there came missionaries,

---

[1] The posthumous name of Iyéyasu.

who conspired with certain rebellious Japanese and plotted to create disturbance. In order to preserve the peace of the country severe edicts were issued, this religious movement was proscribed, the missionaries were driven away, and in the end the visits of foreign ships were prohibited, and Japanese vessels were forbidden to go to foreign countries, trade being permitted with only one or two foreign countries at the single port of Nagasaki. The closing of Japan was a step rendered unavoidable by the circumstances of that time.

Of recent years, however, the conditions of the world have greatly changed, and, an Envoy having come from the United States, the country was opened. The Tycoon of that time, and one or two leading statesmen in the Government realized that in modern times, from the moment when the invention of steam navigation had brought all countries near to one another, it was impossible for one island country in the East to refuse to have intercourse with all other nations in the world. They, therefore agreed (to the Envoy's proposals), and it was decided to establish foreign intercourse and trade, conclude treaties, and generally to revert to the condition of things which existed under the rule of the founder of the line.

This was indeed a great change in the affairs of the country, and people who were contented with the old condition of things became very dissatisfied. Consequently the cry of ' Close the country and expel foreigners ' was heard everywhere. The Tycoon's Government, suiting its action to circumstances, took the excellent and suitable decision above-mentioned; but those who were dissatisfied mistook what was done for submission to foreign demands from fear of hostilities. And they slandered (the Tycoon) to the Court, saying that he was neglecting the military duty entrusted to him. The Court did not understand the state of things, and at once agreed to what was suggested, ordering the Tycoon's Government to break off intercourse with foreigners. Consequently many foreign complications occurred, and indescribable inconvenience was caused. With these the Foreign Representatives are well acquainted, so they need not be mentioned here.

We confess with shame that it cannot be said that since foreign intercourse was established by the Tycoon's Government all its measures have been attended with complete success. But we can say this, that ever since the conclusion of foreign treaties those who have advocated the closing of the country, and have been hostile to foreigners, have gradually been suppressed, and that the Government has never swerved from its fixed intention to carry out every clause of the treaties.

That it has been possible to settle the rules for the opening of the country, and carry out all treaty stipulations, is due most certainly to the fact that our present energetic and sagacious Tycoon, who is endowed with heaven-sent intelligence, has filled the post of ruler of Japan in succession to his ancestors. The Foreign Representatives know well what cordial feelings he manifested to them when in the course of this year he received them in audience in the castle of Ōsaka, what sincere friendship he showed, how careful he was to respect treaty engagements, and how many obstacles, incidental to his duties as Tycoon, were met and overcome before the present position was attained.

The form of administration under which (the Tycoon) has governed the country, holding a rank one degree below that of the Emperor, is one peculiar to Japan, which is the natural result of circumstances, and has lasted for the last six hundred years. By virtue of the authority thus wielded tranquillity was maintained, but now that relations have been established with the whole world much inconvenience is caused owing to the name under which this intercourse is carried on. Moreover, the fact that, at present, men's minds throughout the country are in a state of confusion, and are not in harmony, is due chiefly to the same cause. Therefore our enlightened Tycoon, making up his mind of his own accord, has arrived at the momentous decision to restore the administrative authority to the Mikado, and convoking a council of the heads of the great houses, and inquiring fully into the present condition of affairs, to set up a suitable Government, and establish a political constitution which nothing in the future can disturb, and in this way enable the country to hold its own with other nations, and become rich and strong. Of a surety never has such great solicitude for the welfare of a country been shown before.

Matters have thus arrived at the present situation. But it is unnecessary for us to give an assurance that the change will in no way affect unfavourably our relations with foreign countries, and that everything will be arranged quietly and harmoniously as before. There is no reason for anxiety.

All the provisions of the treaties concluded with Foreign Powers have been carried out by the Tycoon, and he has thoroughly recognized the importance of foreign relations. The Council of feudal nobles, great and small, which is shortly to assemble, will, as soon as the circumstances of foreign affairs have been explained to them, all respect what has been done. And in view of the fact that eight or nine in every ten persons have enjoyed the benefits conferred on them by the Tokugawa rule, although there may be some people who are in favour of old institutions, there is no chance of their being able to gain the day. We earnestly trust, therefore, that the Foreign Representatives will support our views with their usual friendliness, and will in the spirit of the exertions already made by their countries for the prosperity of all concerned look at things as they really are.

We have ventured to undertake this explanation of the past. With regard to other matters, as was stated in our recent letter, we shall communicate with you again as soon as we have heard from Kiōto.

APPENDIX 23

PROTEST PRESENTED BY EX-SHŌGUN TO THE COURT ON
JANUARY 7, 1868.[1]

(Extract from the *Sanjiūnen Shi*, ' History of Thirty Years,' p. 753.)

I BEG to acknowledge with respect the receipt of the Imperial Orders stating that the matter of the Chōshiū princes has been arranged in accordance with the Imperial wishes ; that no objection to this arrangement has been made, but that it is desirable, in view of the Emperor's youth, and the importance of not alarming His Majesty or prejudicing the Imperial authority, to take every precaution against the outbreak of disturbances, and that therefore I am to exert myself to preserve order.

I had taken careful steps for guarding the Imperial palace, but now extraordinary changes have been made, so that I am greatly distressed about preserving order. Careful instructions have been given to all officials, but I find it difficult to control so large a number of people—[an allusion evidently to the numerous bodies of clansmen who had entered Kiōto]. I have tried to do my duty by the Throne, but I fear that my efforts will be brought to naught by the rude action of common fellows. I have therefore decided to retire to Ōsaka for a short while. I trust that the Emperor will understand that I am doing this solely in the interests of the Throne, being anxious that order should be preserved, and tranquillity maintained, in the precincts of the palace. I ought to have asked leave of the Throne before quitting the capital, but this would have taken time, and I was afraid that in the interval, through some fault of those low rascals, a grave national crisis might be precipitated. I am therefore leaving for Ōsaka at once.

---

[1] Both in the book from which this document is taken, and in the *Kaikoku Kigen*, the date given is Jan. 27, 1868, which is manifestly an error.

APPENDIX 24

MEMORIAL SURRENDERING THEIR FIEFS TO THE CROWN
PRESENTED IN MARCH, 1869, BY THE DAIMIŌS OF
SATSUMA, CHŌSHIŪ, HIZEN, AND TOSA.

(Taken from Parliamentary Paper (Report on Taxation and Land
Tenure by Mr. Gubbins) published in 1884.)

'YOUR servants again venture to address Your Majesty
with profound reverence. Two things are essential to
the Mikado's administration. There must be one central
body of government, and one universal authority which
must be preserved intact. Since the time when Your
Majesty's ancestors founded this country and established
a basis of government, all things in the wide expanse of
heaven and all things on the earth to its furthest limits,
have belonged to the Emperor from generation to generation. This is what is known as " one central government ".
And the sole power of giving and of taking away, which
renders it impossible for the nobles to hold the people in
subjection by virtue of their land, or to deal with the
smallest piece of ground at their pleasure, or to seize and
treat despotically any single individual of the humbler
classes ; this is what is understood by the term " one
universal authority ".

'The administration of the Emperors was conducted
entirely on this principle. They conducted the government in their own persons, the name and the reality of
power were combined, and consequently the nation was
tranquil and contented. But from the time of the middle
ages the administrative system became lax, and the
authority of the Emperors came to be a plaything. All
men fighting for power, changes of government followed
each other in rapid succession, until half of the country
fell into the hands of men who dealt with the people and
the land at their pleasure ; and in the end a state of
things was reached where there was nothing but open

contention and acts of violence. The Government having no body of administration to protect, and no effective power, were unable to control matters. Everywhere men of influence, but of unprincipled character, took advantage of the existing disorder to promote their own interests, and the weak became food for the strong.

' The most powerful barons took possession of fourteen or fifteen provinces, while those of less influence collected bodies of armed retainers to the number of five and six thousand. Successive Shōguns seized land and people arbitrarily wherever they thought fit, and by this means extended their influence. Finally the Mikado's Government lost all real authority, and was entirely dependent on the will of the Shōgunate. The boundless despotism of the Shōgunate lasted for over 600 years, and during this interval violent dealings with land and with the people were carried out by stealth under pretence of the Imperial Authority. And these acts were rendered possible owing to the existence of people who could not dissociate themselves from the time-honoured observances of the past, and were still guided by the reverence due from a subject to his sovereign, and by a proper sense of the relations which should exist between high and low.

' The ancient family of the Tokugawa dynasty of Shōguns and their relatives held half of the country ; as a natural consequence fresh families were constantly springing up ; and it became a precedent founded on long custom which has lasted up to the present day for these numerous branches of the Tokugawa family to take no heed of the question as to whether their lands and subjects had been received in grant from the proper Government or not. It was commonly said by members of these families : " These possessions of ours were gained by the military power of our ancestors." But there is little doubt that these ancestors had originally raised forces, plundered the Imperial storehouses, and laid forcible hands on the treasures contained, and that they had braved the penalty of death in the execution of their designs. Those who break into storehouses are commonly termed robbers, but no suspicion was attached by the nation to those who seized upon the land and the people. It is terrible, indeed, this confusion of ideas between right and wrong.

' It is now sought to establish an entirely new form of government. Care must, therefore, be taken to preserve intact both one central body of government, and one universal authority. The land in which your servants live is the land of the Emperor, and the people whom they govern are his subjects. Neither the one, therefore, nor the other can belong to your servants.

' Your servants accordingly beg respectfully to surrender to Your Majesty the registers of the population, and beg Your Majesty to deal with everything as you may think fit, giving what should be given and taking away what should be taken away. They entreat Your Majesty to issue such Imperial decrees as may be deemed necessary with respect to the lands and the people of the four clans represented in this Memorial, and to make such changes as Your Majesty may think proper. They also beg that all laws, decrees, and military regulations, extending even to military dress and accoutrements, may be issued by the Central Government, so that all matters of state, both great and small, may be decided by one and the same authority. In this way both name and reality will be secured, and this country will be placed on a footing of equality with foreign powers.

' Your servants share the responsibility which the present critical condition of affairs entails upon the Mikado's Government. It is this which has led them to present their foolish views for the consideration of Your Majesty.'

GLOSSARY

AIDZU. Name of clan whose territories were in the old province of Mutsu (now Iwashiro). The castle-town was Wakamatsu. It was one of the clans which supported the Shōgun in 1868 up to the last.

BAKUFU. The Shōgun's Government. The term, which means literally ' camp-office ', dates from the establishment of the feudal system by Yoritomo in the twelfth century.

BUGIŌ. A word of frequent occurrence in the titles of Tokugawa officials who were governors of towns, or in charge of certain branches of the administration. Its exact rendering in English depends on the context. Thus when joined to the name of a town, as in the titles Fushimi-bugiō, Nara-bugiō, Nagasaki-bugiō, it meant the governor of the town named ; but *jisha-bugio* was a superintendent in charge of temples and shrines, and *fushin-bugio* was a commissioner of works.

CHIŪNAGON. An official title conferred by the Court.

CHŌSHIŪ. Name of clan whose territories comprised the two provinces of Nagato and Suwo at the south-western extremity of the main island.

CHŌTEKI. Rebel. The literal meaning is ' enemy of the Court '.

DAIDZU. A kind of large bean. The word occurs in the Dutch treaty of 1857, where it is spelt *daitz*.

DAIKWAN. Literally ' representative official '. A term applied to the governors of the Shōgun's domains and other territories ruled by the Yedo Government.

DAIMIŌ. Literally ' great name '. A term applied to all territorial nobles the annual assessed yield of whose lands was not less than ten thousand *koku* of rice.

DAINAGON. An official title conferred by the Court, ranking above *Chiūnagon*.

DAIZEN NO DAIBU. An official Court title, hereditary in the family, borne by the Prince of Chōshiū. It may be rendered Superintendent of the Imperial Kitchen.

DAJŌKWAN (also pronounced Daijōkwan). Name of Council of State established in 1868.

DZUSHO NO KAMI. An official Court title, which may be rendered Chief Librarian.

FASSAK. See Hassaku.

FUDAI. Literally 'successive generations'. The term was applied by Iyéyasu to the daimiōs who joined him before the battle of Sékigahara in 1600, as distinguished from the *tozama* daimiōs, who submitted to him after that battle. Two-thirds of the feudal nobility (some 176 daimiōs in all) were of the *fudai* class. The term was also applied to *hatamoto, gokénin,* and *kerai,* who were hereditary vassals.

FUYO. A term applied to daimiōs dependent on an overlord.

GIŌBUKIŌ. An official title conferred by the Court. It may be rendered 'Minister of Justice'. The title was held for a time by the last Shōgun.

GISŌ. Court officials at Kiōto, five in number, who were associated with the *Tensō* in the transmission of the communications which passed between the Throne and the Shōgunate.

GOKÉNIN. A section of the military class created by Iyéyasu, and ranking after the *hatamoto.*

GOKINAI. The five provinces round Kiōto, namely, Yamashiro, Yamato, Kawachi, Settsu, and Idzumi.

GOSANKÉ. The three princely Tokugawa families of Kishiū, Owari, and Mito. They ranked first in the territorial nobility, and members of the first two were eligible for the dignity of Shōgun.

GOSANKIŌ. The three princely Tokugawa families of Hitotsubashi, Tayasu, and Shimidzu, the members of which were eligible for the dignity of Shōgun. They were a later creation than the Gosanké, and were not members of the territorial nobility ; they had neither clans, nor castle-towns ; and their lands were, like the Shōgun's domains, administered by special officials.

GOYŌSHI. See Goyōsho.

GOYŌSHO. An official place of business. The term occurs in the earlier American treaties, where it is misspelt *goyōshi.*

HANSHI. A kind of thin rough paper in common use.

HANSOTSU. A clan *samurai* belonging to the lower or *sotsu* class.

HARAKIRI. Suicide by disembowelment. There were two kinds, one voluntary, the other compulsory, the latter being imposed as a penalty for certain offences. The Japanese rarely use this word, preferring the Chinese form of the word, *seppuku*.

HASSAKU. A term which occurs in the earlier Dutch treaties, where it is spelt *fassak*. As there used, it refers to the annual presents given by the Dutch factory to the local authorities of Nagasaki.

HATAMOTO. A section of the military class created by Iyéyasu. They and the Gokénin were known by the collective name of *Shōmiō* ('small name') in contradistinction to the *daimiō*.

HIDÉYOSHI. The regent who ruled Japan before Iyéyasu.

HIRADO. An island off the north-west coast of Kiūshiū, where the Dutch and English factories were established in the seventeenth century.

HIZEN. Name of province and clan in Kiūshiū.

INKIO. Abdication, or a person who has abdicated.

ISÉ. Province in south of main island near Owari Bay, noted for its national shrines.

IYÉMITSU. The third Tokugawa Shōgun, who closed the country.

IYÉYASU. The founder of the line of Tokugawa rulers, who became Shōgun in 1603.

IYÉYOSHI. The Shōgun who died in 1853.

JIMMU TENNŌ. The mythical first sovereign of Japan.

JŌDAI. (1) the custodian of a castle ; (2) the term applied to the Shōgun's representative at Ōsaka, who was custodian of the castle.

JŌ-I. Literally, 'expel the barbarians,' the cry of the anti-foreign party.

JŌSHIU. Literally, 'lords of castles.' The term applied to third class into which daimios were divided.

KAMI. This word was used in two ways in person's titles. (1) When it followed the name of a province, it signified the prince of the province named. But the title might be, and very often was, borne by a noble who had no connexion with the province in question. (2) When it occurred in what were known as official titles bestowed by the Court, the word had the general sense of 'chief' or 'head', the English rendering in these cases depending on the context.

KARŌ. Literally 'house elder'. The chief retainers (several in number, and of two classes) of a clan who managed the clan's affairs. The office was usually hereditary. There were also *karō* in *hatamoto* families.

KERAI. A feudal retainer.

KII. See Kishiū.

KISHIŪ. Name (1) of a province in south of main island bordering on Kii Channel, and (2) of the clan (the head of which was one of the Gosanké) to which the territory of the province belonged.

KIŪSHIŪ. Name of the southernmost of the islands comprising the Japanese Empire before the annexation of Loochoo in 1879.

KŌGISHO. The first deliberative assembly, or parliament, established in 1869.

KOKU. (1) (of rice) a measure equal to about five bushels ; (2) (of ships) one-tenth of a ton.

KOKUSHIU. Literally, 'lords of provinces.' A term applied to some eighteen of the feudal nobility, who formed the highest of the three classes into which daimiōs were divided.

KUGÉ. Court nobles residing at Kiōto, as distinguished from the feudal nobility.

KUNSHIU. Sovereign, or ruler. A term used occasionally to designate the Shōgun in the earlier treaties and official correspondence.

KUWANA. Name of castle-town in province of Isé, and of clan of same name.

KWAMBAKU. The post of Prime Minister in the old Kiōto Government. The minister holding this office was regent (*Sesshō*) during the Emperor's minority. Occasionally, as in Hidéyoshi's case, a *kwambaku* was virtually regent. After the establishment of the Tokugawa Shōgunate, this office, like all the other Kiōto posts, became a sinecure. It was abolished in January 1868.

KWANSEI (also called Kwansai). Literally, 'west of the barrier.' General term applied before Restoration to country west of the guard-house, or barrier, on the Hakoné Pass.

KWANTŌ. Literally, 'east of the barrier.' (1) General term

applied before Restoration to country east of guard-house, or barrier, on the Hakoné Pass ; (2) the Shōgunate.

MATSUDAIRA. One of the surnames of the Tokugawa family and their descendants. Before the Restoration more than fifty peers bore this surname. The privilege of using it was also conceded to nine of the eighteen *kokushiu* daimiōs, including the Prince of Chōshiū.

MÉTSUKÉ. A class of officials subordinate to the *Ōmétsuké*, q. v., and charged with similar duties.

MIKADO. Literally, 'Honourable Gateway.' A term applied to the Emperor of Japan.

MINO-GAMI. A kind of thick paper originally made in the province of Mino, and used for wrapping purposes. (Mentioned as an article of commerce in the Dutch treaty of 1857, where it is referred to as paper-' mino '.)

MITO. Name of one of the Gosanké, of a clan, and of the town of Mito in province of Hitachi.

NAKATSUKASA-TAIYŪ. Vice-Minister of the Imperial Household (an official Court title).

ŌMÉTSUKÉ. Chief *métsuké*, a class of officials, created under the Tokugawa régime in 1632, whose functions, as defined in the *Tokugawa Kinreikō*, included the duty of seeing to the strict observance of the laws, watching the administration of justice, and reporting any irregularities which might occur. They were charged also with a general supervision of the country, and were regarded as ' the ears and eyes of the Shōgun ', who was enabled, through the information thus received, to ascertain the actual working of the administration.

OTOKODATÉ. A term applied to the members of bands, or guilds, of apprentices which were formed in later Tokugawa times in the chief cities of Japan. See p. 127.

RI. One Japanese *ri* is equivalent roughly to $2\frac{1}{2}$ English miles.

RIŌSHIU. Literally, 'lords of territories ; ' the term applied to the second class into which daimiōs were divided.

RŌNIN. Literally, ' wave-man.' A general term applied to *samurai* not attached to any clan ; see pp. 126 and 127.

SAIKOKU. A term applied before the Restoration to the provinces, or clans, in the country west of the Hakoné Pass.

Sankin Kōtai. Literally, 'Attending in turn to perform duties.' The term applied to the compulsory attendance of daimiōs at Yedo.

Satsuma. Name of a province, and of a clan whose territories comprised the provinces of Satsuma, Ōsumi, and a portion of the province of Hiūga in the island of Kiūshiū.

Sayemon-no-jō. Left Warden of the Palace Gates (an official Court title).

Sekké. The term applied to the five leading *kugé* families (Ichijō, Nijō, Kujō, Konoye, and Takatsukasa), from one of which the Empress, and the *Kwambaku* and *Sesshō* were always chosen.

Sesshō. The regent during the minority of the Emperor in the old Kiōto Government. Under the Tokugawa Shōgunate the post was a sinecure.

Shimoda. The port in the province of Idzu where the Additional Regulations attached to the American Treaty of 1854 were agreed upon.

Shōdzu. A kind of small bean. The word occurs in the Dutch Treaty of 1857, where it is spelt *schoods*.

Shōgun. Literally, 'the general commanding an army.' The term applied to the administrative rulers, as distinguished from the sovereigns, of Japan. Also known as Taikun.

Shōmiō. Literally, 'small name.' A term applied to those members of the nobility and gentry the annual assessed yield of whose lands was less than ten thousand *koku* of rice. The class comprised the *hatamoto* and *gokénin*.

Shoshidai. The Shōgun's official representative, or Resident, at Kiōto.

Sōshi. A term first applied some years after the Restoration to a class of political rowdies who to some extent took the place of the former *rōnin*.

Taikō. The title given to a *Kwambaku*, who, on retirement from office, was succeeded by his son.

Taikun. Literally, 'great lord.' The term employed by the Japanese in the earlier treaties, and in their official correspondence with foreigners, to designate the Shōgun ; sometimes also, though rarely, used in the closing days of the Shōgunate in official correspondence between Kiōto and Yedo. It was first used in connexion with intercourse with Corea.

TAIRA. The family which administered Japan in the twelfth century, and was eventually crushed by the rival family of Minamoto.

TAIRŌ. Literally, ' great elder.' The term applied to the minister appointed under the Tokugawa Government to the presidency of the Council of State in Yedo in times of emergency. The position was equivalent to that of regent.

TENSŌ. Literally, ' transmitting and presenting to the Throne.' The term applied to the two officials at Kiōto through whom communications from the Yedo Government were transmitted to the Throne.

TŌGOKU. The provinces, or clans, to the east of the Hakoné Pass.

TOKUGAWA. The family and line of Shōguns founded by Tokugawa Iyéyasu.

TŌSHŌGU. Posthumous name of Iyéyasu.

TOSA. The name of a province and clan in the island of Shikoku.

TOZAMA. Literally, ' outer gentry '. The term given by Iyéyasu to those daimiōs, one-third of the whole number, who submitted to him after the battle of Sékigahara (1600). Their position was more independent than that of the *fudai* daimiōs, but on the other hand they were not, like the others, eligible for official employ.

TYCOON. See Taikun.

URAGA. The port in the province of Sagami where Commodore Perry arrived in 1853.

YAMATO. One of the names for Japan. *Yamato-nishiki*, Japanese brocade.

YASHIKI. A general term applied to the residence, in town or country, of a daimiō or hatamoto. It was also applied in a special sense to the residential establishments maintained by the clans in Yedo, Kiōto, and Ōsaka. The leading clans had two or more of these residences in Yedo itself.

DATE DUE